The Book of Jeremiah

THE BOOK OF JEREMIAH

The Life and Ministry of Jeremiah A. Wright Jr.

SUSAN WILLIAMS SMITH

Dedication

This book is dedicated to my children, Caroline and Charlie, to my mother, the late Mary Lee Kidd Simmons, to my sister and brothers, Pamela Reeves and Harold and Bruce Simmons, and to Gwen Edwards and Ida Edmondson, two of the best friends a person could ever ask for.

The Pilgrim Press, 700 Prospect Avenue, Cleveland, Ohio 44115
pilgrimpress.com

Printed in the United States of America on acid-free paper

17 16 15 14 13 5 4 3 2 1

Library of Congress Cataloging-in-Publication Data

Smith, Susan Williams, 1954–
The book of Jeremiah : the life and ministry of Jeremiah A. Wright, Jr. / Susan Williams Smith.
pages cm
ISBN 978-0-8298-1935-9 (alk. paper)
1. Wright, Jeremiah A., Jr. 2. United Church of Christ—Clergy—Biography. 3. African American clergy—Biography. I. Title.
BX9886.Z8W75 2013
200.92—dc23
[B] 2013040005

CONTENTS

Acknowledgments . . . **vii**

Preface . . . **x**

Introduction . . . **xxi**

1 · In the Beginning: Young and Black in America . . . **1**

2 · The Country, College, and Contradictions . . . **16**

3 · What Then Shall We Say? . . . **26**

4 · Unashamedly Black and Unapologetically Christian . . . **38**

5 · Removing the Mask . . . **52**

6 · Not Here You Won't! . . . **71**

7 · Wright and Preacher and Prophet . . . **90**

8 · The Peculiar Role of Wright as Prophet/Preacher . . . **104**

9 · Teaching a Theology of Freedom . . . **115**

10 · Anger Is Not Hate . . . **129**

11 · The Oppressor and the Oppressed, United . . . **154**

12 · Preaching and Reaching for Liberation . . . **174**

13 · Wright and the Would-be President . . . **194**

14 · At the End of the Day: Is Wright's Message Relevant Today? . . . **223**

15 · A Tragedy of Shakespearean Proportions . . . **250**

Notes . . . **261**

Acknowledgments

My first encounter with Jeremiah Wright Jr. was when I was a student at Yale Divinity School. He had preached a stirring sermon and given a presentation, but it was during dinner with him and the president of Yale that evening that I became fascinated with this man and his work. Even then, I knew that "regular church," meaning Sunday morning worship and Wednesday evening Bible study and prayer meeting (in the black church tradition), wasn't enough for me. In my very soul, I felt that God wanted us who were called to ministry to do something more, to try to get people to "get" that the essence of Christianity was serving serve "the least of these." At that time I had not had much exposure to churches and/or ministries carrying out such work . . . but as I listened to Wright that evening, I knew his ministry was something of which I wanted to be a part. Chicago's Trinity United Church of Christ was reaching out to "the least of these" in all kinds of ways. As Wright spoke about what Trinity was doing, it wasn't with even a hint of arrogance; to the contrary, he was humble and quiet, yet clear about the vision God had given him. When he talked about his church having a "Bible Study Institute," where students learned not just verses of the Bible but their historical contexts and significance, and where there was a curriculum to which students had to adhere in order to really learn the Bible and its significance, I was done. I asked him that evening if there was a way I could get to his church as an intern, and Trinity, with help and cooperation from the then extant Board for Homeland Ministries of the United Church of Christ, made that internship happen. I worked at Trinity for two years as an intern and became an associate pastor there upon my graduation from YDS.

To say that my experience there was life-changing is an understatement. For the first time, there was no disconnect between being an African-American and a Christian. For the first time, I, as an African-American and as a woman, felt I had a voice in the life of the church. For the first time, I "got it," the connection between the life and death of the Christ and the work we as Christians were called to do. It was fascinating and exhilarating. As I learned about the African presence in the Bible, as I experienced American history being stitched to theology and religious history, I felt an affirmation of my very being, the likes of which I had never felt before.

I must, then, acknowledge the time I spent at Trinity UCC as a major inspiration for writing this book. Not only Rev. Wright, but the late Rev. Barbara Allen and her beloved husband, Sam; Val Jordan and his wife, Ethel; "Papa Joe"; the late Jeffrey Radcliffe; and the amazing Trinity UCC choir helped shape my early ministry and my perception of life. My Trinity family, as well as Rev. Wright, were maligned when the debacle of the 2008 presidential election attempted to shatter what had been an amazing, life-saving, and life-affirming ministry to literally thousands of people, black and white. I felt in my spirit a need to at least try to tell the story, and to embrace those who had embraced me, by writing this book.

Leaving Trinity and traveling to Ohio to become a pastor myself, I was blessed to have an amazing congregation for twenty-two years, a fact for which I am and will be eternally grateful. My sense of the need and importance for social justice was shaped not only by my time at Trinity, but also by my time working with BREAD (Building Responsibility, Equality, and Dignity) under the leadership of John Aeshbury, which sharpened my awareness of how important the work of justice is in ministry. John's leadership, in a different yet equally important way as Jeremiah Wright's, has had a profound impact on my life.

There have been friends and supporters too many to mention, but I must name a few: Dick Wing, pastor of First Community Church, who always said to me, "Keep showing up for life!"; Frank Thomas, former pastor of Mississippi Avenue Christian Church in Memphis, who reminded me weekly that what I was going through was "not an illness unto death"; James Pope, a deacon at my former church, who always loved and supported me; Stephanie Rogers, who, with my daughter, gave up a Friday night to help type the endnotes for the text; Rev. April Blaine, pastor of Summit UMC, who has shown love, support, and compassion; Pam Highlen, who, when I was at my lowest, offered love and support (and good wine!); Ida Edmondson and Gwen Edwards, two of the best friends a person could ever ask for; "Aunt Jane," who prayed with me and counseled me; and all of my sister-friends, who have been a constant source of inspiration, reminding me to write when I didn't want to.

My friend Rhoda McKinney Jones is an angel in the flesh. The editor of my book *Crazy Faith: Ordinary People; Extraordinary Lives,* she has always "been there" for me, even when she has not agreed with me. She has loved me when I've been strong and, more importantly, when I have been weak. And as I have struggled through some fairly difficult times over the past year, she has prayed with me, cried with me, . . . and stuck with me.

I have to acknowledge my Pilgrim Press editors, Kim Sadler and Kristin Firth—Kim for her patience as I wrestled at the beginning with whether or not to write this book, and Kristin for her precise and careful editing of the text. I am grateful to the Pilgrim Press for taking me on as one of their authors.

I acknowledge my mother, Mary Lee Kidd Simmons, who died when I was a teen, yet whose spirit is ever with me. She was a profound woman who died far too soon, but her presence has never disappeared. Somehow I feel she is, from wherever she is, looking down on me and sending her love.

My final acknowledgements must go to Caroline and Charlie Smith, my children. I think that every book I write shall be dedicated to them. Rarely does a parent have two amazing children who are kind and compassionate, independent and smart, patient yet tenacious, but I have been blessed to have exactly that. If I have done nothing else right, I have raised two children who will make an impact on this world. They will never know how their love and commitment has helped me over the years, as they have walked with me and stood with me in my work as a pastor. I am deeply blessed.

Preface

I can remember the day the preaching of Rev. Dr. Jeremiah Wright changed my life.

He was preaching about racism, as he often did, and I was only half listening. But it seemed that, out of the blue, I heard something that rattled my soul to its core. He was relating to us that the United States Supreme Court, in its historic *Dred Scott* decision, had made the position of this nation as concerns race unequivocal: Chief Justice Roger B. Taney, Wright said, had written that "there are no rights of a black man that a white man is bound to respect."

I was stunned. I was too old to be naïve about America or the difference between the myth of a democracy where "all men are created equal," as Thomas Jefferson had penned, and the reality of a capitalistic society where "the least of these" were too often ignored, but for some reason, I had not thought, or had not studied, the role of government and the justice system in keeping the oppression of African Americans alive and well. I had learned about the *Dred Scott* decision in school but had never been taught that the Chief Justice of the nation's highest court had said such a thing. I had learned that Abraham Lincoln freed the slaves, but only much later did I learn that not even my beloved Lincoln believed African Americans were equal with whites . . . but for some reason, I believed that in the court system, ultimately, there was justice to be had for black people.

I don't remember what Wright said after I heard those words. I was stuck. When I left church, I went to the library to look up the speech, and, sure enough, there were the dastardly words:

> In the opinion of the court, the legislation and histories of the times, and the language used in the Declaration of Independence, show, that neither the class of persons who had been imported as slaves, nor their descendants, whether they had become free or not, were then acknowledged as part of the people, nor intended to be included in the general words used in that memorable instrument. . . . They had for more than a century before been regarded as beings of an inferior order, and altogether unfit to associate with the white race, either in social or political relations; and so far inferior, that they had no rights which the white man was bound to respect; and that the negro might justly and lawfully be reduced to slavery for his benefit.[1]

The words stung . . . and my hunch was that Wright had meant for those words to sting *someone*. This being a Christian was not supposed to be a milquetoast experience. Oppression of people had existed from the beginning of time, and it had not stopped just because Jesus had been dead for more than two thousand years. Wright taught that Jesus knew oppression well; during his lifetime it was the Romans who oppressed . . . and Jesus' firsthand and experiential knowledge of oppression helped shape and define his ministry. Those who followed Jesus had to know that. If we were to "imitate" the Christ, as Paul had written, we had to know what we were imitating.

We were forced to take the blinders off our eyes and look at the world "face to face," and not "through a glass, darkly," as Paul wrote.[2]

Because of the profound wisdom I gleaned from Wright's preaching, I was disturbed and angry at what happened in 2008. The presidential election of 2008 was as exciting as it was historic. An African American man was running for the highest office of the land in a nation where the color of a person had most often been used to hinder his or her progress and define him or her as inferior to whites. From the time of slavery, and probably some before that, blacks had been relegated to second-class citizenship in America, but now, in spite of the biting words written by Justice Taney in 1857, Barack Hussein Obama was taking the country by storm. It was nothing short of exhilarating for those who said they thought they'd never live to see the day when this would be America's reality.

But Mr. Obama was not the only African American man with whom Americans became familiar in 2008. He was thrust up against his pastor, the Rev. Dr. Jeremiah A. Wright Jr., with the force of a deadly and unwelcome tornado. Obama's political opponents were looking for a way to bring him down, and once a couple of clips from sermons Wright had given years ago were found, the two men were pitted against each other, the powers-that-be salivating at the carnage that was sure to result. How would the man who would be president of the United States justify his relationship with a man, his pastor, who had said, "God damn America"? Those words were unconscionable for any American to say; people needed to be patriotic, especially in the aftermath of 9/11. "God Bless America," belted out through the voice of Kate Smith, was a national anthem in its own right. The words and sentiment contained in the song were held sacred. That Jeremiah Wright would say just the opposite, and base it on events that happened in the Bible, with God damning or cursing those who had broken covenant with Yahweh and the laws of God, was unacceptable. That he had likened what was happening in modern-day America to biblical times was doubly unacceptable.

Wright's words were only part of the problem, however. *This was Obama's pastor!* It was widely known and reported that Mr. Obama and his family had attended Trinity UCC for some twenty years; it was also known that Rev. Wright had married Barack and Michelle Obama, and had dedicated their two children, Sasha and Malia. Thus, Wright, it was thought, had had plenty of time to "teach" Obama the anger of a black man. This clip would be Obama's Waterloo, his opponents felt.

While the drama unfolded, those who had been touched and liberated by Wright's sermons writhed in agony and anger. For years, he had preached as powerfully as had prophets in the Hebrew Scriptures, who had railed about injustice, specifically the injustice done by government. Rev. Wright had drawn attention to the fact that racism was real and that democracy in America had not been so "democratic" for African Americans nor for other marginalized groups. His message had never changed; for Mr. Obama to have said that he had never heard some of what his pastor had reportedly preached seemed a bit disingenuous.

The fury over Wright's sermons, however, was misplaced. The representation of Wright as incendiary and hate-filled was painfully incorrect. Those who had listened to Wright for years knew better. His sermons were informational, instructional, biblically based, and theologically sound. Many of them were critical of American government, for sure, but that criticism served as a source of inspiration to a group of people who had historically been marginalized in this nation. In many churches, the disconnect between what God mandated and what government dished out was ignored. But that was not true of Wright's sermons. His ministry was one that encouraged people to have a religion that was not one merely and solely of personal salvation with Jesus Christ, but to have eyes that saw as did the Christ—to see "the least of these" in spite of having been part of that group themselves. Wright nudged his listeners, whether they were black or white, to move from pat and incomplete opinions about God and government and to study both deeply.

God, he taught, was not one who would be pleased with people who had not a clue about what was going on in the world; part of being a Christian was to "go" into the world and bring good news, but to do that, one would have to know one's world. In addition, he taught his congregants that democracy had a "de facto" and a "de jure" component. Just because Thomas Jefferson had written that "all men were created equal" did not mean that that was the way our democracy worked. People knew that, but it wasn't often talked about in church. Wright, however, would not let his listeners sink into a disinfected reality. God had requirements—of individuals, surely, but also of governments! In order to be a viable Christian, one would have to see God as one who exacted accountability from those who said they loved God, seeing not only their situations but the situations of others as well. He taught that God's people would also have to leave the comfort of their pews and walk into the lion's den called American democracy with eyes wide open, seeing not what had been spoon-fed in lopsided history lessons, but what was actually the case.

What Wright dealt with, and what African American preachers deal with in general, was a group of people who really suffered and still suffer from a sort of post-traumatic stress syndrome caused specifically by racism in America. Post-traumatic stress disorder (PTSD) is defined by the U.S. National Library of Medicine as "a potentially debilitating anxiety disorder triggered by exposure to a traumatic experience such as an interpersonal event like physical or sexual assault, exposure to disaster or accidents, combat or witnessing a traumatic event."[3] The *New England Journal of Medicine* states that PTSD comes about from an event that has a "capacity to provoke fear, helplessness, or horror in response to the threat of injury or death."[4] Evidence suggested that people exposed to such trauma were, or are, at "increased risk for major depression, panic disorder, generalized anxiety disorder and substance abuse."[5]

Wright knew that the members of his congregation, members of an oppressed and marginalized group, had all dealt with and were still dealing with emotional, physical, and spiritual trauma caused by racism. Years of discrimination and oppression had deadened the hearts and spirits of many African Americans and lessened their capacity to hope—and they were feeling that in spite of being Christians. William Sloan Coffin said that many of God's people are victims of "psychosclerosis," or hardening of the spirit.[6] The people had God, had Jesus . . . but time had eroded the sharpened edge of a religion that challenged injustice. Instead, it seemed that religion was a tool with which people hammered away at the bleakness of their lives; in all actuality, religion for many African Americans had become a numbing agent. It did not seek to empower people to deal with their daily trauma. Necessarily, religion for African Americans had long been eschatological in nature, encouraging blacks to sing and pray for the afterlife: "Soon-ah-will-be-done-a-wid-de-troubles-ob-de-worl"[7] is an old Negro spiritual which, not unlike many other spirituals, encouraged African Americans to look for peace and blessings not while they were alive, but after they were dead! Countless spirituals conveyed the thought that "over there," in "Egypt land," there would be peace and fairness and, finally, an end to unjust suffering on the part of black people.

Wright's ministry, however, his teaching and preaching, challenged this eschatological worldview, as well as religion that seemed to have become complacent. His teaching and preaching let people know that their pain was real, that the trauma they experienced was not being imagined, but also let people know that because of their God and God's son Jesus they were not helpless in the face of oppression and that in fact they had the power to overcome it. There was, in fact, reason to hope for empowerment and release from oppression while they were yet alive.

His teaching and preaching would also not allow those who heard him to be concerned merely with their own circumstances and suffering. There was injustice throughout the world, and a Christian, even one oppressed in America, was simply not allowed to sit and complain about his or her own suffering and not be concerned with the suffering of others. Hence, Wright's ministry broadened the worldview of those who heard him, even as he connected the dots between religion and the political and economic systems in America. He preached about racism in America, but also about apartheid in South Africa and the present-day conflict between the Palestinians and Jews. His "Free South Africa" sign in front of Trinity UCC in the 1970s and beyond offended some, but he was clear in his vision and understanding of Jesus. We were to be brothers and sisters and we were to fight oppression everywhere it existed. He taught that Jesus had fought against exactly what oppressed people were fighting against in the present day.

His preaching and teaching, then, was not unlike that of the Hebrew prophets. Isaiah, Ezekiel, Jeremiah, Hosea, Joel, Amos . . . all were men who challenged the government and even the religious elite as they railed against governments that seemingly did not have the best interests of "the least of these" at heart. Though it might not have been called "capitalism" in Jesus' day and before, the agrarian societies common during that time were as guilty as is our society today of allowing way too many "have-nots" compared to the "haves." It seemed that in the days of the prophets, as well as in the time of Jesus, governments and individuals were unable and unwilling to consider the plight of the poor. Wright's preaching followed in the footsteps of not only biblical prophets, but of modern-day preachers as well, including William Sloan Coffin and Martin Luther King Jr.

His work was never about hatred.

Perhaps one of the most powerful components of Wright's ministry was his ability to empower African American men. One former member said, "Rev made it okay to be a black man. He didn't emasculate us." Black men were often criticized and ridiculed by other black men who called Christianity "the white man's religion," but Jeremiah Wright's ministry pulled black men in, affirming them and empowering them. "You could be comfortable being a man," this member said. The black men who flocked to Wright's ministry appreciated being taught that Jesus was not a white man, kind of effeminate, with curly hair. Jesus, they were taught, was a powerful male, who came from the continent of Africa, and who changed the world.

In order to be a Christian, one didn't have to reject one's maleness. "Rev was a regular guy," this ex-member said. Prior to his coming to Wright's ministry, this former member said he had been taught a "Christian" way to live that was problematic. He didn't fit the mold. Jeremiah Wright, though, a "regular guy," let him and others know that it was okay to smoke or drink; doing those things didn't make one less Christian. By accepting black men "as they were," Jeremiah Wright was able to draw black men into the folds of a religion that, it seemed, they had always wanted to embrace but couldn't because they felt unworthy, and unable to embrace a Jesus who was so not like them. Even men who had been members of the Nation of Islam because it had allowed and encouraged them embrace their "maleness" were drawn to Trinity.

Black men who called themselves a "man's man" felt like they had a place in the world under Jeremiah Wright's tutelage. These were men who had seen, or whose ancestors had seen, American terrorism in the form of lynching, KKK cross burnings, and worse; they had been forced to be quiet while they watched their lives and the lives of their families being destroyed. These were men, or children of men, who had been challenged and punished for speaking up for themselves and their families. They had been prevented from voting because they flunked literacy tests that those giving it could not have passed. They had been told all that they could not do and should not expect to do . . . and their church experience had not offered them anything much different. The Jesus and church experience they knew instructed them to be meek and to back down. Never mind about racism; they were born "unfree" in the land where freedom was supposed to be guaranteed to all its citizens. Some of them had migrated to Chicago from the South; others had been children and grandchildren of those who had migrated, and thus, they had seen and heard much that was painful and troubling to them. They didn't have a way to release the tension they felt within, however. Nowhere had Jesus been presented to them as a symbol of strength. Quite the contrary—the Jesus of their parents and grandparents seemed weak; he was one who taught people to acquiesce to injustice. Black male preachers, they soon realized, were unable to connect to their pain. To some, black preachers were like roosters in the hen house. They were less interested in teaching sound theology than they were in controlling their flocks. They liked it that their congregations were female-dominated; the females worshiped the pastors as much as (or sometimes more than) they did Jesus and didn't seem to mind being controlled; and men, many of them the husbands of these church members, were often marginalized so much that eventually, many stopped attending church altogether. But under the leadership of Jeremiah Wright, black males who had heretofore rejected church, God, and religion were now eager to worship.

The African origins of the Bible were taught; it was likely that Jesus hadn't had wavy brown or blonde hair and blue eyes after all. Jesus was not meek at all. This Jesus, the Jesus of the Bible, was not the cultural creation of a race that needed to remain dominant. The Jesus they learned about under Wright was bold and revolutionary in the way he challenged injustice. He was *masculine*. The former member interviewed said, "There was no shame attached to that image. . . . Rev made being a black man okay. That reality made us empowered, spiritually. It was safe to be in the world and not have to reject being Christian."

This book is going to examine the work, words, and ministry of Jeremiah Wright. Perhaps the greatest tragedy of 2008 is that what Wright was working to achieve—for African Americans to rise above racism, discrimination and oppression, was ultimately realized and then crushed in the person and candidacy and ultimate victory of Barack Obama. The thirty-second sound bites of Wright's sermons—taken and presented out of context to have exactly the effect that they did—were effective in an effort to feed enough fear into people about Barack Obama, but they did not derail Obama's victory. They did a terrible disservice, however, to the life-work of Wright, skewed the perception of his work by people who knew little to nothing about him, and caused some who had previously supported him to back away.

The sound bites damaged Wright's ministry from the outside; Wright perhaps damaged his own ministry somewhat by his appearance at the National Press Club, but his anger at that event was justified, even if his presentation was troubling to some. He had given a brilliant presentation on the black church, a topic about which he has lectured much, but the questions presented to him afterward ignored his presentation altogether. All the moderator of that event wanted to do was grill him on the sound bites that had caused so much of a stir, and Wright reacted.

However the damage came about, it was sad to see; it was truly a tragedy of Shakespearean proportions. The world grabbed onto the sound bites and labeled Wright a man who spewed hatred, an observation that cannot be supported from listening to and/or reading his sermons, including the ones from which the sound bites were taken. Following the National Press Club event, Obama the politician had to distance himself from Wright the pastor/preacher/prophet as the fear of Wright being a racist bubbled and brewed and threatened Obama's chance for victory. It was not only whites who turned against Wright; many African Americans, some of whom he had helped much in their ministries, turned against him as well. It was sad and painful to see, because anybody who knew Jeremiah Wright and who had learned under him knew that the charge of him being a hatemonger was an outright lie; nothing could have been further from the truth.

Because of the tragedy that lay underneath the amazing victory of Barack Obama in 2008, the jubilation of some was tainted. It seemed that one great man had been elevated at the expense of another. It should never have been that way.

The experience with the media in 2008 profoundly affected Wright, his family, and his then congregation. The media was brutal in trying to prove or uncover proof that Wright was a racist and that consequently the nation was in jeopardy because one of his protégés was headed to the White House. The strategy failed; Obama won, but not without great cost to both men. There was carnage, and it has not yet all been cleaned up.

This book is not a biography of Jeremiah Wright. In fact, Wright refused to grant interviews for this book, and so the biographical information has been pieced together from sermons and conversations with people who knew him and who were willing to talk. As with any of us, Wright's childhood and early life experiences profoundly affected his work and ministry; I have tried to show what some of those effects were.

Neither is this book a history of Chicago's Trinity United Church of Christ. Although Wright had an amazing and powerful ministry in the church he built from eighty-seven members to more than five thousand, there will be others who can and will write that story. Wright himself has written its history in a book called *A Sankofa Moment: The History of Trinity United Church of Christ*. The history of the transformation of lives that took place inside the walls of Trinity is yet to be written.

This book also is not a book about the relationship between Barack Obama and Jeremiah Wright; that story will be told, I am sure, by expert biographers and historians. This book is, however, an attempt to show what the ministry of Jeremiah Wright was, by showing what he preached and why, by relating and connecting his words to the historical and cultural context out of which he and those to whom he preached came. The book will compare and relate his prophetic voice with the prophetic voices of biblical and modern-day prophets, and it will attempt to show how powerfully his theology impacted the way he perceived and taught about the inequities of our socioeconomic system in juxtaposition to the words of the Bible and the precepts of the United States Constitution.

It will drive home the point that there is a difference between anger, or passionate anger, about a system and hatred for people. It will try to describe the unique and peculiar struggles around theodicy faced by people of color and, in fact, anyone who is oppressed and living in a Christian nation, and it will examine how Wright's words and work addressed that issue.

In the course of this book we will examine some of the sermons of Wright, including the ones that were so infamously used to try to discredit him, and we will look at the sermons of other prophets, ancient and modern-day. We will examine some of the reasons why a message of liberation is vital, even now, almost 150 years after the Civil War. At the heart of the assault against Jeremiah Wright was the elephant in the room: racism. Hopefully, by the time one has read this book, the elephant will have been moved over, just a bit, toward the door. It is far past time for racism to stop being the seedbed of oppression it has been for far too long. And it is time for the truth of Jeremiah Wright's ministry to gain some discussion. In fact, it is past time.

This work will not be exhaustive, by any means, but hopefully it will whet curiosity about the work and ministry of Jeremiah Wright in the hearts of those who did and did not decide, on the basis of two thirty-second sound bites, who Jeremiah Wright is and what he stands for and has in fact always stood for. Jeremiah Wright's ministry impacted people from all over the world. This book will not even begin to touch on his international legacy.

How did that day that I heard Wright quote the words of Chief Justice Taney change my life? It made me aware of the historical lack of justice in this country, aware of the breadth and the depth of it, and it made me understand that the struggle to work for "the least of these" can never really end. It gave me a deeper appreciation for the words of the biblical prophets and for the work and the struggle that Jesus had while he was on earth. It made me understand that to be a Christian is a dynamic and not a static experience, and that what Jesus taught, though controversial, was life-changing and life-saving. It made me want to know history a little more, and not be content with the very limited knowledge I had. It made me want to know Truth.

Someone said to me that Jeremiah Wright is so hated as a result of the 2008 election that nobody will read this book. My prayer is that person is wrong, and that perhaps some of the pieces of truth that shattered in 2008 will be picked up and put back together. Politics is brutal, and racial politics is the most brutal of all. That is but one of the messages Wright taught throughout his life. Sadly, the truth of his teaching raised its ugly head at the moment when a great victory should have been savored. That the moment was stolen from history is a sad fact indeed.

Introduction

Had Shakespeare been alive during the 2008 presidential election, he would have relished the making of a true American tragedy.

At the heart of the drama was Barack Obama, running a hard campaign against Hillary Clinton, and Obama's pastor, the Rev. Dr. Jeremiah A. Wright Jr., who was the pastor of Trinity United Church of Christ in Chicago. Obama had met the minister during his days as an organizer in Chicago and had noted Wright's talent "to hold together, if not reconcile, the conflicting strains of black experience—upon which Trinity's success had ultimately been built."[1] Young Obama, the son of an African father and a white mother, was doing work which, it seems, immersed him in parts of African American culture that were fairly new to him. Obama found out from his first meeting with Wright that he, Wright, and his church, had at best mixed reviews from fellow clergy and churches; "Some of my fellow clergy don't appreciate what we're about," Obama recalled Wright sharing. "They feel like we're too radical. Others, though, feel we ain't radical enough."[2] Obama heard Wright shrug off the criticism that the church was "too upwardly mobile," and also heard from Wright his opinion that the life of an African American man was perilous: "Life's not safe for a black man in this country, Barack. Never has been. Probably never will be."[3]

The future president wrote that he studied the vision of Trinity, the "Black Value System," which contained ten points that Wright wanted Trinity to address and be involved in, and at the top of that list was "commitment to God." The vision clearly stated that the members of Trinity would be committed to God, "who would give them the strength to give up 'prayerful passivism.'"[4] The Black Value System was written in 1981 by a member of Trinity, Manford Byrd, who was an educator who became the superintendent of Chicago Public Schools. He was committed to teaching children to aspire to excellence, and he saw adherence to the principles contained in the Black Value System as necessary for those aspirations to take place.

Obama grew to respect Wright for his vision, for his dedication to "the least of these" with whom Obama was working and organizing for social change. In spite of the criticism that Trinity was too upwardly mobile, Obama quickly noticed that "the bulk of its membership was solidly working class," and that the church had programs designed to meet the needs of working class families, everything from legal aid to tutoring to drug and HIV/AIDS programs.[5] This was a church that welcomed all, including and especially "the least of these."

But Obama also noticed something else: in spite of the church's mixed socioeconomic membership, there was a sadness, a feeling of a "spiritual dead end."[6] It was as though he were seeing Coffin's "psychosclerosis," or a hardening of the spirit, something that happens when one is disappointed in God and tired of trying to make sense out of an unkind world. Obama had seen it before among the people he worked with, good church people working hard to change an unbending system, and he found in Trinity that that it was not uncommon among African Americans. It seemed that God was in some regards woefully insufficient, and oppression—racial, economic, sexual, and otherwise—was one of those areas. People went to church and "did" church but often with a sense of hopelessness.

That is perhaps one of the reasons Wright's ministry influenced Obama. Wright was able to identify the sadness; he was able to meld different socioeconomic classes of African Americans into a more or less working whole, and he was able to infuse and inject them with a sense of hope. In his book *Dreams from My Father*, Obama recalls a sermon, "The Audacity to Hope" preached by Wright, which brought him to tears. In that sermon, recalls Obama, Wright preached about a harpist who was sitting atop a mountain. Wright shared that one cannot see until looking closer that the woman sitting there is tattered and worn and bruised. In the world upon which she sits, there is famine and destitution and poverty and things that make no sense, like cruise ships "throwing away more food in one day than most residents of Port-au-Prince see in a year, where white folks' greed runs a world in need, apartheid in one hemisphere, apathy in another hemisphere. That's the world! On which hope sits!"[7]

As Wright continued his description of life in a world filled with contradictions, where the "haves" ruled and manipulated the "have-nots," Obama was moved. This was something he knew about; he saw the lack of fairness and opportunity in the lives of the people with whom he worked every day. He saw the contradictions between the ideals and the reality of American democracy. And yet, if there was still hope—if people could and would have the audacity to hope—in spite of that, then perhaps his work was not in vain.

He joined Trinity United Church of Christ and continued to be influenced by his pastor, a man who encouraged him and reminded him that in all things, because there was God, there was hope.

But nothing prepared Obama for the attack against his pastor when the presidential election got into full gear. He knew that, though Wright's sermons criticized the government, and rightly so in most instances, Wright's messages were not about hate. He had heard hate-filled sermons before, sometimes obvious and sometimes more muted, and nothing in Wright's sermons approached that. But those running his campaign understood the nexus of fear and distrust among American whites, and some blacks as well. Obama's handlers knew politics, and how words and phrases were used and manipulated in order to bring an opponent down. Wright was trouble, and Obama's people knew it. And so it began, this "tempering" and isolating of Jeremiah Wright. Right at the beginning of his campaign, when Obama was in Springfield, Illinois, to announce that he was running for president, Wright, who had been invited by Obama to give the invocation, was "dis-invited."[8] According to Wright, he traveled to Springfield and was prepared to give the invocation, when, at the last moment, he was told it might be better that he not do it, and so, as one black man stood on the steps of the State Capitol Building to announce his candidacy for president of the United States, another black man, the man who had probably most helped him get there by helping him to develop his spirituality and understand his place as an African American man in a hostile country, stood in the basement of the capitol building, alone.

It was only the beginning. As it became apparent that Obama was not going to go away, Obama's handlers' fear seemed to increase. In lieu of any record of national policy with which to beat Obama down, there had to be something else that his opponents would use, and Wright, they feared (correctly), would be that "something." Wright was known nationally and internationally; his critique of America's racism was no secret, and he made no secret of respecting and being friends with Louis Farrakhan, though not always agreeing with him. Just the mention of Farrakhan's name in the same sentence as Wright's would be enough to make people wary, Obama's handlers knew, and they began to brace themselves for the certain storm that was to come.

And come it did. Like an EF-5 tornado came sound bites with Jeremiah Wright, "Obama's pastor," preaching a sermon in which were the words, "no, no, no . . . not God bless America. God damn America!" The clip was devastating to the Obama campaign and devastating for Wright as well. There was Wright, full of passion and fury at a nation that had done its share of oppressing people, saying words that Obama's handlers knew would enrage voters they desperately needed in order for Obama to win. The Obama camp knew that Americans, especially white Americans, were and are very protective of their country. No warm-blooded American gives a darn about misdeeds this country has done or political, moral, or ethical things it has not done. At the end of the day, one is to remain faithful, loyal, and patriotic, no matter how he or she has been treated, and to be patriotic one had better not talk poorly about the "land of the free and the home of the brave." Although America celebrates the Constitutional right of free speech, it is a fact that sometimes speech here is not all that free, especially if that speech includes scathing criticism of the government. In other words, there is an unspoken culture of censorship. The censorship cannot be blatant; we have, after all, the First Amendment, guaranteeing freedom of speech. But it is clear that one does not talk badly about America, especially not publicly. To do so is to be unpatriotic, and to be unpatriotic is almost worse than being agnostic or atheist. The United States Constitution is a sacred document to many Americans, probably more sacred for some than the Bible. One can get away with disputing much or some of the Bible in this country, but few people can get away with criticizing America, freedom of speech notwithstanding.

Thus, when Wright was heard saying, "God damn America," though the words were taken completely out of context, the move to use him to get rid of Obama was on. How could anyone be trusted to be president of the United States when his pastor, of all people, had said such awful words? It didn't matter what that sermon was about. What mattered is that Wright had presented himself as an enemy of American democracy. Not only had Wright said "God damn America," but it was brought up that he had also had the audacity to declare that he would not disown Louis Farrakhan, because Farrakhan was not his enemy. Here was a black man who was as honest as he was clear that he was not so enamored with America's legacy of democracy and freedom that he was unable to see or willing to ignore how America had historically treated "the least of these." Wright, an American who had served his country as a United States Marine, had not been taken in by the romantic myth contained in the words penned by Thomas Jefferson, "We hold these truths to be self-evident, that all men are created equal." History had shown otherwise, and Wright knew it.

Americans were furious that Wright would say that "America's chickens had come home to roost." The words seemed traitorous. In his sermon "The Day of Jerusalem's Fall," written and delivered after the tragic events of September 11, 2001, Wright clearly expressed his pain at what had happened in America on that fateful day, and at the end of that sermon, he shared how the 9/11 debacle had pulled into focus his need to live and to preach the love of God more than he had ever done before. That sentiment was lost, however. The words "America's chickens have come home to roost" sounded sacrilegious to many. From their perspective, it was a horrible thing to say, and they were not about to let him off the hook, no matter what else Wright had expressed in that sermon. If many more of Wright's sermons had been scrutinized, it was not clear that that had happened in the 2008 campaign; had there been more scrutiny, perhaps the venom against him and Obama would have been lessened, That didn't matter, though. With these two clips, the move against Wright was on; it was like a political necrotizing bacteria; it even caused many who had previously fully embraced Wright and his message to question everything he might have preached.

The goal of African Americans was to get Obama in the White House, and many probably hoped they would be able to connect with the would-be president in ways they had not been able to connect with the federal government in the past. African Americans were caught up in the profound symbolism and history that was being made; no matter what, they wanted Obama to win. It seemed that they were completely forgetting that should Obama win, he wouldn't be "America's black president," suggesting that perhaps he would do more for black people than previous presidents had done. No, Obama would be the president of the American people, of whom black people were a part. Prior to this election, there was a sort of drunken ecstasy, it seemed, among black people, and mounting unrealistic fears among white people. A different type of emotion than ever before—caused by race, not reality—swirled around this election. Obama's race made both African Americans and whites giddy with unrealistic expectations; blacks, it seemed, were expecting that Obama's election would mean relief for the race economically, socially, and politically; whites, it seemed, expected that his election would cause America's slow descent into hell. The unrealistic expectations of both races, exacerbated by the fears of many whites, made people distance themselves from Wright, and made some whites distance themselves from Obama. African Americans were angry at Wright for possibly "messing up" the opportunity for a black man to win the presidency; whites were angry at Wright for being less than nobly patriotic. Both blacks and whites wanted Wright to go away. This writer heard some say that Wright was "hurting the black race" and they were clearly irritated at the thought. If whites were frightened by the clips, blacks were mortified. Both blacks and whites felt the pull of this historical moment, but neither group knew quite what to do with it. The country was in disarray.

The clips were bad enough, but when Wright spoke at the National Press Club, a milestone was placed solidly in American political tradition. A line was drawn in the sand: if Obama could not and would not disown his pastor, then Obama was not right for the job of President of the United States. Period. End of discussion.

It had to be hard for Obama because he knew this man. Obama had heard his sermons and knew that the character assassination that being done on Wright was wrong, but the movement to use Wright to destroy Obama had garnered momentum and would not stop. The infamous sound bites were played over and over again, on Fox News and on the so-called "mainline" news stations, including the major networks and CNN. There seemed to be no attempt to find out and expose the context of Wright's words. Instead, the clips were aired with little more than a brief "this is Obama's pastor," over and over, playing into the fears of people who wanted to believe they were past their fear of black people and the way black people think, but who realized, upon hearing Wright, that they were not quite as far along as they had thought. Obama tried to ignore the ruckus; prior to Wright's National Press Club speech, he compared Wright to an old uncle or relative who is a mainstay in all families, prone to beliefs that younger family members consider outdated and with which they do not agree. The president even compared Wright to his own grandmother, a white woman, who had obviously had her share of racist thoughts and beliefs and whom Obama had heard spout off a few times on the subject of race.

But those who would be riled would not be quieted. Wright came off as an angry black man, and people shuddered. Was Obama as angry as was his pastor? Anger was not permitted. If Obama was as angry as Wright seemed to be, what did that mean for America? Obama's political opponents were gleeful that they had apparently found "the thing" that was going to push this man out of contention for the nation's highest office, and his supporters were nervous. Obama's explanation of Wright being like "an old uncle" didn't cut it for them. Too much was at stake. America couldn't afford to have an angry black man in the White House. Obama was going to have to be the president of all of the people, not just of black people who felt they had been wronged by America's policies for too long. His agenda would have to be inclusive to a fault. No favoritism; the presidency was no place to make up for lost time or blatantly unfair policies and practices. White people had to feel like they would not be punished by this black man, and Wright was making it hard for them to feel that type of reassurance. Wright might not be what the media was playing him up to be, but nobody really cared about that.

This was politics and the stakes were high. Obama was going to have to choose: his pastor or the presidency. The distancing that had begun in Springfield increased and intensified; it was solidified at the National Press Club. Wright's words that day in April of 2008 changed everything for Obama. Some say that following the National Press Club event Obama threw Wright under the bus; others say that Wright, in that same appearance, threw the young presidential hopeful under the bus first by not being more careful about what he said and how he said it.

Contrary to what some have said, Wright did not schedule his appearance at the National Press Club during the height of the 2008 election. His appearance had been planned and confirmed long before Barack Obama announced that he would run for president. Wright is a co-founder and a member of the Board of Trustees of the Samuel DeWitt Proctor Conference, Inc., a group dedicated to helping African American churches form and implement social justice agendas by providing them capacity to do so and the necessary resources. It was named after the late Samuel DeWitt Proctor, a well-loved and well-respected preacher known to African Americans and others, who had a special gift and affinity for getting people to see the need for the church to be engaged in social justice ministry.

On that day, April 28, 2008, Wright gave a brilliant presentation on the black church. This was not new for him; he has a love for the black church and knowledge of how it has helped African Americans survive racism in America. His presentation that day was typical, vintage Wright: sweeping, yet detailed in its historical scope; illustrative on the role of the black church in history; and intense in its message that the black church must never cease to be. He told the gathered group that for the two days that the SDPC conference would be meeting beginning later that day, the "various streams of the black religious experience" would be addressed,

> streams which require full courses at the university and graduate school level, and cannot be fully addressed in a two-day symposium, and streams which tragically remain invisible in a dominant culture which knows nothing about those whom Langston

> Hughes calls "the darker brother and sister." It is all those streams that make up this multilayered and rich tapestry of the black religious experience. And I stand before you to open up this two-day symposium with the hope that this most recent attack on the black church is not an attack on Jeremiah Wright; it is an attack on the black church. . . . The most recent attack on the black church; it is our hope that this just might mean that the reality of the African American church may no longer be invisible.[9]

Wright was concerned about the black church; by this time, the infamous sound bites had been played ad nauseum, and he was afraid that the purpose and historical power of the black church was being compromised.

In that speech, Wright stayed away from politics, from Obama, from mentioning the sound bites; he talked in depth about the black church, about liberation theology having started "from the vantage point of the oppressed":

> I call our faith tradition . . . the prophetic tradition of the black church because I take its origins back past Jim Cone, past the sermons and songs of Africans in bondage in the transatlantic slave trade. I take it back past the problem of Western ideology and notions of white supremacy. I take and trace the theology of the black church back to the prophets in the Hebrew Bible and to its last prophet, in my tradition, Jesus of Nazareth.[10]

Wright, the scholar, was on a roll, and his audience, made up primarily of African American preachers, sat spellbound. He reminded everyone there how Sunday morning is the most segregated hour of the week; he told of how the black church had survived becoming an invisible church because of the Black Codes of America (legal statutes and amendments passed by ex-Confederate states after the Civil War designed to limit the freedom of black people and make it legal to use black labor cheaply) and later racist policies. The black church was to be respected and admired because it had endured, he said; the meetings that the Samuel DeWitt Proctor Conference would have over the next two days would serve to preserve and enrich the black church.

Wright spoke of the elephant ever present "in the room" in America: race.

> Now, as an honest dialogue about race in this country begins, a dialogue called for by Senator Obama and a dialogue about to begin in the United Church of Christ among 5,700 congregations in just a few weeks . . . maybe now, as that dialogue begins, the religious tradition that has kept hope alive for people struggling to survive in countless hopeless situations, maybe that religious tradition will be understood, celebrated, and even embraced by a nation that seems not to have noticed why 11 o'-clock on Sunday morning has been called the most segregated hour in America.[11]

Wright laid it out that the black church had been a cloth that, for many African Americans, served as a shield from the sharp winds of oppression. He talked about God's desire being for a "positive, meaningful and permanent change."[12] He cited Luke 4:18, where Jesus quotes Isaiah 61: "The spirit of the Lord is upon me, because he has anointed me to bring good news to the poor. He has sent me to proclaim release to the captives and recovery of sight to the blind, to let the oppressed go free, to proclaim the year of the Lord's favor."

Wright showed his passion for what he believed to be the will of God. Oppression, racial or otherwise, was not, could not be pleasing to a God who had created us all. This God, who embraced us all, also embraced liberation theology, said Wright. This God wanted reconciliation:

> God does not desire us, as children of God, to be at war with each other, to see each other as superior, inferior, to hate each other, abuse each other, misuse each other, define each other or put each other down.
>
> God wants us reconciled, one to another. And that third principle in the prophetic theology of the black church is also and has always been at the heart of the black church experience in North America. . . . The prophetic theology of the black church is a theology of liberation; it is a theology of transformation, and it is ultimately a theology of reconciliation.[13]

Because God had made us all in God's image, Wright continued, regardless of religion or color, God wanted us reconciled, and he acknowledged that reconciliation "is where the hardest work is found for those of us in the Christian faith . . . because it means some critical thinking and some re-examination of faulty assumptions" that we had, all of us, carried for far too long.

The speech was brilliant, hitting all the points that Wright felt that concerned theologians, pastors, and preachers should be seriously considering, but it wasn't what the press wanted. When the questions from the National Press Club moderator began, it was as though she had not heard a word that he had just said. Her first question was about Wright's statement that "America's chickens have come home to roost," something that had been played in the sound bites. She and the gathered press didn't want to hear about the black church, about liberation theology or reconciliation of God's people. Wright hadn't been controversial at all in this presentation; though he had been hurt and, frankly, angered by the way the sound bites had been used to malign him and his ministry, mischaracterizing him as a man who preached hatred, he clearly wanted to move on. The press, however, was after ratings; they wanted to see and hear the man who had been labeled "incendiary," the one who it was said used "divisive" language. Wright's presentation had been anything but that, and the press might have been disappointed.

Wright wanted to move on, to do the work he had been doing for years. His message was about people being liberated, not held prisoner by a hostile culture. That was one of the things about which he had preached for years—a culture that had no interest in including all of America's citizens in reach of true liberation and freedom. To be manipulated and controlled by the dominant culture was just another way of being enslaved, something Wright knew all too well. As he had preached to his congregants to recognize this manipulation and to not be ensnared by it, he now had to do the same himself, as he had, undoubtedly, done many times before.

But the press tasted blood; there was Wright, in their midst. They could "have at him" and, they thought, expose this man who had been Obama's pastor, for who he was. So, it was not surprising that the moderator of the National Press Club was not interested in the speech Wright had just given about the black church and the important role the black church had at this time in history, but it was certainly annoying to the embattled preacher and pastor. Immediately upon the completion of his remarks, the moderator began her questioning, making it obvious that whatever Wright had just said was unimportant.

"You have said that the media have taken you out of context," she began. "Can you explain what you meant in a sermon shortly after 9/11 when you said that the United States had brought the terrorist attacks on itself? Quote, 'America's chickens are coming home to roost?'"[14]

Clearly irritated, Wright asked her, "Have you heard the whole sermon?"

The moderator replied, "I heard most of it," to which Wright responded sharply, "No, no the whole sermon, yes or no? No, you haven't heard the whole sermon? That nullifies the question."[15]

It seemed clear to all who had heard the whole sermon that Wright had caught the moderator in a bad place, which Wright illumined.

"Well, let me try to respond in a nonbombastic way," he said quietly, yet decisively. "If you heard the whole sermon, first of all, you heard that I was quoting the ambassador from Iraq. That's number one. But, number two, to quote the Bible, "Be not deceived. God is not mocked. For whatsoever you sow, that you also shall reap. Jesus said, 'Do unto others as you would have them do unto you.'"

"You cannot do terrorism on other people and expect it never to come back on you. Those are biblical principles, not Jeremiah Wright bombastic, divisive principles."[16]

We will examine that sermon, entitled "The Day of Jerusalem's Fall," in a later chapter, but Wright's points were well-taken. Neither this woman, nor the press, which had latched onto the sound bites, had heard or read the sermon in its entirety. This was a political battle, a manufactured creation of and about an "angry black man" who also happened to be the long-time pastor of the man who might be president. Truth did not matter, and that bothered Wright, who, though he had criticized the government for its socioeconomic oppression of black, brown, and poor people from the beginning of his ministry, had never preached hatred. If anything, he preached awareness so that people could be empowered to fight the oppression they faced. That, it seemed, was the basis of his liberation theology message. That he was being characterized as a hatemonger was particularly offensive. All he had ever done was preach that the "good news" was good for blacks and others as well as for the dominant culture. He had taught his listeners to become aware of the self-hatred they had internalized as the result of having been hated by this same dominant culture, and had taught them that it had kept them in a dark place.

He wanted anyone who would listen to know that slavery in America had not been of God or from God, in spite of theologians having used the "Ham Doctrine" for years to justify their theology of oppression.[17] There had been something wrong with a religion that allowed oppression and the claim that the oppression was biblically sanctioned. Wright had been a careful teacher, not relying on opinion, but rather on careful biblical and historical scholarship. Wright wanted black people to stop being in pain because they were, in fact, black. He wanted them to know that God loved them as much as God loved everyone else. He needed black people to know that they had a place in God's world and in God's heart. And in the midst of all this, he also wanted them to know that God did not sanction hatred against anyone, even against those who had been so unfair to others.

Did he hate racism as an American anomaly? Yes. Did he hate economic and social oppression? Yes! But although racism in all its ugliness had been the work of white people in America, he did not hate white people. He would preach, "Everyone who is white ain't your enemy, and everybody black ain't your friend." Hatred for anyone was out of the will of God. More than anything, Jeremiah Wright grasped the essence of God's will: that in the midst of all things, good or bad, there must be love. That the moderator seemed not to have the slightest interest in who Jeremiah Wright was, or what his message was, or what those sound bites were about, was particularly painful for the man in the eye of the storm. The situation was all the more maddening because it felt so contrived, so political, an effort to shift the course of history, which, even after all of this, would not be shifted. As Wright addressed the moderator's questions, those in the room who knew how this was going to sound to the millions watching and listening, cringed in pain. A tear rolled down the cheek of one of Wright's "daughters" in the ministry. This was going so badly! This was supposed to be a glorious time for the pastor who had helped nurture a young African American man to the point where he was today. This was supposed to be a time to celebrate what Wright's ministry had been about from the beginning, and instead, his work, his ministry, his message, all seemed to be crashing and burning.

After the National Press Club event, which was followed the day after by then-Senator Barack Obama officially distancing himself from his pastor, it was hard to hear anything positive about Jeremiah Wright. People in his own denomination, people who had supported him, now turned against him, angry because they believed he had ruined the chance for the first African American to become president of the United States. Instant arguments could be ignited just by mentioning Wright's name—and the description of him always came out as a hateful man. Over and over, he was called "incendiary" and "divisive." Some churches that had extended invitations to him withdrew those invitations; some people whom he had nurtured in his ministry shunned him, saying, he had "undone" the work done by blacks over the years.

Some people in his own denomination turned against him, in spite of the fact that his church, Trinity UCC, had been one of the largest contributors to that denomination's "Our Church's Wider Ministry" fund for years[18] and that he had been one of the most sought-after preachers at the denomination's events. All his life he had worked to teach about how to use religion to combat a society that had little regard for "the least of these"; all his life he had worked to teach an oppressed people how to thrive in spite of that oppression, and now the oppression was swallowing him up.

The comforting thing, if there is to be any comfort, is that Jeremiah Wright remained and remains a prophet, preaching with the same point and purpose as did the biblical prophets, as did people like William Sloan Coffin and Martin Luther King Jr. He remained and remains committed to preaching a message that challenges injustice, in spite of opposition from the powers that be. Jesus said that a prophet is without honor in his own country (Matt. 13:57; Mark 6:4). The 2008 presidential election thrust Wright into that category—a prophet without honor—but yet, he has held onto his understanding of "the good news." The late Rev. Peter Gomes, the chaplain at Harvard University at the time of his death, said, "The good news for some people is bad news for others."[19] He talked about the "reticence of the pulpit," characterized by clergy who are more interested in maintaining the status quo than in confronting that which is out of alignment with what Jesus would have us do.[20] Jeremiah Wright was never reticent, not even after the assault upon his ministry was launched. He preached and still does preach in the tradition of the Hebrew prophets, who riled feathers and threatened kings with their words of warning against those who "forsake God."

And so some watched in horror as what should have been a glorious moment of triumph for Jeremiah Wright turned into a debacle. It is and was a tragedy of Shakespearean proportion. More importantly, it is a tragedy that should never have been.

I

IN THE BEGINNING
YOUNG AND BLACK IN AMERICA

A community is democratic only when the humblest and weakest person can enjoy the highest civil, economic, and social rights that the biggest and most powerful possess.

—A. PHILIP RANDOLPH

In the year 1941, the war in Europe, spawned by a ruthless tyrant named Adolph Hitler, was in full gear. Winston Churchill, the prime minister of Great Britain, was anxious for the United States to join the war effort, with "boots on the ground," but President Franklin Delano Roosevelt was not so eager to oblige; he had all but promised his nation that it would not participate in the war. Nevertheless, the world was in an uproar because of the war. It was a year in which events would happen that would change the course of history forever.

On January 6, 1941, FDR gave his "Four Freedoms Speech." Said the president:

> In the future days, which we seek to make secure, we look forward to a world founded upon four essential freedoms.
>
> The first is freedom of speech and expression—everywhere in the world.
>
> The second is freedom of every person to worship God in his own way—everywhere in the world.
>
> The third is freedom from want—which, translated into world terms, means economic understandings which will secure to every nation a healthy peacetime life for its inhabitants—everywhere in the world.
>
> The fourth is freedom from fear—which, translated into world terms, means a world-wide reduction of armaments to such a point and in such a thorough fashion that no nation will be in a position to commit an act of physical aggression against any neighbor—anywhere in the world.[1]

There were other important events for and affecting African Americans in 1941. Duke Ellington recorded his hit song "The A Train," the National Gallery of Art opened in Washington, D.C., and Richard Wright and Paul Greene's *Native Son* premiered in New York. In May of that year, the movie *Citizen Kane* premiered in New York, the fragrance Chanel No. 5 was released, and Joe DiMaggio began a fifty-six-game hitting streak. Joseph Stalin became the premier of Russia. FDR signed the "GI Bill of Rights and later issued Executive Order 8802 forbidding discrimination against African Americans in government agencies and defense industry plants. Roosevelt signed the order as part of a deal with A. Philip Randolph; the latter was threatening to call a March on Washington, and the president, fearing racial violence, would not agree to the march but offered the executive order instead.

In 1941, Cook Third Class Doris "Dorie" Miller, USN, aboard the *USS West Virginia* when the Japanese attacked Pearl Harbor, defended his ship and his fellow soldiers on that fateful day by firing a 50-caliber Browning anti-aircraft machine gun, though he had never been trained to use it. He was an African American, and African Americans were generally not allowed to engage in combat, making Miller's actions all that more heroic. . . . In the same year, Congressman Arthur Mitchell (D-Illinois) successfully argued to the United States Supreme Court that African Americans were entitled to have interstate seating privileges equal to those of white passengers. Mitchell had been the only African American, a Democrat, up to that point to have been elected to Congress.

Jesse Jackson Sr., whom we know as the Rev. Jesse Jackson—was born in 1941. And on September 22, 1941, Jeremiah Alvesta Wright fell violently and brutally from his mother's womb, so much so that he was not expected to live. He came three months early.

He was born into a world that was roiled in conflict and into a nation that had still not fixed its "race problem." In spite of FDR's eloquent "Four Freedoms" speech, at least two of those freedoms—freedom from want and freedom from fear—were elusive pipe dreams to far too many black people. Jeremiah Wright, thrust into this world before he was fully developed, was born apparently tagged by God to meet this "race problem" head-on.

In his book *What Makes You So Strong?* Wright recounts the miracle of surviving his traumatic birth. In a sermon entitled "Faith in a Foreign Land," Wright remembers the faith of his father, a powerful presence in his life, who taught him how to lean on God, no matter what. On the day of his birth, Wright writes, his father was returning from a ministerial meeting. When he arrived home that Monday afternoon in September of 1941, he got word that his wife, who had had a difficult pregnancy, had passed out. The baby had come out of her and landed on the floor; his umbilical cord was wrapped around his neck. His wife had been rushed to the hospital; the infant was near death and was not expected to live.

Wright's father rushed to the hospital, where his tiny son had been pronounced dead. He remembered that "they weren't trying to save his life," recalled Wright. He writes: "My daddy didn't call on no 'Babylonian' theology; my daddy didn't look up no 'Babylonian' Christology; my daddy got down on his knees right there on the floor next to his wife's blood and called on the God of Abraham and Sarah, Isaac and Rebekah, and said, 'Lord, if you can and if you will, I know you will save my boy.' And fifty-two years later, here is the one that was pronounced dead on arrival. Don't you tell me what God can't do!"[2]

Jeremiah Wright was one of two children born to Jeremiah Alvesta Wright Sr. and Mary Henderson Wright. Though both his parents were from Virginia, young Jeremiah and his sister, Mary LaVerne, called LaVerne, were born and raised in Philadelphia, Pennsylvania, where his parents moved after finishing college in their native state. Jeremiah is the younger of the two children, by sixteen months. Nobody seems to know where the name "Alvesta" came from; the elder Wright was given the name by his aunt, Hattie Sharp, who helped raise him after his mother was tragically killed in an electrical storm.

Wright the son said that his Aunt Hattie was profoundly spiritual and was a force throughout both his father's and his own life. It might be safely assumed that Aunt Hattie had something to do with the name "Alvesta" being handed down to the tiny, struggling infant at his birth. Wright says that neither he nor his sister ever thought of Hattie as their great-aunt, which she technically was. "She was our aunt and her love for learning in spite of the racist environment in which she was nurtured has helped me keep my eye on the academic prize when forces around me could have very easily distracted me and kept me from reaching my goal," Wright wrote of her, years later.[3]

Not only Aunt Hattie, but both Wright's mother and father instilled in him the value and importance of education from an early age. While Wright's father was the only one in his family to attend college, Mary Henderson was just one of the Henderson children who attended and completed college and graduate school. Whatever this little boy did, getting a good education was going to be front and center. That was a determination made even while his parents depended upon God to save his life at birth.

Wright's father was born and raised in Caroline County, Virginia, the son of a tobacco farmer. He worked hard on the family farm but always had a love for books and education. From the beginning, he walked to and from school every day—no small feat, as the school was literally miles away from the farm—and though he would get home late and had to do his chores, he never let anything get in the way of his studies. He had a hunger to learn, and he let nothing dissuade or discourage him.

When Jeremiah Wright Sr. finished high school, he announced that he was ready to go to college. The family was proud of young Wright and supported his desire to go to college, and so his father took him. He had no idea of how expensive college was, however. He gave his son a quarter with which to begin his college education.[4] While they must have been mortified to learn just how much college would cost, there was no turning back. Wright's grandfather was a preacher; for years he had taught from the scriptures words of hope to a people for whom hope seemed impossible and illogical. Wright the son had heard from Wright the preacher-father that they could do all things through Christ.

And so the journey began. It took Jeremiah Wright Sr. years to complete college because he would have to work a semester, and then take classes, then stop classes again so he could go back to work to earn his tuition. His grandparents were proud of him; they knew how significant it was for black people to get an education, period, and to go to college was an almost unheard-of opportunity. His grandmother Mamie Henderson, who had taught him to read before he got to kindergarten, beamed with pride. Not racism, not a legacy of slavery, not the lack of funds was enough to keep her grandson from doing what he wanted to do.

His college time was precious to him. He was able to study under Carter G. Woodson and Sterling Brown, among others. He read everything he could and absorbed even more, and graduated from Virginia Union with three degrees. It had taken him seven years, but at the end of his time at Virginia Union, he had earned bachelor of theology and bachelor of arts degrees, and then went immediately to seminary (still at Virginia Union) where he earned a master of divinity degree.

Recalls his son: "My daddy used to be an embarrassment to me until I found out a few things. He came straight off the farm. His father sent him to college with twenty-five cents, and Daddy had twelve earned letters behind his name: a B.Th., a B.A., an M.Div., and an S.T.M. He had four degrees: one undergraduate and two graduate degrees from Virginia Union University, a black school, and one from the Lutheran School of Theology."[5]

It was while he was in college that he met the woman who would eventually become his wife. Mary Henderson was a serious student, and

Wright was enchanted by her. From the beginning, theirs was a classic love story; to him, she was always his "best girl," something she reminded him of even as she kissed him good-bye as he lay dying years later. Mary was clearly the love of his life, and he was hers.

Mary was a passionate student. According to Wright, his mother had also been an embarrassment to him sometimes because she seemed "country."

"My mama used to be an embarrassment to me. My mama finished college at an earlier age than Martin Luther King finished. She had a master's degree at eighteen and a second master's degree at twenty-one. She earned a Ph.D. from the University of Pennsylvania, and my mama, with all of that education, would say every time somebody preached or prayed, 'Well! Well! Well!'"[6]

Mary got to know Jeremiah as he continued to attend school off and on; had he not had to attend school like that, for so many years, they might never have met. Nevertheless, they did meet, dated, and married, and after they finished school, they headed to Philadelphia in 1938, where Wright began to pastor a church. Though he had three degrees, and though there was always the belief that life was better "up North," the young pastor did not find that to be the case, at least when it came to making a living for his family. The new husband and highly accomplished college graduate had to work several jobs in order to make ends meet. Nevertheless, he did it. Working several jobs was no more difficult than walking miles to and from school every day in all kinds of weather, or earning college degrees between having to stop every other semester to work. The elder Wright had been prepared for his life in Philadelphia by his time in Caroline County and in his quest for an education.

It was not surprising that the Wrights would instill their love of and ideas about the importance of education in their children too. Young Jeremiah and LaVerne were pushed toward academic excellence. Television was a relatively new phenomenon in American culture; the Wright family got a TV when Jeremiah was almost a teen, but his father was unimpressed; he saw no inherent value in it and refused to let his children watch too much of it. They were allowed to watch it one hour a day. The rest of their "down time," that is, time when they were not doing homework, had to be filled in other ways.

Young Jeremiah took to reading. His father had an extensive library, filled with books that were, according to his own recollection, far too difficult for him. Yet he read. He read books written by Carter G. Woodson, W. E. B. DuBois, and other African Americans, but also books on biblical criticism, theology, church history, and American history. He was fascinated, and reading those books helped shape the trajectory of the rest of his life.

His parents kept a close watch on both their children and monitored their educational progress. His mother was an algebra teacher (a fact that made Jeremiah laugh when he remembered flunking a math course in college.); his father, in addition to being a pastor, was also a substitute teacher in his English class. Wright recalls:

> We had a ritual every night at the dinner table. My parents wouldn't say, "How was school today? If you ask your children that, they can get off real easy—"Fine." One word, and you go on with the rest of your life. But my parents would ask, "What did you do in school today? They would start with the first period and work all the way to the last period.
>
> They would ask my sister first because she was older, and she would go from first period through gym and all the way up through the last period. "What did you read in study hall?" (she would be asked.)
>
> Then they came to me. Daddy said, "And you, young man?" We started in first period and talked about history. Then we talked about math. We went on and got to English. He said, "What did you do in English?" I said, "We're doing Shakespeare."
>
> He said, "Oh, I like Shakespeare. What are you doing, his plays for his poetry?"
>
> "Oh, we're doing his plays." He said, "Which play are you on?"
>
> "*Midsummer Night's Dream.*"
>
> He said, "No, that was yesterday. We're on *All's Well That Ends Well* today.'"[7]

Young Wright's attempt to put something over on his father failed, and, as was the case after this particular conversation where that attempt failed, when that happened he would get a spanking.

Because Wright's mother worked a great distance from the family's home, causing her to have to leave early in the morning and get back very late, Wright's father was more of a "hands-on" father than was the norm of that time, and, though Jeremiah balked at some of his father's involvement in his life when he was a boy, he grew to appreciate the rich lessons his father had given him. He recalls having been angry at his father because he wanted a cap pistol, and his father would not allow it:

> God put a daddy in my house for whom I will go to my grave being thankful. But when I was little, I did not understand this. I did not understand what I had right there in front of me. My daddy would not let me have some cap pistols that my uncle brought (sic) for me. All the other boys had guns, so I didn't understand. I thought it took a gun to make a man, and my daddy was trying to teach me that it didn't take a gun to make a man; it took God to make a man. My peers were teaching me that being a man was a function of my sexuality, and my papa was trying to get me to see that being a man was a function of my spirituality.[8]

Wright's father continued to powerfully impact him; he says his father went "from the tobacco fields of Caroline County, Virginia, to a municipal board seat, the only black on the Juvenile and Rehabilitation Board for the city of Philadelphia . . . but he never got too grand to seek God's guidance."[9]

Wright has fond memories of his father's interactions with him. In a personal letter sent to this writer, Wright recalled a memory that, he wrote, brought a smile to his face and put a smile in his heart:

> Do you remember what "slats" are? That term might date you just a little bit, but those are the pieces of wood that used to be underneath the mattress and box springs on our beds. My father would take a slat, cut it in half, and make me a scooter when we were too poor for our family to afford a "store-bought" scooter.
>
> Daddy would take a roller skate (the old kind of skate that was "one-size fits-all!") This was long before the shoe skates came out. Daddy would separate the skate and put one set of the

> wheels on the front of the slat and the other set of the wheels on the back of the slat. He would not only nail the wheels to the slat. He would also take an orange crate and nail that to the front end of my "scooter" so that it would look like the "Harley Davidson" of ghetto scooters!
>
> I, of course, would decorate the orange crate with bottle caps, foxtails, aerials and anything else I could find. My dad's chest would swell with pride as he saw me "tooling around" the neighborhood on the scooter he had made for me.[10]

As a child, the younger Wright played little league baseball, soccer, and fast-pitch softball. He loved music and was immersed in it from an early age; in school, he played in the jazz band, marching band, and concert band, and also in the school orchestra. He took piano lessons from the time he was in kindergarten until high school but would not practice because he was mercilessly teased by his friends. It is, or was, a common occurrence in African American neighborhoods for children, especially the boys, to strive to fit a certain image, as macho as could be. There was no place for a piano-playing, excellent student in that image, and so young Wright, though he loved music, would not practice. His classical piano playing ended with his playing Chopin in the eleventh grade.

He also grew up surrounded by love. His was a day where neighbors were like family, with permission to spank him if he got "out of line" in their view. Of course, such a spanking from a neighbor meant more trouble for him when he got home, but Wright recalls that the closeness of the neighborhood was a given in that day, where the smallness of the African American community meant they were more like an extended family than mere neighbors.

Wright says his parents sheltered him and his sister from the bad things of life, including racism. They knew racism well, but would not dwell on it. Wright noticed, though, things that his parents did. When the family would visit Virginia in the summer, they would always pack a lunch. That puzzled young Jeremiah, because there were restaurants all along the route. He wondered why they just didn't stop in one or two of those on the way. That's when his father began teaching him that things below the Mason Dixon line were different for black people. Any eating or going to the bathroom had to be done before they crossed that line because his father "refused to subject his children to segregated facilities." The elder Wright explained the Mason Dixon line so well that young Jeremiah recalls looking for it as the family car ambled down the highway.[11]

His father was generous with his love and serious about impressing upon his son values that would be necessary for him to make it in life in general and in America in particular. His father had lived within the folds of racism. He would tell his son how it felt when, growing up, for example, he had seen white kids being transported to and from school in busses while he walked. Seeing acts of racism had left an impression in both his parents, but they wanted Jeremiah and LaVerne to know that racism hadn't been strong enough to keep them from getting a good education and having a good life. After all, they had always had family, a family that was close, stitched together by love and the capacity to hope. He was glad he and Mary had moved "up North"; presumably life would be easier for his children than it had been for him . . . but it was clear that he had loved his life in Caroline County. His talks included vivid stories about what it had been like "back then" in the country, a place where there was no electricity, where there were cows to milk and chickens to feed. There had been nothing wrong with that, his father would share. In fact, it had been good; it had helped build his character. Young Jeremiah would listen, fascinated, to his father's stories; it was as though his father's world was another world. Perhaps in reality it was, but this father cherished his past, racism notwithstanding.

His father was not particularly excited about integration. As he talked about the *Brown vs. Board of Education* case of 1954, he said that it was dangerous. His words confused his young son; he thought that integration was what the "old folks" wanted. Why in the world, then, would such a landmark case be "dangerous?" Wright's father said that the care that African Americans had been able to show to each other in their segregated communities would disappear. . . . As black people sought to assimilate into white culture, much of what had bound them together in community would be sacrificed. It hadn't happened yet, Wright's father said, but it surely would, in time.

His father also tried to shield him from the ugliness of racism; one of the reasons he and Mary had moved north was so that their children would not have to see or experience what they had. So Jeremiah's parents were shocked and saddened when they felt the bitter reality of race and color-consciousness in Philadelphia. There, the elder Wright could see how years of being hated by whites because of who they were had caused black people to hate themselves. There was competition between blacks, sometimes as if blacks were trying to see who could be "less black" in their white world. Jeremiah said that when he was growing up, "folks used to buy a bleaching cream called Nadinola to try to change what God had done. Our dads wore stocking caps to make their hair lie down smoothly like somebody else's."[12]

Black women yearned to have "good hair," which was a euphemism for straight hair, like white women, and went to great lengths to make sure they had it. Chemical relaxers were used by black women, but also by black men, who wanted "good hair" as well. It didn't matter that these chemicals damaged the hair or that they often left horrible burns on the scalps of those who used them. The goal was to leave the relaxer on one's hair for as long as one could tolerate it, because the longer the relaxer stayed on, the straighter one's hair would get. Once done, the process had to be repeated; black men and women and young girls put themselves through this agony every six to eight weeks. Young black girls would just about panic at the mere thought of their hair getting wet, because if it did, the straightened locks would curl up and retreat to their natural state. The goal was to be as "white" as possible. The lighter one's skin, the better; there were some churches and social clubs where only the lightest-skinned blacks could become members. There existed the infamous "brown paper bag" test: if one was darker than a grocery store bag, he or she could not be a member of some organizations.

Racism ran rampant, even in Philadelphia.

The reality of the pervasiveness of racism hit home for Wright in an incident he relates. Another boy, with whom he eventually became friends, had fought him every day for years. Wright didn't understand why, until, after Wright had finally fought him back and thus ended the daily beat-downs, he asked his friend, "Why did you fight me every day like that, beating me up?" He was told, "My mama say we don't trust yellow people." Wright said his friend "was very big and very dark."[13]

When Wright told his parents about what his friend had said, they were saddened: "They thought they had left all that foolishness down in Virginia, with the house slave, field slave stuff. They told us all about the color problem within the African American community. They thought they'd never have to teach us that in Philadelphia, but they did. And the whole time we were friends, I was never allowed in his house. I could go on his porch, but I couldn't go in his house because of what his mama said."[14]

Later, when Wright turned twenty-one, he found out from this friend that the guy had never really liked him anyway; he had befriended him because he liked Wright's sister.[15]

There was no place, it seemed, for a black person to go without racism stubbornly following. Wright's grandmother had been raped by a white man, and the family had endured the pain of remembering that horrific incident. There was no justice for black people injured or wronged by white people, in the South or elsewhere in the country, in spite of the myth that the North was good and the South, bad. When it came to racism, North and South ran neck to neck. Wright's father had hoped that wasn't the case, but he was wrong.

Wright's father taught him the values that he carried through life, including a love for Christianity, though with an ability to see its flaws. He took his call to Christian ministry seriously and taught the values of Jesus the Christ as he saw them. He was a man of deep faith, Wright recalls, a man who could be seen and was seen by his children on his knees praying, either alone or with their mother. His father's values, including his deep love for his family and for God, were values that would stay with his young son.

Wright's mother, Mary Henderson Wright, had a twin who had died at an early age. She grew up in Surrey County, Virginia, also "the country." Five of her siblings had died. Her brother James had died by drowning and, for that reason, Mary never took to the water. She was a woman who came from a family that was deeply committed to education. Wright's grandfather on his mother's side was kept on a plantation until he was twenty years old. Naturally, he had no education when he was freed . . . but that didn't stop him. He began attending elementary school at age twenty and continued through school until he had earned a college degree. Once he had his education, he and his wife taught other blacks who had no education. Education was part of the quilt of the legacy from which Mary Henderson Wright came.[16]

While Wright's father was serious, Mary was a free spirit who loved to laugh and who, even after Wright was grown, would call him on a daily or weekly basis with a savory joke. She "raised us to have a sense of humor," Wright recalled, a humor that one could see and hear in Wright's sermons later in his life. She taught her children how to play pinochle, something their grandparents would never have permitted, because cards were thought to be "of the devil." But they only played when they were away from their grandparents.

Although she was fun-loving, Mary exacted obedience and respect out of her children. Wright recalls a time when he met his mother's wrath head on:

> We didn't have rap when I was young. We had something called "doo-wop." When I was young, the musicians sang music instead of talking it. But all of our songs weren't that good in terms of content, either. We had forty-fives, and they cost less than a dollar. I bought a forty-five RPM called "Cherry Pie." It was a very simple little song. It didn't have a lot of words, but it was one of those good "grinding" (slow, sensual dancing that was fashionable in the fifties) songs. I took it home and began playing it: "Cherry, cherry pie. Cherry, cherry pie. Oooo, so good." The second verse came on: "Gimme, gimme some. . . . "
>
> That's as far as the record got before my mama was in my room and taking the needle up off my forty-five. There wasn't any discussion. She broke my forty-five and said, "If I ever catch you playing it in here or listening to it again, I'm going to beat you from an amazing grace to a floating opportunity."[17]

Mary was strict, as was Wright Sr. She would sometimes grow exasperated with her young son, who alternated between being mischievous and rebellious.

When he was fifteen, Wright remembers that he got into trouble. It was when he was in full rebellion mode and he and his friends decided they'd steal a car. They thought they had gotten away with it, but of course, they had not. Police showed up at the Wright home and took young Jeremiah off to jail in handcuffs. Mary Wright was beside herself. Both she and Jeremiah's father were well-respected members of the community. The incident was embarrassing to them but perhaps more important to Mary was a fear that her son was taking "the wrong turn" in life that would lead him away from all she and his dad had tried to make possible for him. She was furious when he got home from jail and wanted to spank him, but the elder Wright said no. Mary fumed, but her husband was able to calm her down. Their son would be all right . . . even though he had embarrassed them and made a profound impact on his own life. Wright recalls that evening:

> When I go to speak at various churches, there's a nice biography on me on the back of the program and a nice blurb in the newspapers, but what these don't tell you is that at fifteen years of age, I was busted for grand larceny auto theft. And the night after my father got me out of prison and took me home, I was waiting for the whipping I knew I had coming. I heard him and my mother in their bedroom singing, "I thank you, Jesus. . . . " Now it seems to me that they were thanking God because we were financially in a jam; they were thanking him because we didn't have any money; they were thanking him because we didn't have enough food; or they were thanking him because I was messing up. But I was just looking at the horizontal dimension. I could see the vertical hookup that my mama and my daddy had. I did not know back then that they were thanking him in advance for all that they had the audacity to hope for. . . . I did not know they were thanking him for how they hoped God would intervene and for what he would one day do for and through their son . . . "[18]

That night and his parents' reaction to what he had done had more of an impact on the young teen than any spanking or "whipping" could have had. Before his parents retreated to pray, Wright's father, so sad because of what his son had done, said out loud that perhaps Jeremiah didn't want to be a part of their family. The battle, however, was not theirs, and Wright's father knew it. The most effective weapon his parents, and their parents before them, had ever used in their lives, facing and fighting not only racism, but all of its attendant problems, was their relationship to God. With God, all things were possible.

A spanking could not have bored its way into his soul as did the realization of how deeply connected to God his parents actually were. He did not stop rebelling; he did other things that caused his parents angst, but young Jeremiah Wright was being fed the lessons of faith that he would need to navigate an unkind, racist world. A black man, he was learning, needed God, not guns, prayer, not false pride. Jeremiah was learning from his parents what he needed to know in order to be what God had called him to be. He was growing up in an era where fewer and fewer African Americans were willing to be silent and take what racism doled out. It is a tribute to his parents' understanding of the gospel that Wright's anger as he left his parents' fold was one expressed within the stories and lessons of the Bible; his ministry was one that was geared to set the captives free, as Jesus declared his ministry would be in the Gospel of Luke. His childhood was one where he saw his parents on their knees praying out loud, and he knew that their faith was not for show but was just the most important tool they used that kept them sane and full of hope in a world that seemed determined to drain African Americans of both.

2

THE COUNTRY, COLLEGE, AND CONTRADICTIONS

Ministers are called to recognize the sufferings of their time in their own hearts and make that recognition the starting point of their service. Whether we try to enter into a dislocated world, relate to a convulsive generation, or speak to a dying person, our service will not be perceived as authentic unless it comes from a heart wounded by the suffering about which we speak.

—Henri Nouwen[1]

Not even a praying, devoted, dedicated, and loving father and mother could shield young Jeremiah from the realities of life. The son of the preacher man, shielded a great deal from racism while he was at home, not only experienced racism when he left home, but also some troubling contradictions between what he thought religion was supposed to be and what it actually was.

His father was a kind, sincere man who did not gossip, who prayed even as he advised others to pray. He worked hard to make sure his two children received the love and attention they needed; he sheltered them as much as he could from the racism he had seen and experienced growing up in Caroline County, Virginia. To young Jeremiah, his parents, but perhaps especially his father, was the prototype of what a Christian should be, and, as his father was, he believed all people were, or at least should be.

But as he grew older, he saw that not every clergy person was as sincere and honest as was his dad. He saw that commitment to social justice did not seem to be the norm among clergy or church-folks in general. The civil rights movement was in full gear, and Wright was becoming keenly aware of the division between the Christ that his father had taught him and preached about, and the practice of Christianity by "believers." He had read Dr. Martin Luther King's "Letter from a Birmingham Jail," in which King addressed white clergy who urged African Americans to back off and be patient. Eight prominent white clergymen in Alabama had published an open letter, criticizing King for the sit-ins and demonstrations, and had so moved King that he responded to them while being held in jail in Birmingham. Some clergy had actually criticized the nonviolent movement and blamed it for the violence that was erupting all over the country, and King responded, "Injustice anywhere is a threat to justice everywhere. We are caught in an inescapable network of mutuality, tied by a single garment of destiny. Whatever affects one directly affects all indirectly. . . . You deplore the demonstrations that are presently taking place in Birmingham. But I am sorry that your statement did not express a similar concern for the conditions that brought the demonstrations into being."[2]

Young Wright was finding it hard to come to grips with what his father had taught him, what he had understood the Gospels to mean, and what he was now seeing with his own eyes. He knew white people; he had grown up in Germantown, Pennsylvania, where he came into contact and was friends with many white and Jewish people. He had attended Central High School, where out of two thousand students, only sixty were African American. And he knew black people, or so he thought. He had grown up around white people, but had been loved and nurtured by black people. He had been graced to have a father and mother who nurtured and affirmed him and who based their lives on the theology of Jesus. He thought that all clergy were like his father: sincere, honest, truly connected to and convicted about the gospel, and that gave him a measure of peace, because his father for him represented the truth about God and religion and the capacity of humans to do "good," shunning all that was evil or in any way detrimental to "the least of these." He knew Matthew 25 well, how Jesus separated the sheep from the goats and said that those who took care of "the least of these" were embraced by Jesus because they were in effect doing to Jesus what they were doing for those in need. It was a gospel he could live with. His father had been his role model and had taught him well.

But when he left his parents' house, the breach he saw and experienced between what he thought "should be" and what actually occurred was nearly overwhelming. If the gospel were true, if it were compelling, which he believed it to be because of his father's life and example, then the world should reflect the same. If religious people, if Christians, followed the Christ and Christian precepts, the problems of the world should be on the decrease, not the reverse. Instead he was seeing people who professed to know and to love God but whose way of thinking absolutely stunned him. Now he saw white clergy who hated blacks just because they were black, or white clergy, like those King addressed in his letter from jail, who professed to be champions of and for racial justice, but who opposed the civil rights movement and wanted blacks to stay in their place. He also saw black clergy who were afraid, it seemed, to own up to being black. He could almost get over the injustice against blacks by whites; he knew, at least, that that kind of thing was part of history. But what stunned him more was how black people treated other black people—and the mistreatment was done, many times, by those who said they loved God. He saw people who witnessed injustice but chose to ignore it. It made no sense; it did not connect with how he had been raised.

"I was angry at people in church who weren't doing anything. I was mad at the church. I was mad at colored preachers,"[3] he said. By this time, he was participating in sit-ins in downtown Richmond, Virginia, to protest racist department store policies, like those that let black people buy garments but not try them on; the stores didn't even have fitting rooms for black people. He remembered being appalled when black people, whose rights the sit-ins were being staged to protect, would not support what the students were doing, and in fact criticized them. He was miffed that when he went home to Philadelphia and, with a group of students, tried to organize sit-ins and boycotts against Woolworth's, a national chain, black people, some of whom were members of his father's church, pushed past the students, saying out loud that racism was a Southern problem. As he got older, he saw more that bothered him, not less. People were not "getting it," including clergy.

Jeremiah remembers sitting on the front steps of a church, drinking wine with some friends. With the help of the wine, they laid out their complaints. Jeremiah remembers that day: "I was angry at people in church who weren't doing anything. Many people in the black church 25 years ago would not take part in the Civil Rights Movement. They weren't addressing racism. They had all of these European pictures of Bible characters hanging up in churches—biblical people with blond hair and blue eyes—like Norwegians. I didn't want anything to do with that type of church."[4]

Jeremiah knew from his time spent in his father's library as a little boy and from reading the Bible that the story of creation and the events of Jesus' life had taken place in Africa, at a place where rivers he had been taught about as a boy merged:

> Now the Lord God had planted a garden in the east, in Eden; and there he put the man he had formed. And the Lord God made all kinds of trees grow out of the ground, trees that were pleasing to the eye and good for food. In the middle of the garden were the tree of life and the tree of the knowledge of good and evil.
>
> A river watering the garden flowed from Eden; from there it was separated into four headwaters. The name of the first is the Pishon; it winds through the entire land of Havilah, where there is gold. . . . The name of the second river is the Gihon; it winds through the entire land of Cush. The name of the third river is the Tigris; it runs along the east side of Asshur. And the fourth river is the Euphrates. (Gen. 2:8–14 NIV)

How in the world could there be racism, how could there be such blatant disregard for what was written in the Bible describing the geographical origin of all creation? How could anyone, white or black, ignore what was written in the text, a text they all said they revered, and still condone racism and white supremacy? Why did white folks, and apparently black folks as well, ignore what was written? What was described in Genesis 2 happened in biblical Ethiopia, (designated by the name "Cush"), which was also the general term for Africa. Today, what is described in Genesis would be happening south of Egypt, or present-day Sudan. Why didn't people know that, Wright wondered? *Did* they know it? Had they—both black and white clergy—just chosen to ignore what was in their beloved Bible? Wright grew sullen, and then angry.

He was beginning to see the religious and biblical foundation of racism . . . and it caused a violent tear in his soul. Nobody had the chutzpah, it seemed, to challenge an obvious oversight at best, a blatant lie at worst. Wright was still struggling to come to terms with his feelings about church, God, and Christian people. He was also dealing with himself as a young man in rebellion mode. He had always been a good student, yet at Virginia Union he ended up flunking a math course (his parents, but especially his mother, a math teacher, was mortified) and got a "C" in zoology. He hadn't earned grades like that before, and it bothered him some . . . but the conflict he felt within because of his confusion about church and God and the presence of racism was more pressing. He was involved in music; he was the president of the choir, and he had a lot of friends. But inside, he was unsettled. He was disturbed. Black people, good church-going, college-attending black people, seemed confused and full of self-hatred.

He had grown up around music and loved all kinds, but in college he was shocked to learn that a student could be put out of the choir if he or she dared try to sing Gospel music. Even in a black school, the Eurocentric model of what "should be" was dominant. Why would God allow a people to hate themselves like that? Perhaps it can be said that he was trying to define God, even as he tried to figure out how God really worked. Was God really good? If so, how come God allowed people to treat others so poorly—primarily on the basis of race? What was up with that? Did not God love the very people God had created? Hadn't God created everyone, and weren't all people children of God? Had God intentionally created a race of people forever destined to be stepchildren? Did God care for them as much as God seemed to care for white people? Where was the compassion and the love that he had always been taught were the trademarks of God and of those who loved God? He saw religious people treat other people miserably, and he could not understand why God let it happen. Suddenly, it didn't feel right to hear people talk about God, and shout and praise God in worship on Sundays, only to come out of church and treat each other miserably.

Jeremiah was on a track to complete his undergraduate degree and then enter seminary, but now he wasn't so sure. That he saw problems between blacks and whites was problematic enough; but seeing it *between blacks and other blacks* was too much. His soul was tearing, little by little. Finally, carrying pain, confusion, and frustration, he quit college. His mind had been challenged academically, but his soul had been trodden upon. The pieces of the puzzle were not fitting; the life he thought was common to all—the life of the caliber of his father—was not so common after all. He had come to college wanting to be like his father; when he left, it is not clear that he was sure what or whom he wanted to like. It was too confusing. He admits that at the time he left Virginia Union, he was bitter. "As a senior, I could not in good conscience go to seminary," he said.[5]

Jeremiah Wright needed time to think, and so he enlisted in the military.

But being in the service didn't help much. The year was 1966 and the nation was in the throes of the civil rights movement. In Birmingham, the so-called "Children's March" had brought young black children and young adults to the streets in droves to protest racism and discrimination. They showed remarkable resolve and courage in spite of Bull Connor's fire hoses and police dogs. It was hard to watch, but his anger grew as white soldiers laughed and poked fun at images of African American women and children being hosed down by police officers and attacked by dogs. *Many of the scoffers were Christian.* Wright could not understand what he was seeing, and could not accept it.

It happened that one weekend he found himself with some of his soldier buddies discussing the issues of the day. They sat on the steps of a church drinking wine and were soon joined by a man who, he learned only four hours later, was the pastor of that church. Rev. Houston Brooks, listened patiently: the spinelessness of clergy, the dishonesty and/or ignorance of clergy, and the break between the real and the ideal in terms of Christ-like behavior was too much.

Wright recalls that the pastor allowed him to vent and rant, his only response being, "You're right son. You're right." Wright told the pastor that he didn't like the church, but the pastor challenged him and eventually said to his now-drunk rebel that he believed Wright, in fact, loved the church. He offered his insight:

> I don't think you're mad at the church. I think you're mad at white racism and what colored Uncle Toms have done to the church, but I don't think you're mad at the church. I don't think you've got anything against Jesus. I don't think you have anything against God. Let me just ask you this: Where do you think you can do the most good? On the outside of the church, throwing stones at it? Because you've got an eight-inch Howitzer and you're blowing it to bits. Can you do the most good out here shooting the church down, or can you do the most good on the inside working to change that which you love with all your heart? Don't answer me right now . . .[6]

The following morning, Wright attended Brooks's church and joined, and it seemed that perhaps he was making his way back "to that which he loved." But the journey would take a little while longer. There were just too many questions and too much disappointment he saw to embrace fully his beloved black church. He simply needed more time.

Wright had joined the military in 1961 and served a total of six years. The Vietnam War was going on, but he was never deployed there. He was stationed in Camp LeJeune after he had spent time doing basic training at Montford Point, the place where all African Americans were sent for combat training before President Truman desegregated the troops.

This was yet another critical time in the shaping of Wright's worldview. It was while he was there that he learned troubling information from military intelligence sources about things that happened and why. He remembers being shocked when he learned that America had entered World War II under less than honorable circumstances. "The United States knew that the Japanese were going to attack Pearl Harbor," he said. President Roosevelt needed a reason to get into the war, as there was a fair amount of opposition to the United States becoming involved. FDR knew that an attack on American ships on American soil would make entering the war a no-brainer. The revelation was devastating to Wright. "Men lost their lives," Wright recalls thinking. Their lives and the lives of their families were not paramount in importance. A few lives lost because of this strategic plan of the Executive Branch of the government was the cost to be paid for democracy. It made Wright sick.[7]

He learned during that time that the Vietnam War was yet another war that was causing mass loss of life, not for democratic ideals, but for other reasons. By the time that war broke out, Wright was working in military hospitals. He saw men who had gone to Vietnam whole but who came home mutilated, physically and mentally: "I started talking to the guys in Intel, to see if there was any military proof (to things he had read in history books about the war) and found out stuff that was like common knowledge now. . . . United States, up to the Executive office, knew the Japanese were going to bomb Pearl Harbor. That's why the fleet was sent away, so we'd have an excuse to get into that war. . . . I said, you mean to tell me, they knew those Japanese planes were coming and we were gonna lose people. They said, 'Yeah, you know. You lose some for a greater good.'"[8]

The revelations angered Wright. "We're not in this war (Vietnam) for any democratic purposes. We're not in this war for anything noble. . . . I'm in the naval hospital, I'm talking with guys whose lives are mangled forever, and whose stories make this movie *Apocalypse Now* seem like a cake walk." He continued:

> To find out what our military was doing, there was something in *Time* Magazine . . . about My Lai. My Lai wasn't anything. We did stuff so much worse than My Lai. We—the United States military—that it would literally, well it literally turned my stomach. I couldn't eat for . . . guys coming home with penises and ears cut off . . . stuffing their pockets. . . . That kind of reality was what was going on in Vietnam because it was a war that we knew we couldn't win.[9]

The wars America had fought, Wright learned, were about business, power, and money. "The war in Vietnam had nothing to do with democracy," he said. Democracy was the catch-word used, the word to make Americans rally to the war cause, but democracy had very little to do with any of the wars America had fought, Wright was learning, and it had a deep impact on him.[10]

As Wright worked in military hospitals (he had been trained as a cardiopulmonary technician), he would have conversations with the wounded vets. He would listen as they shared with him what the Vietcong would say to Americans at night, words that hit hard every soldier who was not white. Wright said they recalled the Vietcong saying, "Hey, black GI, why you (sic) over here fighting for the white man when you know you can't live next to him when you get home? We will write your obituary tonight; you can read it in the morning. It will say, 'Here lies a black man, killed by a yellow man, fighting for the white man, who stole his land from the red man.'"[11] What the African American blacks were doing was puzzling to the Vietcong. They were fighting for a people and government that had historically had little regard for people of color. "Why are you fighting?" the Vietcong wondered. The question jarred Wright because its apparent truth was piercing.

In spite of his disillusionment, Wright continued to serve . . . and to read about his country, its politics, and its history. He says that for six years, he was reading two to three books a week.[12] While in the military he heard, over and over again as concerned the Vietnam War, that it was a war that we could not win. Guys there, he said, were counting time, counting the days, before they would be finished with their deployment. Nobody understood, least of all Wright, why the United States was in a war that had nothing to do with democracy. "It (had) nothing to do with democracy as we knew it or as we were then to embrace. These fights (were) about business and about people getting rich, not us. Why are we here? It was not . . . good."[13]

He had joined the military because he needed someplace to go, something constructive to do, and someplace to sort things out after he quit college. But he had also joined because *he was an American* who wanted to serve his country. He wasn't against America because of the racism he saw and was experiencing; he wanted to *understand* America. He didn't want to leave America; he was clear and glad that he was an American citizen, but he wanted to figure out how to navigate the difficulties caused by racism. He wanted a citizenship with full rights and benefits, like white people had. He wanted to understand where God was in all of this as well. Turning his back on his country was not his goal nor was it his desire. He was not unlike African Americans who had fought in the Revolutionary War, or in the Civil War. Blacks had historically *wanted* to serve America, and had done so, even when, as in the case of the Civil War, they were denied weapons and properly fitting boots.

While Wright did not serve in combat duty, he would have, had he been called to do so. He was not against his country; he hated, though, what he was learning about imperialism and about the motives of the powers that be. He was looking for answers; he was trying to find his place in the world, both secularly and spiritually. He was defining his dreams and trying to hear God's voice, even as he struggled with Christians participating in racism and with black Christians being apathetic to it. He was angry and confused, but he was still an American and he was still a child of God. His experiences in the military did nothing to make him believe that racism would go away; the treatment he received there and the behavior of some of his white colleagues convinced him that racism was deeply embedded in America's soul. It was a sobering reality.

The tension that Wright felt between what he thought *should be* and what was did not decrease while he was in the military. As he read, and thus continued to learn things that bothered his soul, he remembers being stunned as he learned that many of the "great minds" in American culture had been voices for the upholding of racism and white supremacy. In a book called *Slavery, Defended,* he read that a Yale-educated scholar posited that the snake that appeared in the story of the Garden of Eden actually represented "a Negro gardener," for everyone knew a snake could not talk. This scholar, among others, used religion to justify racism. It was nothing new; the Babylonian Talmud, the Holy Koran, and other holy books had done the same. Nonetheless, the more Wright read and learned the more concerned he became. Going to the military had only sharpened his vision so that he could see the reality of human behavior as concerned race and religion. The myths with which he had grown up were slowly going away, fading into a cavernous past. Wright, like Jacob in the Bible, was now wrestling as he never had before.[14]

Who was God? What was God's plan and vision for black people? And how did Wright fit into God's plan? These were the questions nipping at Wright's spirit and helping shape what would become his ministry.

3

"WHAT THEN SHALL WE SAY?"

*What then shall we say? Is God unjust?
Not at all!*

—ST. PAUL, LETTER TO THE ROMANS 9:14 NIV

The impact of Wright's father and his "house rules" that included only an hour of television a day was more profound than Wright realized. Though Wright Sr. had worked hard to shield his son from the harsh realities of racism, his son was encountering those realities head-on. He had not been prepared for what he had experienced in college or the military. From his father, he learned that Jesus was a savior of all people; he had internalized the message that God had and distributed a love that knew no favorites, something buoyed by words in the Bible: "So in Christ Jesus you are all children of God through faith, for all of you who were baptized into Christ have clothed yourselves with Christ. There is neither Jew nor Greek, neither slave nor free, male nor female, for you are all one in Christ Jesus. If you belong to Christ, then you are Abraham's seed, and heirs according to the promise" (Gal. 3:26–28 NIV).

Those words were comforting to Wright on one level but profoundly disturbing on another. Although he had at least for the present moved away from the church and any aspirations he had had to go to seminary, "church" was still in him. By now he had seen enough of what church people did to each other; he had seen how church people, theologians, and scholars had manipulated the scriptures to fit their ideologies, passing the same off as theology. He had witnessed what appeared to be the "silence of God" as concerned the way black people were treated in America. The first line of Psalm 10 came to mind: "Why are you so far away, O Lord? Why do you hide yourself when we are in trouble?" (Psa. 10:1 GNT). He was not thinking in terms of what his ministry would be; he was not thinking he would do a ministry at all, at this point, but the seed was being planted, the outline of what his ministry would have to be for black people was being constructed. Was God against black people? Certainly not. What, then? What should he or any other preacher say to a people who had bought into the hype that God had condoned their marginalization and oppression?

"There will be trouble and distress for every human being who does evil; first, for the Jew and then for the Gentile; but glory, honor and peace for everyone who does good; first for the Jew then for the Gentile, For God does not show favoritism" (Rom. 2:9–11 NIV).

Wright's lessons about God were staunch and sure; his father's teachings had been solid. Supposedly, this was a just God, in spite of the injustice in the world. To be "righteous" was to be "in right relationship" with God, meaning that the human being accepted God (and God's son, Jesus) as sovereign. The goodness of God would be pleased by the righteousness of human beings, and in the end, there would be no "favorite child" or favorite or preferred group of people. The message was a comforting one.

But how did one get past the pain of the contradictions? Where was God in what Wright was seeing? He had a deep faith, but his life lessons were clashing with the love-filled lessons given to him by his father, and he was no doubt wrestling with the God of his youth and remembering what he had read so many years ago in his father's study in a book by Carter G. Woodson called *The Mis-Education of the Negro.* He had been a young boy when he'd read it, but Woodson's observations about the white world, and the participation of "Negroes" in that world, had had a profound effect on him, even if he didn't know it at the time. Woodson was extremely critical of the education received by African Americans in America, saying in effect that they had been educated only to imitate their oppressor. He wrote: "The only question which concerns us here is whether these 'educated' persons are actually equipped to face the ordeal before them or unconsciously contribute to their own undoing by perpetuating the regime of the oppressor."[1]

Woodson had written that "when you control a man's thinking you do not have to worry about his actions."[2] Wright was now fully appreciating the words of Woodson he had read so many years ago as he sat in his father's study. It would seem that Woodson had observed white American culture correctly and the participation of African Americans in that culture, but he was clear he could not allow any system, person, or religious rhetoric—to control his thinking.

But . . . what was he to think, really, about God, about this world, about good and evil, about racism . . . about the church? He came across people, black people, who would rather be white, and again he remembered the words of Woodson, "The difficulty is that the "educated Negro" is compelled to live and move among his own people whom he has been taught to despise."[3] He was now seeing this in ways he had never seen in the South where he had visited his parents' loving families, or even in Philadelphia attending all-white schools. Life was giving him teaspoons of the bitter elixir of racism, and he didn't like it. Nor did he like much the way God was being used to justify racism, and he didn't like it that so many African Americans seemed unwilling, unable, or both, speak up against it. Was the God his father taught him real or not? Was that THE God of all, or were there different "gods" for different groups of people? Was there a universal theology of divine, agape love, or was the God who showed agape love an exclusive entity for people who needed to find and hear comfort in an uncomfortable world?

Wright had dropped out of school and had left the church, but he had not left God. He was in a serious struggle with God and with his faith, trying to make sense out of that which seemed to make no sense. He was trying to understand his own people, who seemed, far too often, to be willing to acquiesce to an unjust system. Their religion was not empowering them but was making them beholden to a God who would ordain racism and racist acts. That was not the God he knew or had been taught to love. Again, the words the little boy had read so long ago must have resonated with him: "The 'educated Negroes' have the attitude of contempt toward their own people because in their own as well as in their mixed schools, Negroes are taught to admire the Hebrew, the Greek, the Latin and the Teuton and to despise the African."[4]

Wright understood what Woodson was saying. He had noticed that black people "up North" seemed to look down upon the type of worship experience he had known "down South." Up North, black worship was more restrained; there was less emotion shown; the congregation was more apt to sing classical music than the "old songs of the church" he had known down South. Was that a part of the self-hatred Woodson had written about? Is that what being "an educated Negro" did to people, made them hate who they were? How could that be? Why would God, who had no favorites, create a race that everybody hated? It was not settling well in Wright's spirit.

There had been nobody who had been better to him or for him than his mother and father, his Aunt Hattie, or his aunts and uncles. The music he had grown up hearing in church had nourished and fed his soul and made him move closer and closer to the God his father preached and taught about. He had grown up among educated people who loved being black; poets Sterling Brown and Oscar Brown Jr. had taught his parents. The professors at Virginia Union had fascinated him with their brilliance and scholarship. He had not grown up being ashamed of being African American. He had grown up seeing his history as much as reading about it, and what he knew was that black people were different, but not deficient, a theme he would carry with him throughout his life. So why didn't everyone know that, black and white? And where was God? Why didn't God clear up the apparent confusion?

God's silence was a theological conundrum with which Wright was struggling, but also something that he grew to understand was a struggle for all people at different times in their lives. Many years later, he was to preach:

> When we want God to say something—anything—yes, no, maybe so, not now, wait awhile, by-and-by—God is silent. And the psalm writer who has been there cries out, "O God, do not keep silent!"
>
> Have you ever been there? Scripture says that God is silent. As much as this goes against the grain of our American under-

> standing of prosperity (God giving us all of the riches we want while South Africans starve to death), and as much as it goes against our treating God as some sort of cosmic bellhop (we tell him how to hop and he just jumps there). Scripture says that, sometimes, God is silent. God reveals himself, yes. God makes himself known to us. But God also conceals himself. Isaiah 45:15 (NRSV) says, "Truly you are a God who hides himself."[5]

As Wright wrestled with this divine silence and with what he was seeing and learning, his life's ministry was being reshaped. Following his time in the military, he had finished his undergraduate degree and enrolled in Howard University Divinity School. He was still feeling wary of "the church," but he still loved the scholarship that surrounded theology, American history, church history, and sacred literature. At Howard, he embraced his original desire, which was to teach in a seminary. Sitting in his father's library had shaped him and developed and enhanced his penchant for scholarship. He loved to learn and loved to teach what he was learning.

It was while he was serving in a small church in Chicago, however, that his mind about what his ministry would be had begun to shift. He had already applied to Chicago Theological Seminary to the "theology and literature" department, in preparation to earn a PhD, concentrating on the treatment of biblical passages in African American spirituals, which he planned then to teach in a seminary. But working in Beth Eden Baptist Church in Chicago, with kids, shocked him. If there was self-hatred among blacks, as he had now come to fully see and appreciate, then there was a reason why. As far as Wright could see, a great reason for blacks hating themselves was because blacks did not know who they were. They had bought into the hype fed to them by white society, which had a vested interest in blacks "staying in their place." It was about power. It had been about power in the days of slavery when it was against the law for blacks to learn to read, and it was about power now. White society had kept its stronghold on scores of black people by limiting what they knew. If black people did not know their history and culture, if they were taught to be ashamed of Africa, the land from which they came, they could be controlled. Wright realized that he was seeing the work of an oppressive society and culture right in front of him in the small church in which he was working.

These kids didn't know their history, he realized. They didn't know who Henry McNeil Turner was. They didn't know who Absalom Jones was, or Zora Neal Hurston, or Maya Angelou. They didn't know about Frederick Douglass or Mary McLeod Bethune. They didn't know much about slavery or about how black people had transcended the worst barriers put before them in order that they could be where they were today. They had not grown up talking about the Mason-Dixon Line; many did not know and had not heard of Emmett Till. There were kids who thought black history began with Martin Luther King! He was learning that many black churches were "white churches in black face," and because of that, he said, "we were about to lose a generation." The history of the black church had been a powerful one, Wright said, but these same kids, who did not know or, apparently, care about their history, did not know the history of the black church, either. He could not bear that thought; deeper than that, God would not let him bear that thought. There were no favorites, the Bible said, but black kids were not getting the message. They were being taught to imitate white people and to believe as white people did, which included a self-hatred of themselves. Wright felt the hand of God upon his shoulder and in his soul in a profound way to minister in the midst of this miry clay in which so many young African Americans were stuck. He knew then that his ministry was not to be in the seminary, but in the church.

Wright was seeing for himself the result of what Woodson had written in 1933. These kids at Beth Eden, many of them, were sons and daughters of college-educated blacks, and yet, they had no sense of themselves and their worth. Woodson had written that students educated by "mis-educated" black teachers were "handicapped," in that black teachers taught them "his black face is a curse and . . . his struggle to change his condition (was) hopeless."[6] That lesson, Woodson concluded, "was the worst sort of lynching."[7] Woodson's thesis was that educated African Americans, taught by prejudiced whites, were ill-suited to teach African Americans; Wright, though educated, knew he was more than suited.

Wright's awareness was undoubtedly helped along by the spirit of the civil rights movement. While he had been in college, first at Virginia Union and later at Howard University, the self-hatred of anything African American was the norm; colleges at all-black schools were not wont to allow their choirs to sing Gospel music. Choirs were allowed to sing Negro spirituals, but other than that, most of what they sang was European music. While at Howard, however, in 1968, the students in the glee club rebelled and demanded that they be allowed to sing Gospel music. Gospel music was not a "niggerism" that should be avoided, the students protested. Gospel music was not *deficient*; it was different. It was wrong to disallow it on campuses filled with students of color, primarily African American, who wanted it and who appreciated and needed it! Moreover, the students were saying, they were tired of being ashamed of who they were. As he looked at the young people at Beth Eden Baptist Church, he remembered the freedom he and others had felt as they became connected to their history and their culture, feeling loved by their God, THE GOD, who had no favorites. The tone and tenor of his ministry had been defined. Wright's work would forever be engaged in resisting the evil called racism.

There was no room for it in religion; there was no room for it in any church, but especially in the black church. Wright believed, as theologian James Cone later wrote, that "to resist evil is to participate in God's redemption of the world."[8] Wright's work was not going to be about spouting aimless anger, but it would be about helping oppressed people see and know that their oppression was not of God or from God. He would be about the business of making people know that God had no favorites. He would show them that their suffering had not been imagined, but that they could and should use God to rise above it. They would resist evil, by embracing who they were and *whose* they were. They would not discredit their education, steeped in European values and history, but they would embrace their own history and culture and thereby enhance their education. They would resist the evil of white supremacy, and in so doing "participate in God's redemption of the world." Wright's work and words would embrace Martin Luther King's concept of "redemptive suffering," and he would teach his followers not to ignore or run from suffering, but to see it and challenge it! They would see the resurrection of Jesus the Christ not as a one-time event, but an ongoing phenomenon for a people who had been stuffed into tombs after being "crucified" throughout history. They would learn that Jesus had "died for their sins," but that Jesus also was on the side of the oppressed, that Jesus fought injustice and spoke truth to power . . . and that Jesus suffered for it, but that the world was better because of his work. If they were to imitate anyone, Wright would teach, it would not and should not be the oppressors, but it should be, as the Bible instructed, Jesus the Christ, who had come, died, and risen, after all, so that they might be free.[9]

What African Americans needed to be freed from was the mindset that they were inferior, unworthy of a good life while they were yet alive. They needed to be lifted from saucers of despair in which they sat as generation after generation suffered setback after setback as they tried to get past the barriers erected by racism. They needed new self-images, and they needed to believe that they were not the "worst of the worst," but were in fact, smart, beautiful human beings created by God. There was a world of knowledge the youth needed to know, knowledge of God and their culture that would set them free and set the stage for those who came after them to be free as well. God had no favorites! They should know *who* they were and what their ancestors had done. They should know, wrote Woodson, that there had been "three thousand Negro soldiers of the American Revolutionary War who helped to make" the presidency of George Washington a reality. They should know about the poet Phyllis Wheatley, and "Benjamin Banneker, the mathematician, astronomer, and advocate of a world peace plan set forth in 1793 with the vital principles of Woodrow Wilson's League of Nations."[10] There was so much the youth needed to know! Wright, the teacher, could feel the energy rising to match his passion for the history he had learned so long ago, from reading books in his father's study to listening to his relatives . . . to studying vociferously as a student.

The youth didn't know it because their parents didn't know it. Wright knew that God was whispering to him to open up their eyes and ears. . . .

It is not clear if what Wright felt God was telling him to do had a *name* for what he was feeling was his ministry, but by the mid-1970s, there was a name: liberation theology. Wright, and all clergy up to that point, had been taught in white seminaries the words and beliefs of white theologians. Woodson posits that those educated in black seminaries had been likewise taught. The oppressor, says Woodson, was making sure that his message was the message received and internalized. Life for African Americans was carefully planned, it seemed, by what African Americans were taught and how they were taught.

The theologian James Cone, however, understood and put pen to paper in 1975 about the reality of liberation theology. He says that the black church had been good; "the black Church taught me how to deal with the contradictions of my life and provided a way to create meaning in a society not of my own making.[11] He further writes: "In the larger, 'secular' black community this perspective on life is often called the 'grace of God.' It is called survival because it is a way of remaining physically alive in a situation of oppression without losing one's dignity. We call it *grace* (sic) because we know it is an unearned gift from God who is the giver of 'every good and perfect gift.'"[12]

There was something consoling in that message that came from the black church, but unfortunately, it was not the message Cone and others received once they left the confines of their churches. Cone writes that in Bearden, Arkansas, he was made to realize "by 800 white people" that "black existence, cannot—indeed *must* (sic) not—be taken for granted." The whites in Bearden, Cone's boyhood home, "tried to make us believe that God created black people to be white people's servants. We blacks, therefore, were expected to enjoy plowing their fields, cleaning their houses, mowing their lawns, and working in their sawmills. And when we showed signs of displeasure with our so-called elected and inferior statues, they called us 'uppity niggers' and quickly attempted to put us in our place."[13]

The theology that Cone and Wright and all ministers were taught up to that point supported the community and, likewise, the community supported the theology. There was something wrong, though. The way God was presented in the Bible, African Americans knew, was not in compliance with what they were being taught. Even the slaves had recognized that there was a disconnect between what they understood of a loving God. Cone writes that he had "encountered head-on the contradictions of my seminary education as I attempted to inform black students about the significance of the theological discourse. What could Karl Barth possibly mean for black students who had come from the cotton fields of Arkansas, Louisiana, and Mississippi, seeking to change the structure of their lives in a society that had defined *bla*ck (sic) as non-being? What is the significance of Nicea and Chalcedon for those who knew Jesus *not* (sic) as a thought in their heads to be analyzed in relation to a similar thought called God? They knew Jesus as a Savior and a friend, as the 'lily of the valley and the bright and morning star.'"[14]

Wright and Cone and others grew up where they saw classic theology at work—and what they saw was that it *didn't* work as concerned African Americans. Classic theology produced clergy who thought the riots were bad but who urged Dr. Martin Luther King to "wait" and to stop making such a fuss. Freedom would come, they would say, if black people would just be patient. Classic theological stances of that sort so disturbed Dr. King that he wrote the *Letter from a Birmingham Jail* in response to a letter written by eight white clergymen who lived in Alabama who also had had a classical theological training. He wrote in that letter:

> I have been gravely disappointed with the white moderate. I have almost reached the regrettable conclusion that the Negro's great stumbling block in the stride toward freedom is not the White Citizen's Councilor, or the Ku Klux Klanner, but the white moderate who is more devoted to "order" than to justice; who prefers a negative peace which is the absence of tension to a positive peace, which is the presence of justice; who constantly says, I agree with you in the goal you seek but I can't agree with your methods of direct action; who paternalistically feels that he can set the timetable for another man's freedom; who lives by the myth of time and who constantly advises the Negro to wait until a "more convenient time."[15]

King and others were concerned about the damage that classic theology had wrought on an already oppressed people. The truth of the matter was that the church, the black church included, was sanctioning oppression. Classic, white theology had taught the clergy, black and white, what to teach. There could be no breakthrough, no "freedom" for blacks unless another theological perspective was offered. Cone wrote that preachers and teachers in the black church had to change; they had to embrace the history and culture of oppressed people.[16] Preachers and teachers, said Cone, had to relate the gospel to oppressed people in a new way, had to ask the question, "What has the gospel to do with the oppressed of the land and their struggle for liberation?"[17]

Many African American clergy had used church to further exploit and oppress their own people, according to some, including Woodson. He believed, in the 1930s, that "Negro preachers must be educated to their people rather than away from them."[18] He wrote: "Ministers with the confidence of the people must above all things understand the people themselves. They must find out the past of their parishioners. . . . Men of scholarship and consequently of prophetic insight must show us the right way and lead us into the light which shines brighter and brighter."[19]

Long before Jeremiah Wright, James Cone, or Dr. King pointed out the weaknesses of the classical theology that was taught to all ministers, Woodson correctly noted that there was a serious problem in what and how preachers were being taught. It was not an education that was uplifting "Negroes," as Woodson wrote. He said, "In theology, literature, social science and education . . . radical reconstruction is necessary. The worn-out theories as to man's relation to God and his fellowman, the system of thought which has permitted one man to exploit, oppress, and exterminate another and still be regarded as righteous must be discarded for the new thought of men as brethren and the idea of God as the lover of all humankind."[20]

The teaching of Wright's father, the mood and spirit of the times, and the very voice of God had moved Jeremiah Wright into the place where God would have him and where God would use him to minister to a people long oppressed—even by religion.

If Jeremiah, during his rebellious phase, wondered about the justice of God in light of the injustice he saw around him, it seems fairly clear that he was able to answer the question. Through his studying, he learned how the scriptures had been twisted and manipulated by white theologians and clergy to sanction racism. He began to study the history of the church, the history of the black church, and American history with a passion. His ministry was being more and more defined, even as he studied. He knew that the people to whom he would preach would have "classic" education, meaning that they would have studied Chaucer and Shakespeare and Faulkner, but he made it his business that they would also know the names Baldwin, Hurston, and DuBois. They would know about Thomas Edison, but they would also know about Jan Matzlinger. They would know about Imhotep as well as Hippocrates. They would come to embrace African kingdoms and would be taught that "Egyptian" civilization was "African." The children would be taught and they would be taught that they had much to be proud of. They would be taught that God had not sanctioned nor did God approve of white supremacy. They would be taught not to hate, but to be able to live in love for all humankind, *including themselves.* Everything Wright would do would be to release the "shackles of slavery," as Woodson had written, from their minds.

Wright would teach them that they did not have to believe the hype—that black children were incapable of learning; in fact, he would *insist* that parents participate in the liberation of black youth from the stigma of feeling inferior. He built a ministry that would build people, a people who had for too long thought they were the scum of the earth. He would get them to see how the majority culture had trained them to despise themselves, but that the majority culture had been wrong. He would challenge them to strive for the excellence God had put in them. He would teach them that they really could "do all things through Christ, who strengthened" them (Phil. 4:13). Woodson had written that "the unusual gifts of the race have not . . . been developed . . ." and he said that "the differentness (sic) of races . . . is no evidence of superiority or of inferiority. This merely indicates that each race has certain gifts which the others do not possess. It is by the development of these gifts that every race must justify its right to exist."[21] Wright worked to build a ministry where African Americans and, actually, anyone who studied under him would learn and embrace the fact that the problem was not an unjust God. The problem was with a sick world. He, the preacher/prophet, had been called to at least begin to set the record straight.

4

UNASHAMEDLY BLACK AND UNAPOLOGETICALLY CHRISTIAN

"And we declare that we are unashamedly black and unapologetically Christian."

—New member liturgy, Trinity United Church of Christ, 1972–2008

With his ministry clear to him, Wright became the pastor of Trinity United Church of Christ in Chicago in 1972. The church had a membership of just eighty-seven and found itself in the midst of social upheaval caused by the civil rights movement. Though Dr. Martin Luther King had been assassinated in 1968, the wave of rebellion and protest that had come from his leadership had not quelled; African Americans all over the United States were not content anymore with the way they had lived or been treated in America. The upheaval spread to churches, or at least some churches.

Trinity United Church of Christ was one such church. The phrase "unashamedly black and unapologetically Christian" had been coined by one of Wright's predecessors, the Rev. Reuben Sheares. Not all of Trinity's members liked the phrase or the identification of themselves as black; many African Americans joined denominations like the United Church of Christ precisely because they were predominantly white, allowing them to run from what they considered to be the primitive nature of black religion. Trinity was no exception.

As the forces out to discredit the candidacy of Barack Obama in 2008 attempted to find something, anything, to destroy him, they jumped on this phrase as proof that "Obama's pastor" was a hate-filled demagogue. Obama had been a member of Trinity for some twenty years; he had been married there and he had had his daughters dedicated there. How in the world could the would-be president of the greatest and strongest nation in the world belong to such a church that supported separation of the races, was the underlying question, ironic in that America had done all it could to keep blacks and whites separate. The fact that there is a black church came about because of the unwillingness of whites to worship with African Americans; the African American church was started when, in 1785, Richard Allen and Absalom Jones, incensed and tired of black people not being able to kneel in prayer with whites, withdrew from St. George Methodist Episcopal Church in Philadelphia, taking the blacks who attended St. George with them and beginning what came to be known as the African Methodist Episcopal (AME) Church. Separating the races had been an American tradition.

Nevertheless, in 2008, a church that openly said its members were "unashamedly black" was criticized as being racist, as well as its pastor, and a would-be president who came from such a church, it was suggested, could not be trusted. He must be racist as well.

Nobody knew, however, the journey Jeremiah Wright had taken, from his home in Germantown, Pennsylvania, taught, nurtured and loved by parents who had come from and experienced the savagery of the racist Deep South. Nobody knew, or researched, Wright's conviction that young African Americans could not be allowed to grow up being ashamed of who they were. Minorities, including women, Jews, gay and lesbians, and African Americans, have had to struggle to find their identity to accept and embrace themselves in a society that did not want them, Wright believed, and it was part of what God had anointed him to do to make sure that the youth not grow up ashamed and unaware of who they were.

In a sermon entitled "When You Forget Who You Are," Wright shared what happens to people and cultures when they assimilate into a culture: "Assimilation is like that. It slowly kills you. You don't even realize what is happening to you because when you assimilate, you forget who you are. As a matter of fact, sin and assimilation are just alike."[1]

In that sermon, Wright gives a vivid description of what an Eskimo shared with him about how Eskimos kill wolves: "An Eskimo takes his knife, coats the blade with human blood, and lets it freeze. Then he adds another coat of blood and lets it freeze . . . he adds more and more. . . . The wolf . . . gets the scent of blood and starts licking. The more feverishly he licks, the more his hot tongue starts melting the frozen blood." In the end, the wolf dies having bled to death, "swallowing his own life."[2] African Americans, Wright knew, had been killing themselves by assimilating into a culture that did not want or respect them.

Blacks were beginning to understand what had been happening to them, thanks to the civil rights movement, in some churches and in society in general. Highlighted by events that had happened as blacks tried to claim their place as American citizens, the ugliness of racism rose more and more to the surface and could not be ignored, and African Americans grew determined to change their status in this country. They were beginning to understand that they were, as Wright would teach, "different, but not deficient." Young blacks, especially, grew defiant as they rejected the society's historic definition of who they were and what they were capable of. The historic Children's March in Birmingham, Alabama, showed the mettle of young blacks determined to be treated as equals; not even the dogs and fire hoses put on them by "Bull" Conner could stop them. There was a movement going on, and nobody, it seemed, was going to stop it. Young blacks who had been ashamed of their identity were no longer willing to buy into the hype of their supposed inferiority; they were no longer willing to be second-class citizens. Black youth were ready to know that their history included more than slavery, but they were also keen and aware that it was their people's labor in cotton fields that had helped make America the wealthiest nation in the world. Historian David Von Drehle wrote in the April 18, 2011, edition of *Time* magazine that "though many want to deny it, the fact is that the labor of black people, slaves particularly, cannot be ignored: the cotton trade made Wall Street a global financial force." "Slaves," he wrote, "built the White House."[3] Indeed, Randall Robinson writes in *The Debt: What America Owes to Blacks*: "To erect the building that would house the art that symbolized American democracy, the United States government sent out a request for one hundred slaves. The first stage of the Capitol's construction would run from 1793 to 1802. In exchange for the slaves' labor, the government agreed to pay their *owners* (sic) five dollars per month per slave."[4]

In spite of the use of slaves to build this nation's symbols of democracy, Robinson noted, in two books in the Capitol's gift shop describing the building of the Capitol, there was no mention of the slave labor used. Robinson describes the work of the slaves, noting that they had hauled arkose sandstone blocks to the site and, he said, "stone blocks that could not be handled by oxen were handled by slaves and pulleys.[5] During the Civil War, he wrote, "slaves dislocated in the turmoil gravitated to Union soldiers, who often brought them to Washington to be put to work on the Capitol. William Allen," continued Robinson, "called them 'spoils of war' and "contraband slaves."[6]

Finally, notes Robinson, it was slaves who were responsible for getting the Statue of Freedom atop the dome of the Capitol. Writes Robinson:

> Atop the dome of the Capitol stands the Statue of Freedom, in the figure of a Native American female warrior clad in a star-festooned helmet and flowing robes. . . . Philip Reed, a slave owned by Mills, was given the responsibility for casting the Statue of Freedom and loading its five sections, each weighing more than a ton, onto reinforced wagons for the slow trip to the east grounds of the Capitol. There, Reed and other slaves reassembled Freedom to make certain that all of its pieces would fit together. The task of assembling Freedom took thirty-one days. The statue was then disassembled, hoisted, and reassembled by slaves on the *tholos*, a pedestal on the dome surmounted by a globe.[7]

Certainly, there was no reason for African Americans to be ashamed, not of being black, not of being slaves . . . and not of being Americans by force.

For all of the excitement of the civil rights era, however, there was much about themselves that African Americans had to learn. In spite of the fact, for example, that slaves had much to do with the building of the nation's Capitol building, most African Americans, as well as whites, knew nothing about that. Most of what they, and whites, and in fact, the world, had been taught was that blacks were stupid and lazy and worthless, and incapable of doing anything but entertaining and playing sports. African Americans were a hated underclass. They had been told that they were not college material, were not intelligent enough to play quarterback on football teams, that their hair was ugly, their skin too dark, and their lips too big. Whites, throughout American history, had tried to "explain" black people. Dr. Benjamin Rush, one of the signers of the United States Constitution and the founder of the American Antislavery Society, thought that there were color differences between blacks and whites because of a "leprous disease . . . a condition which would be corrected once a cure for leprosy was discovered." "Then," he wrote, "black skin would lighten and all would be well."[8]

In spite of the Emancipation Proclamation freeing slaves, the plight of black people did not change. Not only did white people think they were superior to black people, but black people bought into that mindset as well. Because of the demoralizing effects of Jim Crow, the lack of legal protection, and discrimination in every aspect of life, black people began to be ashamed of who they were. Wright talked about the way black people felt about not being liked because they were born black; in a sermon entitled "Unhitch the Trailer" he said, "We don't like it one bit when Europeans set the standards of beauty by telling us that thin lips are pretty and full lips are ugly; when Europeans tell us that thin noses are pretty and broad noses are ugly . . . we don't like it."

That was part of the problem, he said, but he continued, "But what about when it is we who dislike ourselves? Do you have any idea what it is like when your own kind doesn't like you because of the way you were born?"[9]

Wright's solid biblical scholarship allowed him to put the phenomenon of trying to assimilate into context. Esther, in the sermon previously alluded to, and the Jews were in a "strange land," that of the Babylonians, due to the fall of Jerusalem to Babylon in 587–586 BCE. Those Jews who survived, as did she, were surrounded by a "majority culture," which had all of the power and a lifestyle that was foreign to the Jews. They yearned to fit in. In Wright's sermon, "When You Forget Who You Are," he details the work that was done on Esther by her Babylonian captors to make her more like them and less like she was, that is, more like a Babylonian and less like a Jew. Wright preached that "she was letting her behavior be determined by the enemy's expectations."[10]

Wright, wanting to get his listeners to see themselves in this story, wove the tale of Esther's assimilation, relating the story of her captivity to that of Africans having been taken into captivity in America. From the moment Esther, who had been named Hadassah by her Jewish parents, was taken into captivity, the process of assimilation was worked upon her. Because of her beauty, she was "accepted" by the Babylonians, but only partially; they began to remake her into their image of beauty. This, taught Wright, had been done to African Americans in this country. Esther had to keep her religion a secret in order to "fit in." In essence, she became like many light-skinned, straight-haired blacks, "passing" as something and someone she was not.

Most blacks, however, are unable to "pass," and the more "ethnic" one looked, the more ashamed one tended to be. Thus African Americans, no matter how dark, found themselves trying to be as "white" as possible: some put harmful chemicals on their hair to make it straight, like their white sisters; some lightened their skin; some had surgery to remake their noses. Wright saw and lived among people who were ashamed of who they were and who tried as hard as they might to "fit into" a culture that did not want them. He heard African Americans refer to straight hair as "good hair," leaving women (and men) with the kinkier hair believing their hair was "bad." He saw that, given a choice, many little African American girls would prefer a white baby doll over one with brown "skin." African Americans internalized the hype of the majority culture, believing themselves to be "bad," "inferior," and "less than." He realized that African Americans knew little about who they were and didn't care to know; what they wanted was to be white. All they really knew and what they had been taught was that they had been slaves and that that was a badge of shame.

This fascination with the white race as being the "master race" imbued with the acceptable standards of beauty was no accident. In his book *War Against the Weak: Eugenics and America's Campaign to Create a Master Race,* author Edwin Black outlines the work done in America to set Caucasians, most specifically Caucasians with "Nordic features" as the master race. What participants in this movement were *sure of* was that there was, in fact, such a master race. Black writes that "throughout the first six decades of the twentieth century, hundreds of thousands of Americans, and untold numbers of others, were not permitted to continue their families by reproducing. He writes:

> Selected because of their ancestry, national origin, race or religion, they were forcibly sterilized, wrongly committed to mental institutions, where they died in great numbers, prohibited from marrying, and sometimes even unmarried by state bureaucrats. . . . This battle to wipe out whole ethnic groups was fought not by armies with guns nor by hate sects at the margins. Rather, this pernicious white-gloved war was prosecuted by esteemed professors, elite universities, wealthy industrialists and government officials, colluding in a racist, pseudoscientific movement called eugenics. The purpose: create a superior Nordic race."[11]

Black writes that the "victims of eugenics were poor urban dwellers and rural 'white trash' from New England to California, immigrants from across Europe, Blacks (sic), Jews, Mexicans, Native Americans, epileptics, alcoholics, petty criminals, the mentally ill and *anyone who did not resemble the blond and blue-eyes Nordic ideal the eugenics movement glorified.*"[12] (italics mine)

So this "badge of shame" worn by many African Americans was no imaginary burden. Many people in American society were targeted as "less than" because of the eugenics movement, but some of them were able to "fix" or alter their looks so that they would "fit in." African Americans, for the most part, could not do that and so were forced to carry their badges of shame like Nathaniel Hawthorne's character Hester in his classic book, *The Scarlet Letter.* Hester carried her scarlet letter because of something she had *done*; African Americans, however, carried their letter because of who they had been born.

During the 1960s, however, things began to change. With the civil rights movement came also the movement of black pride. Though it seemed sudden, what was gradually happening was that African Americans were beginning to discard the badge of shame they had long carried. More and more, African Americans were rejecting the notion that they were "ugly" or "less than." As the civil rights movement began to crescendo, it was no longer a problem to say one was "black"—and "black" was the accepted term of self-identification for African Americans during this time, after a several different names, including "colored" and "Negro" had been the used monikers. The term "black" was defiant, an in-your-face pronouncement to the world that, yes, the skin color was designated as "black" and therefore, somehow, a problem. Young people were moving away from the practices of their parents and grandparents, away from a time when most black families knew and whispered a popular adage:

If you're white, you're right
If you're brown, stick around,
If you're yellow, you're mellow,
But if you're black, get back.[13]

In this new era of self-awareness, young African Americans were shedding the message and sentiment of these words; they were coming into their own, and with a passion.

Not only were African Americans rejecting the belief that they were somehow deficient because they were "black," they were also struggling against the criticism cast by some that they were in the "white man's religion." Christian missionaries had done much to perpetuate racist beliefs and practices; Christian doctrine had done nothing to promote fair and good treatment of African Americans. In the height of the civil rights movement, members of the Nation of Islam criticized African Americans who would not renounce, then, this religion that had not only done nothing to empower them, but had done, according to many, all it could to keep them enslaved in body and in spirit. Here, too, there was a need for education, and Wright knew it. African Americans needed to know the origin of biblical peoples; they needed to know that Christianity was in Africa long before white missionaries ever arrived there. They needed to know that not only Christians, but Muslims as well, had been involved in the business of trading slaves. Everything that was erupting in the quest for a new identity required education and clarification, and Wright knew it. The dis-ease with which blacks embraced Christianity was not lost on the young pastor.

Though there was a black church, it was fairly easy to see that in matters of theology and religious beliefs and practices, the black church was really a white church in black face. Those who began the black church didn't do so with an urge to embrace their history and culture. To the contrary, blacks were, even in 1785, trying their best to assimilate into the white culture. It is not clear that the preachers of the black church attempted to lead blacks to embrace and love themselves any more than the white preachers had. In effect, black preachers tended to preach that blacks should "hold on and hold out," because they would receive justice and love in heaven. In this sense, the black church, or the theology of the black church, had been historically eschatological in nature. Blacks were in effect told to hush up and do as they were told, to not make waves... Hence, some of the favorite hymns of the church indicated that life would be better "by and by":

We are often tossed and driven
On the restless sea of time
Somber skies and howling tempests
Oft succeed the bright sunshine
In that land of perfect day
When the mists are rolled away
We will understand it better by and by!

Refrain:
By and by, when the morning comes
All the saints of God are gathered home
We'll tell the story how we've overcome
For we'll understand it better, by and by[14]

But African Americans who had grown up in homes where Jesus was the focus of religious faith were not willing to abandon their Lord and Savior, and because of that, some were meek when it came to proclaiming their faith. Even if it was "the white man's religion," it was the only religion they had ever known.

Wright wanted people to know, however, how the Bible had been used as a tool of manipulation and control throughout history, not so that African Americans would abandon the faith, but so they would be able to embrace the faith in a more authentic way. The issue was not God or Jesus; the issue was people who had used God and Jesus for their own purposes. Wright knew that the Bible had also been used to justify anti-Semitism, homophobia, and sexism. Contrary to believing that educating people on the weaknesses of their religion would cause them to lose faith, he believed that it would help them sort out truth from lies, and thereby have a stronger faith. He felt compelled to teach them that they did not have to accept the erroneous teaching that the Bible ordained slavery, which is what many African Americans had been taught, sometimes blatantly and sometimes subliminally.

The use of the Bible to keep black people under control can be traced at least to 1704, when Elias Neau, a French Hugenot who had converted to Christianity, was assigned the task of writing a catechism in a way to "instruct the slaves." Several years later, Cotton Mather, in *The Negro, Christianized,* formalized a method process for teaching slaves:

Question: If you serve Jesus Christ, what must you do?

Answer: I must Love God, and Pray to Him, and Keep the Lords-Day, I must Love all men and never quarrel, nor be Drunk, nor be unchaste, nor Steal, nor tell a Ly, nor be discontent with my condition.[15]

To drive the idea of the divine sanction of their servitude into the minds not only of the slaves but of the white people who used the slaves, to make all believe that this thing called slavery was God's will, the case had to be made that everything that was being done was from God, including the treatment of slaves:

Question: Who gave you a master and a mistress?

Answer: God gave them to me.

Question: Who says you must obey them?

Answer: God says that I must.

Question: What book tells you these things?

Answer: The Bible.[16]

Thus, there was a disconnect between what people thought they knew about Christianity and what Christianity must really be about. After all, the Bible had been taught to black people by white people. This disconnect came because of the subjective nature of interpreting scripture, causing some manipulation of texts, surely, but also some honest mis-teachings based on what one's experiences led one to believe. Scripture was used and taught to maintain the balance of power; those who were "free," according to the United States Constitution, were white, property-owing males. Since the population was not made up solely of white males who owned property, there had to be a means of keeping not only blacks, but everyone, under control. Lessons taught were skewed in favor of the "haves" and at the expense of the "have-nots," but that was not a peculiarly or uniquely an American phenomenon. In the time of Jesus, teachings were skewed in the same manner. The have-nots, however, were left wrestling with the question of the goodness of God. Was God good or not? Did God love everyone or not? Would God create a whole race of people whom God did not like? The questions were troubling, so much so that many pastors, preachers, and teachers would not tackle them. Wright was an exception.

One of the earliest and most powerful biblical weapons used to justify slavery and used by preachers as proof that God intended black people to be slaves, putting into question the ultimate goodness of God, was the so-called "Ham Doctrine," found in Genesis 9:18–28 in the Hebrew scriptures. Noah, builder of the ark that saved some during the Great Flood, was accidentally seen naked by his son, Ham. To see one's father naked (Noah presumably had passed out in a drunken stupor) was against Jewish law, and so when Ham saw him, he ran out of his father's tent and told his two brothers, Shem and Japheth. The two of them were horrified that Ham had seen their father naked, and so they backed into Noah's tent and covered him with a blanket. When Noah awoke and was told what had happened, the Bible says that he got angry and said, "Cursed be Canaan! The lowest of slaves will be his brothers!" (v. 25).

Noah also blessed his other two sons, Shem and Japheth. The way this scripture was interpreted to both black and white people was that "the Bible" said that God cursed Ham and that Ham and his descendants would be slaves. In fact, the text says that Noah cursed Canaan, Ham's son, and said that Canaan should be the slave of Japheth. In addition, those who interpreted this text and biblical justification of slavery posited that Ham was the progenitor of all black people (Canaan in the Bible is the name for Ethiopia); Japheth was the progenitor of all white people, and Shem, the progenitor of all Semitic peoples.

There are two things that inspire immediate attention. First, *God did no cursing of anyone.* Noah did the cursing, and it wasn't Ham who was cursed, but Ham's son. In ancient Israel, a curse issued was meant to last a generation at best. Second, an illogical family structure is suggested, seeing as how Noah and his wife had three sons, all of different races. Because until recently it was considered by most (and probably still today by some) a sacrilege to question the Bible, nobody ever really dealt with the illogicality of this teaching. Some would probably say that there was no need for the story to make sense; it was in the Bible, which meant that "God said it," and that was it. Therefore, there was nothing anyone could do, was the response offered by those who relayed this story to bolster and strengthen their ideologies. It was God's will . . . because the Bible said so. The most intelligent of people bought into the story and the social malady it gave divine sanction to; Dr. Benjamin Rush, commenting on the state of slavery, said that "slavery was a special means of salvation granted to Negroes by God."[17]

Few people understood or even knew the way the Bible had been mishandled and misused as the civil rights movement gained momentum. The Bible had been smugly used to keep many groups "in their place." The Pilgrims used the Bible to bolster their belief that "God had cursed the Indian population in order to prepare New England for his children."[18] Even then, those in power sought to make people assimilate into the white culture; the Puritans believed that "conversion did not mean a simple declaration for Christ, but, rather, required the savage to give up his pagan ways and adopt the white man's habits—in short, to repudiate his culture."[19] Forrest G. Wood writes that Pilgrims believed that *"the heathen do need the gospel. There is no other remedy for them* (sic). "Without exception," wrote Congregational pastor Samuel Worcester, "all other world religions were utterly worthless and their adherents were without hope, salvation or eternal light. If there was a universal component in evangelical Christianity, it was the unshakable belief that everyone else was wrong and that infidels had to be 'rescued.'"[20]

What happened, writes Peter Gomes in *The Good Book: Reading the Bible with Mind and Heart,* was that "in the matter of slavery, each side adapted the context and content of the biblical writings to suit the moral purposes of their own contemporary climate of interpretation."[21]

John Wesley and George Whitefield, early American clergy, made cases against the slave trade, though they said that it was permitted by scripture. Once anyone said that something was or was not permitted by scripture, any disclaimers pertaining to that behavior were negated and dismissed. So, if slavery was permitted and in fact ordained and sanctioned by scripture, and scripture was the Word of God, the case was made. Scripture was not to be questioned. Oppression was said to be of God and from God. Writes Gomes: "In the American South in particular, it was Bible-reading, church-going Christians, chiefly Protestants and largely Baptist, who could and would lynch, castrate, and horribly mutilate errant black men on Saturday night and pray and praise all day in church on Sunday, without a hint of schizophrenia or even of guilt. How could they sustain such a culture for so long? The Bible told them so."[22]

Wright realized what he was up against. He knew that Christians in general, and blacks in particular, were gullible. "Black Christians would fall for anything they saw on television (whether it was from white or black televangelists) . . . [but] they were functionally illiterate when it came to what God's word said."[23] Most African Americans who were feeling and responding to the criticism from members of the Nation of Islam had no legitimate basis on which or from which to defend their faith. Wright sought, then, to enlighten those whom he taught and those to whom he preached. It was a new day; African Americans would know who they were and *whose* they were!

Wright's goals of enlightening any Christian who would hear him had nothing to do with spreading hatred, as some are wont to charge any time racial disparities and situations arise. His goal was to help lift the shackles traditional Christianity and the biblical teachings had put on the minds of black people. Woodson had said that if a person's mind was enslaved, the enslavement of his or her body was not required.

Wright knew how deeply the shackles wrought by Christianity cut into the spirits of the people to whom he was to minister. In all the teaching he did, he always came back to the fact that God was love, and that God's son Jesus was love. Without such love, no relationship with God was valid. It was a lesson he would drive home with every lesson he taught and every sermon he preached.

5

REMOVING THE MASK

In the matter of slavery,
each side adapted the context and content
of the biblical writings to suit the
moral purposes of their own contemporary
climate of interpretation.

—Peter Gomes[1]

Jeremiah Wright's becoming clear that he would be a pastor and not a professor didn't mean his work would be easy. He constructed a ministry that would use the Bible. Moreover, the biblical teaching would include the history of Americans, African Americans, and Africans. The group and individual levels of the system would help educate and free those who had been held captive by their lack of knowledge about the Bible and about who they were. Black folks were not all that interested, if the truth be told, in knowing about themselves or about their history; they had been assimilated into the dominant culture, step by painful step, and many found no need to "keep bringing up all that stuff about slavery." Black people, for the most part, tended to shy away from their history; they knew they were considered inferior; their efforts were to try to lessen that inferiority not by knowing their history, but by pretending that their history did not exist, or at least, was not all that important to get to know.

In addition, black people, for the most part, were not all that interested in hearing anything about history or politics or the effects of politics on their lives from the pulpit. The pulpit was for hearing "the Word." Sunday mornings were a time to forget about the trials due to racism they endured on a daily basis. What they wanted was a moment to breathe, to get away from it all. Sunday mornings have been "the most segregated hour of the week," as Wright and others have long noted. Blacks were fine with that segregation. There were no white folks to worry about, no white folks to have to please. On Sunday mornings, black folks could relax; one friend of this writer noted that Sunday mornings were for "grief release." If that release could come from a song sung or a "shout" given in response to a particularly moving sermon or song, or both, then that's what needed to happen. Nobody went to church to learn about who he or she was.

Many black preachers knew the spirit of the masses of black folks, and, quite frankly, took advantage of that knowledge. They were not wont to mention anything that even got close to being political, or sociopolitical in nature. (This is part of the "reticence of the pulpit" that Gomes described.) They were not particularly concerned with giving accurate biblical scholarship in their sermons, either. What many wanted was for the crowd to respond on an emotional basis. If a preacher got his congregation riled up and excited, that preacher had done his (for the most part, black preachers have been male) job. People would crowd sanctuaries and be willing to stay in church for most of the day. Church was a safe place. If one cried in church, it was okay; if one shouted in church, it wasn't frowned upon, not in most African American denominations. It was "good church," healthy and robust, food for wilting souls that had to go out the next day wearing "the mask" that Paul Laurence Dunbar wrote about:

We wear the mask that grins and lies,
It hides our cheeks and shades our eyes,
This debt we pay to human guile;
With torn and bleeding hearts, we smile,

And mouth with myriad subtleties.
Why should the world be over-wise,
In counting all our tears and sighs.
Nay, let them only see us, while,
We wear the mask.
We smile, but, O great Christ, our cries
To thee from tortured souls arise,
We sing, but oh the clay is vile
Beneath our feet, and long the mile;
But let the world dream otherwise,
We wear the mask![2]

While many African Americans cherished this type of Sunday morning experience, others did not, criticizing the spirited worship for being too full of "niggerisms," and being too emotional. Many also noted that there were preachers who were, frankly, experts at taking advantage of the emotionally drained and hungry crowds they saw each weekend. People who had little money themselves were willing and, in fact, anxious to take care of the "man of God," many times to their own detriment. The preacher was revered in the black community, not for his scholarship or for his efforts to liberate an oppressed people, but for bringing God to the people, a God who loved these despised people. Through their crying and shouting, and through their recitation of the parts of the Bible, the congregants got the hope they needed, and as long as they received hope, they would come back again and again.

Black preachers, not immune to the traps that are a part of a capitalistic economy, many times were able to realize very comfortable lifestyles. Carter G. Woodson expressed disdain for these sometimes educated men who took economic advantage, far too often, of the black masses. Noted Woodson: "We must feel . . . discouraged when we see a minister driving up to his church on Sunday morning in a Cadillac. He does not come to feed the multitude spiritually. He comes to fleece the flock. The appeal he makes is usually emotional. While the people are feeling happy, the expensive machinery is granted, and the prolonged vacation to use it is easily financed. Thus, the thoughtless drift backward toward slavery"[3]

It seems, then, that Jeremiah Wright was swimming upstream in his effort to make his people know "who they were and *whose* they were." Many white people didn't like black people, he knew, but he was aware of how much black people *didn't like themselves* because of what the dominant culture had communicated not only to them, but to the world, about them. He didn't understand fully, not yet, how preachers could be so careless in disseminating biblical information—and that bothered him. Because of his studying, he knew about the Bible, how it was put together, how and when books of the Bible were written, and by whom; but as he learned, he also realized that he had been preached to inaccurately all his life by some of his favorite preachers. He wanted to set a different tone; people to whom he preached would know accurate scholarship. There was so much to correct!

For instance, the Israelites, escaping from Pharaoh, did not cross the Red Sea, but, rather, the Sea of Reeds. In studying Hebrew, Wright had discovered that the appellation for the famous body of water had been handed down incorrectly because the translators had not seen or perhaps not honored the grammatical marking that indicated the name of the sea was "Reed" and not "Red." Surely preachers knew that, he thought, but if they did, they did not bother to correct the famous and beloved story.

The disjuncture between fact and fiction bothered him, and he asked his father, whose life he wanted to emulate, how he handled it. Wright protested to his father, saying that preachers should tell the truth, but the elder Wright taught his son a lesson he would take with him and remember for the rest of his life. "There is a difference between biblical studies and the book of faith," his father told him. Peoples' faith stories were far more important, his father said. It was a lesson the son internalized and used, even as he sought to teach and preach in his own style. He would honor the faith stories of the people, but he would also enlighten them. He would juxtapose the way they had heard things, or learned things, against the truth. He would strengthen them, not by tearing down what they had always been taught, what had brought them through their "Red Seas," in effect, but he would open their eyes and let them see the same stories in new ways.

He would push the need to *study* the Bible and not just read it. People would know the truth, both about the Bible and themselves, and it would set them free. They would be taught to put their faith in a historical context and understand where African Americans had been in order to understand where they were now. They would learn that the God they served was not a God of oppression, that this God really did not have favorites. In learning who they were and whose they were, they would be equipped to handle the world and its racism in a profound and powerful way.

Wright's preoccupation with wanting black people to know who they were and to not be ashamed of it was not ill-conceived. Black people had suffered ignominiously, at the hands of both the government and religion. Neither the Bible nor the United States Constitution offered safety, fairness, or solace. When Joy Degruy Leary, PhD, visited South Africa not all that long ago, she writes that coming back "home" to the United States jostled her: "I simply needed time to adjust to having been in a place where, for the first time, it felt perfectly normal to be black. It felt odd returning to America, to a place where being black is frequently a life sentence of cultural isolation and social invisibility."[4]

Race has always been an issue in America. In fact, as mentioned in the previous chapter, America was at the forefront of trying to create a "master race," which, in the eyes of the researchers and writers of the eugenics movement, was a "Nordic" white. So intent were some to create the perfect physical, racial prototype that "mandatory sterilization laws were enacted in some twenty-seven states to prevent targeted individuals from reproducing more of their kind."[5] In the "first six decades of the twentieth century, hundreds of thousands of Americans and untold numbers of others were not permitted to continue their families by reproducing.[6] The targeted people were not just African American, but were indeed anyone who was deemed "deficient" in any way. Thus, Jews, Italians (or anyone who was too dark or swarthy), people with epilepsy or other diseases thought to be genetically transmitted, people who had been born with birth defects were targeted to be eliminated in this country. So expansive and comprehensive was the eugenics work in this country that, Edwin Black writes, American eugenics "spawned similar movements and practices throughout Europe, Latin America, and Asia."[7] Black says that eventually "America's eugenics movement spread to Germany . . . where it caught the fascination of Adolph Hitler and the Nazi movement."[8] After Hitler took the concept of eugenics to a horrifying level, resulting in the extermination of six million Jews, Black writes that American eugenics institutions "rushed to change their names from *eugenics* to *genetics*."[9] Clearly, even though this work to create a master race seems to have originated in America, the world was and concerned with race, and horrible genocide has occurred in other countries, with racism at its core.

But America's fascination with race was troubling, primarily because America claimed to be a Christian nation and a nation that believed in "freedom and justice" for all. In a Public Broadcasting Stations (PBS) presentation of the documentary *Race: The Power of an Illusion,* it is noted that there really is no such thing as race; it is a social construct that has no biological basis in fact. And yet, from the beginning, white Americans have held a fascination and a disdain for African Americans. Blacks, first arriving in America in 1619, were said to be an ideal source of labor for the burgeoning new nation, but, according to Ira Berlin, "the founding fathers wrote certain people out of the population."[10] That included not only blacks, but women and Native Americans.

From the beginning of America's history, then, there was an uneasy relationship between blacks and whites. Blacks were seen as "objects" and not people, which, argue many sociologists and psychologists, made it easier for whites to treat them as property. Thomas Jefferson, certainly one of the most beloved of American heroes, himself owned 175 slaves, but penned "all men are created equal." He didn't know what to make of blacks as a "species" of people; what he did know, he said, was that they were "certainly" inferior to whites. In his *Notes on the State of Virginia*, he writes that blacks themselves favored whites, who had "flowing hair, a more elegant symmetry of form . . . " and he said that the Oranootan (sic) had a preference for "the black woman over those of his own species." Continued Jefferson:

> The circumstance of superior beauty, is thought worthy of attention in the propagation of our horses, dogs, and other domestic animals; why not in that of man? Besides those of colour (sic), figure and hair, there are other physical distinctions proving a dif-

> ference of race. They have less hair on the face and body. They secrete less by the kidnies (sic) and more by the glands of the skin, which gives them a very strong and disagreeable odour. (sic) This greater degree of transpiration (sic) renders them more tolerant of heat, and less so of cold, than the whites. Perhaps too a difference of structure in the pulmonary apparatus, which a late ingenious experimentalist has discovered to be the principal regulator of animal heat, may have disabled them from extricating, in the act of inspiration, (sic) so much of that fluid from the outer air. . . ."[11]

The future president continued his observations, saying that the griefs of the blacks were transient, and that they were "more ardent after their females." He ended up this portion of his discourse on blacks by writing, "Comparing them by their faculties of memory, reason and imagination, it appears to me, that in memory they are equal to the whites; in reason, much inferior."[12] Later he writes:

> Let me add, too, as a circumstance of great tenderness, where our conclusion would degrade a whole race of men from the rank in the scale of beings which their Creator may perhaps have given them. . . . To our reproach it must be said that though for a century and a half we have had under our eyes the races of black and or red men, they have never yet been viewed by us as subjects of natural history. I advance it therefore as a suspicion only, that the blacks, whether originally a distinct race, or made distinct by time and circumstances, are inferior to the whites in the endowments both of body and mind. It is not against experience to suppose, that different species of the same genus, or varieties of the same species, may possess different qualifications.[13]

Jefferson was not the only one of America's patriarchs who wrestled publicly with "what" blacks actually were and how they came to be . . . black. Of the fifty-six signers of the Declaration of Independence, several owned slaves (even though some freed them not long after the revered document was signed), including George Washington, James Madison, John Monroe, John Jay, Benjamin Franklin, and Charles Pinckney. Samuel

Morton was a Philadelphia physician who wrote an entire book about the innate differences among humans; Josiah Nott, a Philadelphia physician, pushed a theory of polygenesis, which held that different people came from different sources, and believed that blacks were a different species.[14] (Polygenesis held that because different species came from different "gods," meant that the Bible only applied to Caucasians.[15]) A culture of white superiority was as much nurtured as was the culture and ethos of freedom, and few, if any, saw or appreciated the irony. Howard Zinn writes that "the system was psychological and physical at the same time."[16] In 1847, Louis Agassiz posited that there were an "indefinite number of original and distinctly created races of men. . . . There are superior and inferior races whose distribution would only have come about by multiple origins," pushing the theory of polygenesis.[17]

There was no release of bigotry from pulpits, sadly. Rev. Francis Wayland, a Northern Baptist, preached that "what God sanctioned in the Old Testament and permitted in the New, cannot be sin."[18] A Southern theologian, James Henley, who was also the president of South Carolina College and editor of the *Southern Presbyterian Review,* said, "Where the Scriptures are silent, (the church) must be silent too. What the Scriptures have not made essential to a Christian profession, she does not undertake to make so. What the scriptures have sanctioned, she does not condemn."[19] The biblical defense of slavery (and therefore of white supremacy) came from distinguished educators, including William Andrew Smith, the "president of Randolph-Macon College who conceded that slavery was a great evil, but not a sin." Samuel Blanchard How, a pastor in New Jersey, said much the same: "Slavery is an evil much to be lamented . . . but we deny that it is a sin against God and a crime against man."[20]

Not even one of the most famous preachers of the eighteenth century, Jonathan Edwards, hailed as he who heralded in "The Great Awakening," was able to wrest himself from the privilege of being white and able to own slaves. He who preached the fiery sermon, "Sinners in the Hands of an Angry God" was apparently not worried about the anger of God in the matter of owning slaves; it is said that he owned several over his lifetime.

Thus, there was a seedbed, carefully tilled and harvested year after year with a crop called racism and white supremacy. Federal, state, and local laws upheld the prevailing social and religious beliefs that were spreading throughout the nation as fiercely as was the concept of democracy. The concept was flawed from the beginning. There was no real freedom unless one was white, male, and wealthy enough to own land. Everyone else had to fight to win his or her freedom, be that person from Ireland or Italy, a female or American Indian . . . or an African American.

Alexis de Tocqueville, who traveled to America to study democracy, made an eerily correct prediction when he said, "If there ever are great revolutions there, they will be caused by the presence of the blacks upon American soil. That is to say, it will not be the equality of social conditions but rather their inequality which may give rise thereto."[21]

Tocqueville noted not only the disparity based on color between blacks and whites, but also the disparity in class. Aristocrats, he noted, have a hard time "mingling with the masses" and said that "those who hope that the Europeans will one day mingle with the Negroes seem to me to be harboring a delusion. . . . Hitherto, whenever the whites have been the more powerful, they have kept the Negroes down in degradation or in slavery. Everywhere where the Negroes have been the stronger, they have destroyed the whites; and that is the only reckoning there has ever been between the two races."[22] Tocqueville, writing in the 1830s, said that "slavery is in retreat but the prejudice from which it arose is immovable."[23] Where "Negroes" were free, he noted, they could not "share the rights, pleasures, labors, griefs or even the tomb of him whose equal he has been declared; there is nowhere where he can meet him, neither in life nor in death."[24]

The cloud of inferiority was thus created and hovered over African Americans from the moment of this country's inception, or at least shortly thereafter. The lingering effect was what Wright was seeing: a group of people who had bought into the carefully constructed and nurtured opinion of them. African Americans were a people who did *not* know who they were and they most likely understood little about a God who could create a people who could be so despised and abused just because of their color. Yet they hung onto this God; it was the only God they knew. Though their captors didn't know it, many Africans had embraced Christianity long before the American missionaries got to African soil. They had constructed a fair and merciful, a kind and benevolent

God and Jesus, a God who hated the injustice they endured. They could not, then, embrace the God that the preachers, pastors, teachers, and missionaries told them about, a God who ordained and sanctioned racism and white supremacy.

Their problem was that the God of the missionaries had apparently not made the case for freedom and justice that was clearly evident in the Bible. To add insult to injury, Jesus had been maddeningly silent on it. The Africans who were brought to the New World clung to their God construct, believing that God really did care about them, and that God really did not have favorites—that is, white people. They needed, however, a prophet and a teacher to convince them, and some came. In present day, Jeremiah Wright was that prophet for and to those he reached. It would be part of his ministry to preach and teach black people lessons of hope laced with sound scholarship, lessons that would allow them to pull off their masks and breathe in unpolluted air for perhaps the first time.

Among the problems Wright was going to have to navigate if he was going to empower people to know who and whose they were was the absolute inundation of racism within every level of existence in this country. Black people had ingested and digested the theology and the hermeneutics of the dominant race, and that "feeding" was part of what led to the abject self-hatred African Americans had for themselves and for each other.

The world wanted to be white, and this country was a leader in the propagation of that sentiment. In a book on prayer by renowned preacher Harry Emerson Fosdick, he noted this, albeit inadvertently. Writing that "God had long intended that Africa be evangelized," Fosdick writes that a missionary, Charles Livingstone, "cried 'O God, help me to paint this dark continent white.' "[25] Fosdick apparently believed in the correctness of Livingstone's prayer, as he further wrote, "(Livingstone) did not alter God's intention, but he did alter God's action. Power broke loose that before had been pent. . . . The cooperation of a man's prayer, backed by his life, opened a way for the divine purpose. There was an invasion of the world by God through Livingstone. No one can set clear limits to this release of divine power which the effectual prayer of a righteous man can accomplish."[26]

Later in this same work, Fosdick, who is considered a preacher in support of social justice, recalled the musings of Henry Stanley, an "African explorer," as concerned Africa:

> To relate a little of the instances in my life wherein I have been grateful for the delicate monitions of an inner voice, recalling me, as it were, to my "true self," it would be difficult for me to do their importance justice. I, for one, must not, dare not, say that prayers are inefficacious. Where I have been earnest, I have been answered. . . . In the conduct of the various expeditions into Africa, prayer for patience has enabled me to view my savage opponents in a humorous light; sometimes with infinite compassion for their madness. . . . Without prayer for it, I doubt that I could have endured the flourish of the spears when they were but half-a-dozen paces off . . . prayer made me stronger, morally and mentally than any of my non-praying companions.[27]

Even the most well-intentioned white people, it would seem, had been students of the white supremacy that had become the belief of the world in general and of this nation in particular. The lesson of the superiority of white people, of white thinking, white living, white beauty, and white power . . . had been mercilessly fed to America's population as a whole. That feeding was deleterious to the nation and its people as a whole, because it resulted in a false sense of pride in one race and a diminished sense of pride in others. In a nation that was supposed to be recognizable by its commitment to equality and fairness, there was little of either, due to the twisting of the hearts and spirits of America's people by politicians, theologians, and preachers alike.

There were two problems that Wright would have to navigate in his preaching and teaching: the actual words in the Bible and the way those words had been manipulated and interpreted by those who delivered them. Peter Gomes has said that there is a "poverty of biblical literacy," not unlike the poverty that exists in the areas of finance and, of course, language. That very poverty, however, has allowed people to be manipulated by those in power, and in the area of religion, that poverty has led to the maiming and dismembering of the human spirit. The Bible, though it consistently appears as a best seller, is one of the least understood texts of all time. Gomes says it "remains an elusive, unknown, slightly daunting book."[28] He also says, in spite of the Bible's popularity, the understanding of it has gone down, rather than up. He gives as evidence: "A recent American poll conducted by the Barna Research Groups discovered that 10 percent of the sample of more than one thousand persons polled said that Joan of Arc was Noah's wife, 16 percent were convinced that the New Testament contained a book by the Apostle Thomas, and 38 percent were of the view that both the Old and New Testaments were written a few years after Jesus' death."[29]

There are many Christians who boast that they have read the Bible "from cover to cover," but it is doubtful that they have understood much of what they have read, and if they have read the King James Version (which many African Americans hold to be the only *true* Bible), then the level of understanding is likely even less. It is nearly impossible to appreciate the Bible without knowing the historical context in which it was written, yet that is the way most people approach it. One can interpret the Bible in his or her own way, but a more challenging way, the way Wright learned and respected, wanting preachers to "tell the truth," leads to a more accurate understanding of the words in the scriptures and therefore of the kind of life those words are leading individuals to live.

For example, Psalm 137, the psalm on which Wright's sermon, "The Day of Jerusalem's Fall" was based, is a remarkable piece of writing, poignant and powerful, yet more so, and highly instructive, if one understands the context in which it was written. The psalm (NIV):

By the rivers of Babylon we sat and wept when we remembered Zion.
There on the poplars we hung our harps, for there our captors asked us for songs, our tormentors demanded songs of joy; they said, "Sing us one of the songs of Zion!"
How can we sing the songs of the LORD while in a foreign land?
If I forget you Jerusalem, may my right hand forget its skill.
May my tongue cling to the roof of my mouth if I don't remember you, if I do not consider Jerusalem, my highest joy.
Remember, LORD, what the Edomites did on the day Jerusalem fell.
"Tear it down," they cried, "Tear it down to its foundations!"

Daughter Babylon, doomed to destruction, happy is the one who repays
you according to what you have done to us.
Happy is the one who seizes your infants and dashes them against rocks.

Few listeners hear, in sermons involving this psalm, about the fall of Jerusalem to its enemies, put in place by God because the Israelites had been disobedient to God, over and over again. The fall of the Northern and Southern kingdoms, the North to the Assyrians and the South to the Babylonians, seems to be central to understanding the overall message of the Hebrew scriptures, but that overall message is muddied by this lack of general understanding of the history behind the texts, and further by the fact that the Bible lends itself to interpretation rather than straight instruction.

An instructive text would be more linear; there would be a set of facts that would be the same to anyone engaging in that text. Instruction of the Bible, however, falls in rank and position to interpretation; he or she who interprets gives his or her instruction. Therefore there is no consistent message; what is true for one interpreter is not true for another, and though the same biblical text may be used, he or she who instructs gives his or her interpretation, and that interpretation becomes "the truth." Throughout history, it hasn't necessarily been the Bible itself that has caused problems in issues dealing not only with African Americans, but women and gays as well—it has been the *interpretation*, the hermeneutic of the one who is giving the interpretation of any given text that has caused problems and confusion.

In using this text following the debacle that happened on September 11, 2001, for his sermon, Wright's hermeneutic was American . . . and African American as well. His hermeneutic was based as much on his being a part of an oppressed group, and as one who ministered intentionally to a group of people who knew oppression, as it was based on his being an American, furious that the attacks on the World Trade Center and the Pentagon had taken place. As an African American, he knew what it was to sit "by the rivers of Babylon," asked to give whatever was demanded of him to a group of people who oppressed him and his people. ("By the rivers of Babylon we sat and wept when we remembered Zion. There on the poplars we hung our harps, for there our captors demanded . . . songs of joy. . . .") Here, Wright would understand the sadness, the emotion, the frustration of those who had been exiled. They were no longer home. As an African American, he would be able to relate as one who had been taken from his home.

He may have felt sadness as an African American exile, but as an American, he knew the feeling of wanting to "get back" at those who had desecrated his home. ("Remember, Lord, what the Edomites did on the day Jerusalem fell. Tear it down," they cried, "tear it down to its foundations!" "Daughter Babylon, doomed to destruction, happy is the one who *repays* you according to what you have done to us..Happy is the one who seizes your infants and dashes them against the rocks" [italics mine]). Here would be the hermeneutic expressed from the perspective of an American, race notwithstanding. As a member of an oppressed group, he knew what it felt like to be so angry that one would want revenge for those who had caused pain. He knew the adage "what goes around comes around," which is another way of stating the Golden Rule, found in the Bible. According to that adage, one should expect that he or she will reap what is sown, and it is natural for the one who has been wronged to want to see the payback he or she thinks is deserved.

So when Wright adapted an old adage and said, "America's chickens are coming home to roost," he was sharing his dual hermeneutic—as an American and as an African American. He was expressing a sentiment that oppressed people would have understood and that sensitive Americans familiar with this country's history of exerting its power on lesser nations and peoples would have understood as well. In that one phrase, he was speaking both as a member of an oppressed group and as a citizen of a country that too often had been accused of, and had engaged in, oppressing others. But just because he may have understood the need and desire of other countries to lash out at America, it did not mean that as an American he was happy about it. It was a sad reality of what happens among humans; God notwithstanding, there is always a desire for revenge when one feels wronged. Wright, remember, had had painful revelations from soldiers about what the American military had done, getting into wars that had less to do with the spreading of democracy than it had to do with spreading capitalism and increasing the capacity for materialism. He had heard and he had studied the world from the point of view of the oppressor and the oppressed. He had been heartbroken in learning why America had entered its wars. He instinctively knew that people will fight back after a while. That was not a behavior based on race; it was a given based on human behavior. So, he understood the wailing of the Israelites, oppressed, cast away and out of their homes by the Babylonians. He understood their need and desire for revenge. But he also understood the pain of the oppressor. He was an American, and his sensibilities as an American had been insulted as well. Wright's sermon highlighted this dual hermeneutic. He had to preach to his congregation as an oppressed group who knew the pain of oppression, but also as a group of Americans who were thoroughly offended over what had been done on their native soil:

> Most of us are familiar with just that part of Psalm 137. Most of us are only familiar with the first six verses of Psalm 137. Most of us have not read or heard the last three verses of this psalm, and most of us, I can guarantee you, have never heard a sermon that touched any of the thoughts of feelings expressed in these last three verses.
>
> When Solomon prayed and asked God's blessing on that temple in Jerusalem—you know that story: fire came down from heaven in 2 Chronicles 7—the glory of the Lord filled the temple. The priests could not go in and the people fell down and worshiped. The thoughts of Jerusalem in Psalm 137 are thoughts of reverence. . . .
>
> But . . . keep on reading. The people of faith move from reverence in verses 4 to 6, to revenge in verses 8 and 9. They want revenge! They want somebody to destroy those who devastated them. In fact, they want God to get even with those who did evil. . . . [30]

The tragedy about how America received the snippet ("chickens have come home to roost") is that the dual hermeneutic was missed; nobody, it seemed, understood where Wright was coming from. The irony is that while Americans were furious at what they thought was Wright blaming America for the 9/11 attack, they were missing the fact that he was speaking *their* pain as well. They wanted revenge; they wanted the "chickens to roost" in and on the people who had been responsible for the attacks. They were not able to dissect what they heard but they reacted to what they saw as the anger of a black man, helped along by the media. Wright was vilified for speaking what many Americans were feeling; while they would acknowledge the "rightness" of wanting and seeking revenge on Osama Bin Laden, they completely rejected the "rightness" and humanness of Wright acknowledging that those who had attacked us had wanted revenge on us as well for perceived wrongs done to them and their people.

Peter Gomes notes that after World War II, in light of the executive order signed by President Truman to desegregate the troops, there was a backlash of protest from whites who believed that the president was going against the Bible. Gomes recalls that Senator Harry Flood Byrd of Virginia said that "you can't legislate morality" and "you can't go against the Bible."[31] Many who based their social and political beliefs on the Bible followed a strict tenet: you don't question the Bible. Yet Wright was lifting up painful words that reflected the human reaction to feeling wronged, and they were not only questioning the hermeneutic but rejecting the Bible they would argue should never be questioned. The hermeneutic of the dominant culture in America would castigate anyone who would question the Bible in passages like, "Slaves, be obedient to those who are your earthly masters, with fear and trembling, in singleness of heart, as to Christ" (Eph. 6:5). The reason why was because that hermeneutic placed no blame of anyone for being out of the will of God; in fact, it would be the slaves who would be out of the will of God if they questioned what the Bible said for them to do. But when the hermeneutic offered after 911 suggested that we are all accountable for what we do—as were the Israelites, who had fallen out of favor with God for their disobedience—there was outrage.

Wright had preached from a dual hermeneutic from the time he began his ministry. The Bible has seemingly supported oppression for many, not railed against it, but Wright felt the responsibility of breaking the scriptures open so that there was meaning and empowerment in them for the oppressed, who had only been given the hermeneutic from the perspective of the oppressor for far too long. In "The Day of Jerusalem's Fall," he was offering a sermon, however, that only some would be able to receive. In an interview with Bill Moyers, he said:

> I was trying to show how people—how the anger—and we felt anger. I felt anger. I felt hurt. I felt pain. In fact, September 11th, I was in Newark 'cause when they shut down the air system, I couldn't get back to Chicago. I looked out the window and saw the second plane hit from my hotel window. . . . And I had to preach . . . that Sunday. . . . They came to church wanting to know where is God in this. And so, I had to show them, using Psalm 137, how the people who were carried away into slavery were very angry, very bitter. . . .
>
> Hermeneutic is an interpretation. It's the window from which you're looking. . . . And when you don't realize that I've been framed—this whole thing has been framed through this window, there's another world out here that I'm not looking at or taking into account, it gives you a perspective that . . . is informed by and limited by your hermeneutic. . . .
>
> That the perception of God who allows slavery, who allows rape, who allows misogyny, who allows sodomy, who allows murder of a people, lynching, that's not the God of the people being lynched and sodomized and raped and carried away into a foreign country. . . . Same thing you find in Psalm 137. That those people who are carried away into slavery have a very different concept of what it means to be the people of God than the ones who carried them away.[32]

The hermeneutic offered by preachers from the Hebrew Scriptures has too often been that of the oppressor—preached by black and white clergy alike. There are countless references to slavery that have been delivered in such a way as to honor and support the oppressor, not the oppressed. Ideology has been passed off as theology. Wright, it seemed, always preached from a dual hermeneutic. He had to acknowledge the spirit of African Americans who were proud to be American, yet bitterly disappointed that their citizenship was not as valid as that of the oppressor. Both oppressor and oppressed had to be acknowledged, and then Wright could get to his message of empowerment—in spite of oppression.

"During that long period, the king of Egypt died. The Israelites groaned in their slavery and cried out, and their cry for help because of their slavery went up to God" (Exod. 2:23). For one group of people, whites who supported slavery and white supremacy, the message was clear: slavery was ordained and sanctioned by the Bible. But for another group of people, those who were enslaved, the same passage would most certainly be interpreted differently—as evidence of a beneficent God who *heard their groaning* and who was in sympathy for their need and desire to be set free.

The Bible is maddeningly ambivalent on the issues that have divided this nation. Both the Hebrew Scriptures and the New Testament contain words that those who support the idea of white supremacy have jumped on and used to further their ideologies, and those same words have been seen by oppressed people as evidence of God's opposition to the ideology of oppression. Jesus' silence is a serious problem and has always been a serious problem for African Americans trying to add sense to a senseless practice. The end result is that oppressed people have internalized the lessons of the oppressors! In her essay, "Reading *Her* Way through the Struggle: African American Women and the Bible," Dr. Renita Weems wrote, "Large numbers of religious women (including feminists) still identify with many of the ideals and characters found in the Bible . . . the Bible is still extremely influential in the African American religious life, and . . . scholars are hard pressed fully to explain why."[33]

Jeremiah Wright knew why, or at least believed he did. The Bible was the one book that his parents had read to keep them sane in an insane world. Now he would be able to meld his knowledge of biblical studies with the faith stories of the people to whom he spoke. He was not held hostage by Jesus' silence, nor was he intimidated by the apparent support of slavery in the Bible overall. For example, the Babylonians became the prototype of the oppressor, and characters in, for instance, the story of Esther became prototypes for the people who sat in the pews. Esther was a Jew who forgot who she was because she had been mentally seduced by the oppressor's culture: "Whenever someone asks you to give up your God in exchange for something else, watch out! Something terrible is about to happen. No wonder Esther's uncle, Mordecai, walked back and forth in front of the courtyard of the harem every day to see what was going to happen to this girl he had reared like a daughter. Slowly but surely the metamorphosis came. She changed little bit by little bit into a magnificent monster, created by an alien culture."[34]

Being in a "strange land" where you were forced to assimilate resulted in the "strangers" feeling out of place. Wright assured his listeners, using the same scriptures that had been used to isolate them, that they were *included*, not excluded, members of God's family: "We see prejudicially: 'He doesn't belong to our group.' But God sees paternally, or parentally: 'They all belong to me. Those are all my children.' We see exclusively. We exclude certain types: 'our gang' versus 'them.' We see exclusively, but God sees inclusively: 'All ye come unto me.' God so loved the world that he gave his only begotten son that whosoever—everybody—can come. We only see what we can see right now, our finitude, but God sees infinitely.[35]

Wright applied, and offered, a hermeneutic that assured black people that they were not a mistake, that God had breathed into them the same breath God had breathed into those who had oppressed them. Wright made them understand that God was not the oppressor, but that some of God's people were. It was a message of hope that many more people needed than anyone might imagine. His preaching and teaching made it possible for African Americans to take off the "mask," and be who they were, unashamed and unapologetic.

6

NOT HERE YOU WON'T!

Any people who forgets their story,
any people who does not remember their history,
any people who ignores their past, are people
who are on their way to death.
Psychologists call it social death.
Theologians call it spiritual death.

—JEREMIAH WRIGHT[1]

From the beginning of his ministry at Trinity United Church of Christ in 1972, the tension between African Americans who had grown up in a world where they lived with their shame at being who they were, and those African Americans who were deciding that they would not be ashamed any longer, was evident.

Wright began his pastorate at the church during the fervor of the civil rights movement. When Wright came, the relatively new church had already had three pastors: founding pastor Dr. Kenneth Smith, who began in 1961, followed in 1967 by Rev. Willie Jamerson, who stayed until 1971. Rev. Reuben Sheares was the interim pastor for the church from 1971 until February of 1972, when a young Jeremiah Wright became the church's fourth pastor.

Wright's father was not pleased with his son's decision to become pastor of Trinity; his desire was that his son would assume the pastorate of Grace Baptist Church in Philadelphia when he retired. Wright knew, however, that he and Grace Baptist were a "bad fit." Though he had become a preacher, scholar, and theologian largely by and through his father's teaching, Wright knew that he was much different than his father. His experiences had not been the same as had been his father's. He was growing up, coming to manhood, in the height of the civil rights movement, a time where African Americans were pushing to make themselves known and respected, not standing back and accepting the restraints that a racist culture and society had put on them. He knew his father had had a mission; he also knew that he had one, and he knew that his was different than had been his father's. Though difficult and painful, he had to let his father know that he knew God was telling him to go another way, to do ministry in a different place, with a different focus, than God had told his father.

The other problem, in terms of his father's concern, was that he was not going into a Baptist church. Wright's father had belonged to the American Baptist Conference (ABC), and there were no ABC churches in Chicago, but larger than that, Wright was not wed to any denomination, his upbringing notwithstanding. He said that if he was, or since he was, called to the ministry, he would serve anywhere he could; he said he couldn't find "denomination" anywhere in the Bible. He hated to disappoint his father; he had always wanted to be just like his father, remember, but he was at a point in his life where his father's training had equipped him to move into his own, carrying his father's lessons and spirit with him, yet living his own life and defining his own ministry.

Wright seemed to be in the right place at the right time. The nation was undergoing an upheaval as concerns race; the same spirit Wright had experienced at Howard University by students who rebelled until they could sing gospel music in addition to the classical music and spirituals that had been traditionally sung at the college, he was experiencing in this new church. Trinity was going in a different direction, Wright remembered. The African American members were willing and ready to embrace their own culture. "Being in the black church had meant blacks embraced being "white" for an hour," he said. Some of people at Trinity were not willing to do that anymore, though Trinity had been run in the way most black churches before this time were run. "The worship services at Trinity United Church of Christ were not designed for all kinds of people," he wrote. "The services were designed to be like the services in white churches. Their attempt was to attract educated, middle-class, middle-income, and upwardly mobile Negroes and whites who were 'our kind of people,'" he noted.[2]

Wright knew that he had come into a place that was ripe for change. The phrase "unashamedly black and unapologetically Christian" had been coined by interim minister Rev. Reuben Sheares. African Americans were waking up, it seemed, from a racism-induced state of shame. They were beginning to realize and embrace that being "different" did not mean they were "deficient," a theme Wright would come back to over and over. In his sermon, "Ain't Nobody Right but Us," Wright preached, some years later:

> We tend to classify folks who are not like us as somehow being substandard, below the norm, not quite up to par. They are deficient. In the field of education, the entire Eurocentric educational system was based on the fallacious assumption that every normal person was a left-brain person when it came to cognition and learning styles. Think about the whole Eurocentric educational system. Children in cribs are provided with mobiles of a certain shape. This is a circle. This is a cube. This is a triangle. Leave them with an object because left-brained people are object-oriented; they relate to objects. Later on you can leave them with a book and they will learn from the book.
>
> On the other hand, right-brain people, such as Africans and African Americans, are not object-oriented; they are people-oriented. When integration first came, back in the fifties, and whites had black kids in their classrooms for the first time, the white teachers did not know what to do, because the black kids kept getting in their space. The children wanted to touch them and hang on them and talk to them, because that's how black children are. In Africa, mothers carry their children for two or three years. They're used to contact. . . . They don't care what the book says, because they're people-oriented, not object-oriented. It took ed-

> ucators like Janice Hale Benson to point out that children of African descent (and Jesus was African) have different ways of learning, and different cognition styles because they are right brained. . . . Difference is not synonymous with deficiency.[3]

Although Trinity "was started by a white denomination for Negroes who knew how to worship properly," Wright wrote, it was pulling away from the pack. Many of the original charter members were not all that excited or in support of a "black" presence in their worship space; many of them thought and wanted, wrote Wright, that the whites who "lived across Halstead" would be joining the church and making it an "integrated church" (sic).[4]

Wright believed that the United Church of Christ, a denomination formed in 1957 by the merger of four white denominations, the Congregational Church, the Christian Church, the Reformed Church in the United States, and the Evangelical Synod of North America, was bowing to the pressures of the historical moment to make anything black less distasteful; after the work and death of Rev. Dr. Martin Luther King, it seemed politically correct for those entities that had been all white to at least make gestures toward change. The United Church of Christ (UCC) was no different. An ecumenical movement begun in the 1920s saw several denominations merge, including those that would form the fabric of the United Church of Christ. The Congregationalists and the Christians merged in 1931, and the Reformed and Evangelicals merged in 1934. The Congregational-Christians and the Reformed-Evangelicals merged in 1957 to form the United Church of Christ.

But in their merging there was no rush to change the basic racial makeup of these denominations, not until the height of the civil rights movement and more urgently after the death of Martin Luther King. In the early1950s, writes Wright, before the merger that resulted in the United Church of Christ, "Blacks began to move into what was then the posh neighborhood of Chicago called Park Manor. The Congregational-Christian denomination decided a church was needed in the upper middle class Negro section of the city for persons who could afford to live in those two-story brownstones and those mansions along South Parkway. It is for that reason that the Congregational Church of

Park Manor was started by the denomination."[5] This was after the Congregational Church started a church in 1909 for "Negroes" who had graduated from schools supported by the American Missionary Association (AMA) of the Congregational Church. That church was the first one of the denomination in Chicago; the second one was the Congregational Church of the Good Shepherd. That church started, noted Wright, because "members of Lincoln split out of Lincoln because of the "color problem." Apparently, there were too many darker-skinned blacks joining Lincoln, and so the lighter skinned blacks pulled out and started Good Shepherd."[6]

The civil rights movement brought about an awareness of social problems due to racism; many black churches were firmly committed to working to end discrimination and to bring about integration. They were *not* committed, however, to being "too black." A Congregational pastor, according to Wright, said from his pulpit that he "would not tolerate any niggerisms (sic) in any of his services, and though he reportedly made that statement way before the civil rights movement, the fact of the matter was that that sentiment was not gone by the 1960s. The depth of the hatred of anything black, including themselves, was too deep to be expunged by a mere social upheaval. The spirit of self-hatred had been carefully cultivated over hundreds of years; integration and antidiscrimination measures might soothe the surface of America's racial problems, but would hardly touch its core. Wright says that in 1968 "Dr. King was murdered and Negroes turned *black*!"[7] Some Negroes, maybe, but far from all of them.

ꝏ

Carter G. Woodson wrote of the "two worlds" of blacks and whites; in spite of education, there was still a breach between the two races that was unmistakable. Whites had denigrated blacks and blacks had internalized that denigration. Writing about a white person who was a "director of Negroes," Woodson recounted his words:

"I realize that I have no useful function in my present position as a president of a Negro institution. I do not approve of their aspirations to many things. I cannot accept the students in my house as I would white students because it might lead to an interracial romance. Marrying is such a difficult problem at best that I should not like to see one of my children make a failure in life by marrying a Negro."[8]

Blacks in America knew the sentiment well, and in spite of efforts to end discrimination and to promote integration, the fact of the matter was that many blacks, even as the civil rights movement and the Black Power movement gained momentum, would have rather have been anything but black.

Wright saw this firsthand as he began his pastorate at Trinity. Some of the members were ready for change. Wright recalls how one member paid him a visit on December 31, 1971, and explained that Trinity had a vision:

> He shared with me the vision of the Trinity congregation. He shared with me the painful history of the congregation. He shared with me how the congregation wanted to change the perception that community members had of them. They wanted to be known as a welcoming congregation. They wanted a worship service that was exciting and attracting to African Americans who were now "conscious" African Americans, unashamed of their history, unashamed of their legacy, unashamed of their culture and highly skilled in every profession imaginable![9]

This church was one that wanted a ministry that followed in the footsteps of Dr. King; it wanted to address social problems that affected blacks not only in Chicago but in Africa and in the Diaspora.[10]

Wright became the church's fourth pastor on the second Sunday in February 1972. What this church wanted, he wanted.

But the whole church didn't want the same thing. When Wright chose a hymnal that was not the traditional hymnal of the Congregational Church, the "first congregational fight broke out!" The congregation was incensed that Wright had brought "a Baptist hymnal" to their church.[11] This certainly was not the case even though there were members of Trinity who were not at all "in" with the movement toward black pride. The last thing they wanted was to be identified as a "typical" black church, which, in their minds, was a church with spirited music, as opposed to the traditional hymns found in the *Pilgrim's Hymnal*, used by the Congregational church. They wanted no shouting, no emotionalism, absolutely *nothing* that would make them like blacks they considered to be beneath them. A movement began to get rid of the hymnal Wright proposed the congregation use, which "went nowhere," but the word was out. Jeremiah Wright was taking their church in a direction they did not approve of. Members began to leave.

When Wright sought to introduce black sacred music to his new church, yet another group of members left. The music done by the choirs at Trinity was primarily European anthems, and some spirituals. Wright wanted to introduce black sacred music, that is, gospel music, because he liked it, because he had studied it, and because he knew young blacks liked it as well. Older members of his church were incensed, or at least thrown off-center. What was the big deal with having "black sacred music?" they wondered. Things had been fine as they were.

In the midst of this first movement of the symphony that was to be Trinity's own, twenty-two of the original eighty-seven members there when Wright had started left the congregation. Wright was infused with and inspired by the vision God had given him, however. He was beginning to see how tightly wound blacks were who did not want to be black, and he felt and tasted their reactions to what he was trying to do. They poured into the experience of "becoming black" what they had received all their lives from "being black"—shame.

African Americans had learned to be ashamed of their ancestry; you almost never heard anyone say proudly up until the late 1960s that their ancestors had come from Africa! Joy Degruy Leary noted that young African Americans, in a study she conducted, showed their shame of Africa: "All that they had come to know, think and feel about one of the largest and culturally rich continents in the world was that they were ashamed of sharing a common ancestry with its inhabitants.[12] The United Church of Christ wanted African American members, but only a "certain kind," and those who joined the denomination prided themselves on being "that kind." With this new, lively music Wright was bringing in, the comfortable berth of assimilation was being jostled, and some members simply did not like it and could not take it. The damage done to their psyches was just too deep; writes Leary, "Being told you are inferior for hundreds of years can have lasting psychic impacts."[13]

The young people of Trinity, however, and a fair number of the older ones, worked through their psychic damage. The music was exhilarating to them; it spoke to them and reached them and helped make worship meaningful. Up to this point, there had merely been a Chancel Choir; this new choir, composed mostly of young people and singing in any month where there was a fifth Sunday, was called the Youth Fellowship Choir. The "kids" were vibrant and on fire. Wright notes that some of his members were rudely awakened; they not only sang a "new music," but they wore red, black, and green dashikis and were accompanied not only by organ but by drums and tambourines. The atmosphere was electrifying, according to some who were there at the time.

Eventually, some of the older members wanted to join this new choir, and its name was changed from the Youth Fellowship Choir to the Trinity Choral Ensemble. Interestingly, once the name was changed, more adults than young people joined the Trinity Choral Ensemble (TCE), speaking to their unmet need to hear and sing music that touched their souls. And overall attendance at Trinity was always "up" when the TCE sang. Wright says that members began calling to see which choir was singing and would opt to go when the newer choir was in place. The minister of music was to do something that was unheard of in black churches up until then: teach a variety of genres of music, including gospel music, both traditional and contemporary, West African music, South African music, Afro-Cuban music, Afro-Caribbean music, and what was known as "meter singing."[14]

Clearly, Wright had hit a long-dried-out place in the hearts of his members. The Chancel Choir still existed but refused to sing anything other than their Eurocentric anthems; TCE sang those anthems *plus* the other, new genres the minister of music was charged to teach. Wright says that two different congregations were developing: those who came when the Chancel Choir was singing and those who came only when the Trinity Choral Ensemble was singing. That could not be; it was not in line with the vision God had given Wright. So he dismantled the Chancel Choir and folded both choirs into one; the new choir was to be called the Sanctuary Choir, and it continued to grow in numbers as it sang music that reached the people's hearts.

In spite of the resistance of some of the older members of Trinity, Wright knew he was on the right track. Yes, the membership had lost twenty-two of its eighty-seven members, but more members were coming in every Sunday. Wright says in his book *A Sankofa Moment* that he recalled the words of W. E. B. DuBois as he continued to shape his new congregation: "W. E. B. DuBois said in 1903 that there are three ingredients to every Black church: The preaching, the music, and the Holy Spirit! W. E. B. DuBois also said that if you take any one of those three elements away you would no longer have a Black church! You would have a social club, a mutual aid society or a mutually congratulatory bourgeois Negro gathering, or you would have a social action group, but you would not have a church carrying out the mission of the Lord, Jesus Christ or trying to be what a church ought to be."[15]

Although there was some dissent from older blacks who were so totally assimilated that they found change hard, more and more assimilated blacks began to edge toward Trinity. The music was a draw, yes, but the content of the ministry was also exciting. Wright joined the Joint Educational Development (JED) team, which was comprised of educators not only from the United Church of Christ, but from the Evangelical Lutheran Church, the United Methodist Church, the American Baptist Church, and several other denominations. Its goal was to teach educators the "truth about Africa and Africans in the Judeo-Christian story, and they wanted their memberships to know about the racism in Christianity" that had affected blacks and whites alike.[16] Wright was ecstatic! The JED was meeting during the 1970s, when the civil rights movement was charging full steam ahead. Now, finally, there was a move to teach the Bible, teach the importance and the presence of Africa in the Bible, and thus get to the wounded spirits of black people and the confused "knowledge" of most practicing Christians. He had in his head ideas about what the Christian Education Department could look like, and what it could do.

But when he got back from his meetings with the JED and shared his vision with the Christian Education Department, he found many of them, and many of the parents of children who would attend Sunday school, less than impressed. They said to him, in a nutshell, that they didn't send their children to Sunday school "to learn about Black things or to learn about Black people."[17] Wright's assistant pastor, Rev. Barbara Allen, was actually "censured" by the Church Council because she took some of the Sunday school curricula and colored some of the characters in the stories brown so they wouldn't be all white. Wright instinctively knew that the process of getting to know "who" they were and liking who they were had to start when they were very young. It might be that the children would lead their parents out of the proverbial shame carried by black people. He knew there would be resistance, but he had to move forward. Not only did some parents revolt and rebel against what Wright wanted to do, but some of the Sunday school teachers resigned, as did the director of Christian Education.[18]

It was like they were saying, *"not up in here, you won't!"* A little change to the music might be okay, but it was a bit much to push this "black thing" in church. What the people wanted was what they had always had as concerns church and worship. African Americans, including the members of Trinity United Church of Christ, had found a way to find meaning in a text that was not intended to feed "the souls of black folk." They had found a way to internalize words of hope they found there, and to ignore words that seemed to support their oppression. Most of them grew up with the image of Jesus as a white man, and white men were their oppressors, yet this Jesus was somehow different. They had done something, fixed something, or altered something, so that *this* white man was not a threat, but was, instead, their ultimate hope.

This white man, this Jesus, would "make it all right," as so many songs sung in the black church alluded to. Jesus would make it right, work it out, and make a way out of no way. There was no need, then, to bother this icon. Many African Americans were not interested, did not care, if the biblical stories took place in what is today known as Africa. They did not care if the biblical peoples were black. It didn't matter. In fact, it was immaterial and not important to know for one to be "saved." What one needed to know only was that Jesus "died and rose for our sins." A theologian might be able to unpack that as African Americans internalized and understood it. One wonders if blacks were suggesting that Jesus died for the sins of all people but especially for the sins of the white people who had oppressed them? Was the joyful proclamation of Jesus dying for "our sins" a way for blacks to say that God would "get" those who had so bruised and wounded them?

Whatever they thought, they did not want Wright to change too much of what they had grown up with. Renita Weems notes this same tendency among African American women. She writes:

> The Bible is in many ways alien and antagonistic to modern women's identity, yet, in other ways it inspires and compels that identity. An example of the complexity of this situation is this: How African American women read the Bible is a topic that has to do with not only uncovering whose voice they identify with in the Bible—female as opposed to male, the African as opposed to the non-African, the marginalized as opposed to the dominant. It has equally and more precisely to do with examining the *values* of those readers and the corroboration of those values by the text; it has to do with how the text arouses, manipulates, and harnesses African American women's deepest yearnings."[19]

Wright was attempting to get his members to tap into their "deepest yearnings" as well. Black people did not *want* to be despised and looked down upon; they had gotten used to it, but it is not what they wanted. They had no clue who they were. Black people were used to being told who they were by a group of people who had been taught that they were better. Black people had been taught that they had nothing to little to offer this country. They were not told that, in their slavery, they had made this nation the economic giant it had become. They had not been told of the many African Americans who had been pioneers in many disciplines. Sadly, many black people did not know who Emmett Till was, and they didn't know that Egypt was actually in Africa.

The smallest things, Wright knew, could begin to open their eyes to who they were, and make them curious about who they really were, not who they had been *told* they were. Black people were used to living with being disrespected on daily basis, no matter how hard they worked or how much education they had. Wright himself had tasted it in the military, but many or most of his members had had experiences of the same ilk.

Trinity continued to grow. The music and the preaching were big draws, but an additional lure was the fact that Wright's ministry reached black men, who had for too long felt marginalized by American society but also by the black church. As noted in the introduction of this book, Wright made black men "feel like men." They were encouraged to be themselves, to embrace their protestations about what happened to them in America so that they could get past it enough to be empowered in spite of the barriers they scaled daily. Black men felt their issues being put out front and center by Wright's preaching and teaching. Older men heard their experiences talked about from the pulpit; young men heard their experiences in the streets of Chicago talked about as well. Wright connected with old and young men alike; he knew the words of songs that appealed to the older men, songs from Brook Benton or Nat King Cole . . . but he also knew the current raps. From the pulpit, one never knew what song might come forth, but Wright was letting everyone, but especially the men, know that he was with them. He knew their pain and he knew their world. The men kept coming.

The feeding of a people who had been starved of dignity was having an effect, and it made some in the denomination uncomfortable. Clergy in the Chicago Metropolitan Association, of which Trinity was a member, seemed alarmed by the rapid growth, suggesting that perhaps Trinity was a cult "just two months after the Jim Jones incident in Guyana."[20] Some, both white and black, were uncomfortable with Trinity's determination to be "unashamedly black and unapologetically Christian." Writes Wright:

> Many of the twenty-two folk who left our congregation did not leave quietly. They left complaining. They went running to "Massa" to tell a white man what they thought was happening to their Negro church. . . . I told the Association minister that he was used to Black churches where the worship was not Black. He was used to bourgeois Negroes who wanted to be white. He was glad that the 1960s were over and that the era of confrontation had passed . . . but what he did not realize was that a whole new breed of African American Christians had come out of the '60s who were, as Reuben Sheares defined them, "unashamedly black and unapologetically Christian."[21]

Wright was reaching out to "the community," many of whom had never been to church, but who had certainly been a part of a community and a society that did not support them. The "right kind of black people" that Wright says the UCC was trying to attract were not at first amenable to this goal, but as time went on and Trinity's membership swelled, class seemed to mean little. There was a common denominator among black people, that they were "strangers" in their own land. They had worked and done all the right things, just to be shoved back into their place. Class had nothing to do with it; it was all about color.

Wright's congregation not only swelled in numbers, but in pride. Many members began to wear African clothing as a matter of course. As Wright preached about how blacks had bought into the European definitions of beauty, which included straight hair, many women began to stop getting chemical relaxers on their hair to make it straight, like white people, and instead wore naturals or braids. In front of Wright was a flower that had long been closed tight, opening up, and the people were sewn together by Wright's messages, which blended biblical scholarship, American history, world events . . . and of course, Jesus.

What was happening in Trinity UCC was that a religion was being birthed that worked for everyone, including black people. Jeremiah Wright was presenting to his congregation a God who truly had no favorites, as the scriptures said. Here was a place where the words found in Galatians 3:28 were being lived out, with black people not being on the periphery, looking at scripture from a distance, but with them feeling included in the mix: "There is neither Jew nor Gentile, neither slave nor free, nor is there male and female, for you are all one in Christ Jesus."

Here, in this growing congregation with the young pastor and a lot of people who wore African clothing, there were almost a palpable sigh of relief: they counted, they mattered to God. It was okay to seek and expect God to work on their behalf while they were yet alive. Prior to this time, African Americans used religion as a steppingstone to the afterlife; their eschatological theology was a way to survive in a country with a system of racial inequality that was beyond unfair; it was simply brutal. If there was relief in heaven, then the masses of black people waited expectantly for the day they would pass over and rest safely in the Savior's arms. That had been the gist of black religion.

The reason Sunday morning was a time for grief release was because black people lived very tense lives for the most part in society. Slavery might have been abolished, but black people knew that the *spirit of slavery*, on the part of themselves and on the part of the oppressors, was still very much alive. Actual lynching might no longer be a reality or common occurrence, but young black men, especially, were still in danger of being harassed and socially "lynched" by law enforcement officers, thrown into a justice system that had been anything but just for black people.

What might be called a "boyish prank" if done by a white person could land a black person in the system, perhaps never to get out. The spirit of slavery had even rested inside many churches, as messages preached tended not to be sermons that pushed empowerment on earth, but nirvana in heaven. Ideology—a belief system that clearly supported white superiority—was passed off as theology. The result was that many blacks internalized and believed the message that their best bet was to behave and stay in their place, and if they did that, they would get their reward in heaven. The problem was, however, that such a worldview was damaging to African Americans as they tried to survive on a daily basis. Where was God? What would God say? What had God said throughout history? It was a tension of behemoth proportions.

Wright tackled the tension head on. In his preaching and teaching, he worked actively to identify the spirit of slavery, to expose it, and then help his listeners climb from underneath its grip. He knew the damage that had been done to black people because of this hovering spirit. It wasn't emotion from which he spoke; it was from experiences, his own and those of other African Americans whose dealings in America he had experienced vicariously. He wrote: "In the founding days of the Association of Black Psychologists back in the 1960s, one of their most powerful points about miseducation when it came to Africans and persons of African descent was the issue of false images and the pictures from the Renaissance which became religious icons in the minds of persons of the Christian faith all over the world. . . . The Association of Black Psychologists argued that (those images) were teaching African Americans how to hate themselves. For a little Black boy or girl to want to be like Jesus meant they wanted to be like the white person they saw in those pictures!"[22]

Most people, whatever their ethnicity, believed that God was white and that Jesus was white as well. This was particularly damaging to African Americans, who had ingested and digested the myth that black people were inferior and bad. Even God and God's son, it seemed, were white. African Americans were used to seeing pictures of a Jesus who looked like an Italian sex symbol with his brown or blond wavy hair, his blue eyes and his white to olive-colored skin. Most people didn't question the veracity of what they had always seen. The images created by Renaissance artists including Michelangelo and da Vinci were seen as the "final answer" in the question of what Jesus looked like. Because they had painted the images, their depictions became Truth, and the images and inherent lesson about the whiteness of the world were ingrained into all children in America, including little black children who felt their unworthiness in light of the "Truth."

The "whiteness" of the world was helped along by the media. In Wright's congregation, there were people who had never seen positive images of African Americans on the small or the silver screen growing up; to be beautiful, the images said, one had to look like the "beauties" seen via the media. Black people had tried their best, from straightening their hair to putting skin lighteners on to make their skin less brown . . . and yet, nothing worked. They were not "beautiful" according to the definition of beauty. One never saw (and still does not see very often) a brown-skinned model wearing lingerie. If one brown skinned woman was so depicted, she had to have long, wavy hair. She could not look "too ethnic." To be beautiful was to be blonde and blue-eyed. Remember, the eugenics movement had worked to create this image of the master race, quite intentionally. Blacks were not deemed "master race" material in any way.

At Trinity, because of Wright's awareness of how badly blacks had been damaged by American rhetoric and work to designate who was "in" and who was not, there was a concerted effort to address the issue. His members had to know who they were! They had to know their worth, and the worth of Africans in history. They had to know that they were not scorned by God and had not been damned by God and relegated to the status of second-class citizenship. That was a human undertaking, misrepresenting God, the God of all and the God of inclusion, for humankind's own purposes. Black people had to get a different message, a different perspective.

This observation is found in the "Afterword" of Wright's book *A Sankofa Moment:*

> In many ways what Pastor Wright tried to do was what the Apostle Paul tried to do as he wrote to a people under Roman oppression. The Apostle Paul sought to present Christ to a people under Roman oppression in spite of the harshness of their Roman oppressors. Paul was faithful in this context and Pastor Wright was faithful in his context. . . . You do not have to be a Black person living on the Southside of Chicago to know and accept Christ and develop a personal relationship with Him. You do not have to be a Black person at all to do that. The Gospel of Jesus Christ is preached to all persons of all colors, all nations, all cultures and all ethnicities. Pastor Wright preached that Gospel and persons from four different continents became followers of Christ because of that preaching."[23]

Wright remained true to his vision and stayed close to his passion for wanting young black people to know who they were. Jonathan Alter, author of several books, including *The Promise*, wrote that Wright was dedicated to "rejecting middle class values in favor of authentically African American ones."[24] Alter criticized Wright for that and said that it was "a pose," because a large percentage of his congregation was middle class.[25] Alter's comments showed a complete ignorance of the Trinity UCC community. While Trinity did adopt a "black value system," Wright did not reject middle-class values; what he worked against was the mindset of middle-class black people who did not know who they were, did not want to know who they were, and ascribed to the white world with all of its values and beliefs at the expense of their own!

He wasn't opposed to blacks becoming "middle class;" he was middle class himself, but what he didn't want was for blacks to become middle class and leave the richness of their own culture and history! That had been the way blacks had lived far too often, largely because of the fact that the spirit of slavery forever hovered over them, feeding into their self-hatred. What he wanted, with the black value system, was to give his members some "bullet points," if you will, to look at and ascribe to in order to better their lives in a hostile society. During the Obama campaign in 2008, the "black value system" was talked about as though it were something subversive, but it was really the guts of a new mentality that Wright felt his church members—and anyone else who would listen—needed to have in order to know who and whose they were. Those twelve:

- Commitment to God
- Commitment to the black community
- Commitment to the black family
- Dedication to the pursuit of education
- Dedication to the pursuit of excellence
- Adherence to the black work ethic
- Commitment to self-discipline and self-respect
- Disavowal of the pursuit of "middleclassness"
- Pledge to make the fruits of all developing and acquired skills available to the black community
- Pledge to allocate regularly a portion of personal resources for strengthening and supporting black institutions
- Pledge allegiance to all black leadership who espouse and embrace the black value system
- Personal commitment to embracing the worth and validity of all activity in terms of positive contributions to the black value system. To measure the worth and validity of all activity in terms of positive contributions to the general welfare of the black community and the advancement of black people toward freedom.[26]

On the issue of "middleclassness," the black value system explained that the *mindset* of those who scrambled their way out of poverty must be tempered; the middle-class mindset of America in general had been such that it sought personal comfort and rights over the welfare of any given community. It was "permissible to chase middle income" with "all our might," the system explained, but "we must avoid . . . the psychological entrapment of Black "middleclassness."[27] In other words, an increased income should not lead to a decreased appreciation for and commitment to a race that had been scorned and oppressed for far too long. It is not clear if Alter ever visited Trinity, but his observation that it was predominantly middle class belied the truth, that Trinity drew scores of people from every socioeconomic level, in great numbers. Black people felt like they "belonged," many for the first time. They were involved in a community of faith that actively worked to get rid of their "vacant" self-esteem, as Joy Degruy Leary terms it. A people who know who they are carry a different spirit than those who crouch under a spirit of slavery, which reminds them at every turn what they are *not*.

Wright was shaping a different way for black people to look at themselves. This country, from its very first president to the president who issued the Emancipation Proclamation, had struggled with its perception of black people, and the country's disdain for its imported citizens had bled over into the very souls of those citizens. Abraham Lincoln, commenting on his first inaugural in 1861, said,

> One-eighth of the whole population was colored slaves, not distributed generally over the Union but localized in the Southern part of it. These slaves constituted a peculiar and powerful interest. All knew that this interest was, somehow, the cause of the war. North and South . . . both read the same Bible, and pray to the same God; and each invokes His aid against the other. It may seem strange that any men should dare to ask a just God's assistance in wringing their bread from the sweat of other men's faces; but let us not judge, that we be not judged. The prayers of both could not be answered; that of neither has been answered fully. The Almighty has His own purposes."[28]

For Jeremiah Wright, the purpose of the Almighty, or at least one of God's purposes, was that black people—including those who came kicking and screaming—would pause and be comforted to know that the Almighty had not made a mistake in creating them. God had no favorites. God's people had to know that.

That was his goal, his vision. Although it was his goal, and although he knew his goal was just God's goal spoken into him, his work was not easy. There were times when, because of some of the opposition, he wondered if he had it right, if he were indeed where God wanted him to be. He recalls that he shared that sentiment with a mentor of his, the Rev. Clarence H. Cobbs, who was pastor of the First Church of Deliverance.

As Wright discussed some of his fears and frustrations, Cobbs did his best to reassure the young pastor, but the real moment of a "divine confirmation" came probably some time later when Wright was listening to Cobbs preach. Looking at Wright, Cobbs stopped in the middle of his sermon and addressed him: "Boy, the Lord will give you as far as you can see! If all you see is right here at 95th and Parnell, then that is all the Lord will give you. If you can see beyond here, all the way to 95th and Stony Island or even further, the Lord will give you that. He will give you as far as you can see!"[29]

As Cobbs returned to his sermon, Wright sat startled, yet reassured. God was trying to reach him, to tell him to make the vision that God had given him plain; God was trying to tell him that not all people, *not all black people,* would agree with him and support him; some of his own people would bring him the biggest hurts and disappointments. Yet, God wanted Jeremiah to go forward in the tradition of the prophet after whom he had been named, Jeremiah. His life would not be easy, as no prophet's life is, yet, it is only from prophets that people at least *hear the heart and the will of God!* Prophets ache because the people will not hear, yet this God continues to reach out to the people God created. God, it seemed, had jostled Rev. Cobbs to give a message to young Wright. Wright heard it . . . and knew that he must move in the direction God was leading him.

7

WRIGHT AS PREACHER AND PROPHET

The word of the Lord came to me saying, Before I formed you in the womb, I knew you, before you were born, I set you apart; I appointed you as prophet to the nations.

—JEREMIAH 1:4–5 NIV

Young Jeremiah probably did not know that he would end up being considered a prophet. A true prophet is picked by God and specially equipped to do a specific task—to speak truth to people who do not want to hear it. It is not just any truth the prophet is called upon to speak, but God's truth, breathed into his or her soul, if the Bible is to be believed. Abraham Heschel, in his book *The Prophets*, gives a profound description of what a prophet is. In contrast to great works of literature, he said, which "have a serene look," the words of the prophet are anything but serene. Says Heschel, "[The words of] a prophet suggest a disquietude sometimes amounting to agony."[1] The style of the prophet, continues Heschel, is "charged with agitation, anguish, and a spirit of non-acceptance. The prophet's concern is not with nature but with history and history is devoid of poise."[2] Heschel says that the "life and soul are at stake in what he says and in what is going to happen to what he says":

> The prophet seldom tells a story, but casts events. He rarely sings, but castigates. He does more than translate reality into a poetic key; he is a preacher whose purpose is not self-expression of the "purgation of emotions," but communication. His images must not shine, they must burn. The prophet is intent on intensifying responsibility, is impatient of excuse, contemptuous of pretense and self-pity. His tone, rarely sweet of caressing, is frequently consoling and disburdening; his words are often slashing, even horrid—designed to shock rather than to edify.[3]

The reason the words of the prophet are so stinging is that these individuals thus touched by God are given a clear mandate from God: tell the people what I (God) desire. Throughout the Bible, especially in the Hebrew scriptures, we see a disappointed God, a sometimes frustrated and angry God, who does not understand why the people God created have been so ungrateful, so willful, to the point of ignoring the voice and will of God. The God of the Hebrew Scriptures is the one who said from the outset:

> These are the commands, decrees and laws the LORD your God directed me to teach you to serve in the land that you are crossing the Jordan to possess, so that you, your children, and their children after them may fear the LORD your God as long as you live by keeping all his decrees and commands that I give you, and so that you may enjoy long life. Hear, O Israel, and be careful to obey so that it may go well with you and that you may increase greatly in a land flowing with milk and honey, just as the LORD, the God of your fathers, promised you. Hear, O Israel: The LORD our God, the LORD is one. Love the LORD your God with all your heart and with all your soul and with all your strength. These commandments that I give you today are to be upon your hearts. (Deut. 6:1–7 NIV)

Surely the problem of racism might have been less a reality not only in the United States, but in the world, had that "great commandment" been adhered to, but the wrath and frustration of God shown in the Hebrew scriptures proves that loving God with "all our hearts and with all our souls and with all our strengths," was no easy thing, or at least no palatable or pleasurable thing. When Jesus referred to this great commandment in the New Testament, he added, "This is the first and greatest commandment and the second is like it: Love your neighbor as yourself"(Matt. 22:37–38). There is so much in this "ask" from God that is, frankly, difficult for humans to carry out. One observer, noting this difficulty, took issue with the statement often heard in sermons, "God doesn't make mistakes." "Are you sure about that?" this gentleman asked. "If God doesn't make mistakes, then why don't the people of God act better? If God wants obedience so much, and if God wants people to love God completely and wholly *and* love each other, then why didn't God wire people to be able to do it?"

It is a sound question and observation, one for which it is doubtful that anyone has an answer, but for sure, the prophet is one sent by God to try to get people to get the fundamentals of believing in God right. The prophet is often in agony, as Heschel writes, because God will not release him or her from the burden of trying to get people to see God and understand God in a way that translates something for them, leading them to then love God with an entirety that changes their lives and therefore the lives of people around them. People, from their inception, seemed to be particularly talented at irritating God to the point of, in the Hebrew Scriptures, God throwing a divine fit of rage, resulting in the decimation and destruction of the very people God had created! Religion, for all its good intentions, was often at the heart of the problem, notes Heschel: "The prophet knew that religion could distort what the Lord demanded of man, that priests themselves had committed perjury by bearing false witness, condoning violence, tolerating hatred, calling for ceremonies instead of bursting forth with wrath and indignation at cruelty, deceit, idolatry, and violence."[4]

When the prophets in the Hebrew Scriptures would rail at God's people for their lack of respect, the people would be reminded and would do better for a short time, but would quickly fall back into old patterns. Exasperated, God would sometimes use enemies God's own people (the Assyrians and Babylonians, for example) as an instrument to shake them up, figuratively speaking, into a state of obedience and awareness of God's will. One can only imagine the antagonism, the cynicism, and the outright opposition these prophets picked up from people as they gave the messages God gave them to give, and yet they pressed on. Their faithfulness to God, in spite of their loneliness on earth, was one of the trademarks of the prophets. The Bible shows that they were often depressed and disenchanted with God and the work God had tapped them to do. Complained the biblical prophet Jeremiah:

> O Lord, you deceived me and I was deceived; you overpowered me and prevailed. I am ridiculed all day long; everyone mocks me. Whenever I speak, I cry out proclaiming violence and destruction. So the word of the Lord has brought me insult and reproach all day long. . . . Cursed be the day I was born! May the day my mother bore me not be blessed! Cursed be the man who brought my father the news, who made him very glad, saying, "A child is born to you—a son!" May that man be like the towns the Lord overthrew without pity. May he hear wailing in the morning, a battle cry at noon. For he did not kill me in the womb, with my mother as my grave, her womb enlarged forever. Why did I ever come out of the womb to see trouble and sorrow and to end my days in shame? (Jer. 20:7–8, 14–18)

Dr. Martin Luther King, who is most certainly a modern-day prophet, struggled as did the Bible's Jeremiah. In 1956 he had struggled, sitting alone in his kitchen; God was talking to him, telling him to persevere in this work; later, in 1960, he remembered feeling spent: "At times I have felt that I could no longer bear such a heavy burden, and was tempted to retreat to a more quiet and serene life. But every time such a temptation appeared, something came to strengthen and sustain my determination. . . . God has been profoundly real to me in recent years. In the midst of our dangers, I have felt an inner calm."[5]

Jeremiah Wright had been given a prophetic responsibility. His prophecy would have to reach an oppressed people who were not sure about who and whose they were; he was, in fact, going to prophesy the goodness and love of God for them, in spite of their living in a hostile country. And he would have to speak to the oppressors, speaking "truth to power," as it were, trying to get them to open their clogged hearts and plugged ears. Some would not want to hear him; some would not be able to hear him, at least not for a while.

For Jeremiah Wright, the voice of God had instructed him to deal with race, not in isolation, but in conjunction with American history, African American history, and the word of God.

Although for some the idea of melding history and the Bible was antithetical, for Wright, it was not only right, but necessary. America's history was dotted with racial tension, too often covered or justified by the word of God. It was maddening that so many Americans, blacks included, wanted to act as though racism was not an issue, and had always been an issue, when racism had accounted for the hovering "spirit of slavery" that had spiritually, emotionally, and psychologically incapacitated or limited black people and concurrently given white people a sense of superiority that was innately false.

Even if slavery was no longer an accepted entity, everyone knew that slavery, for all intents and purposes, was as alive as was racial discrimination; the two fed each other. Even though segregation had technically been eliminated, it still in fact existed. Discrimination in housing, jobs, and education was still a reality. So, in spite of looking different from the outside, America was still the same America, rotted through with racism. African Americans, including Wright's members, felt it and lived it. Peter Gomes wrote that "racism was the mother of slavery and that segregation was its child."[6] In fact, in spite of the fact that the Civil War had long ended, this nation was still "North" and "South" in spirit. Sometimes, it seemed that in everyday dealings the mindset of the South, angry that it had lost the war and its right to own slaves, was the predominant emotion of American life, albeit nobody wanted to say it. There was no escaping it.

In Wright's congregation, as in all black institutions, there were people who not only lived with the ugly reality of racism, but who had grown up with mothers and fathers, grandparents, aunts, and uncles, who had lived through some horrid times and experiences due to racism. Some of his members had landed in Chicago during the Great Migration; others were sons, daughters, or grandchildren of people who had fled the South looking for freedom and dignity, only to find things different but not much better if one's skin was black. In her book *The Warmth of Other Suns*, author Isabel Wilkerson describes the experiences black people had had in the South which had encouraged them to leave; one such account was offered about basketball great Bill Russell's parents:

> Bill Russell was born in Monroe (Louisiana) in 1934 and watched his parents suffer one indignity after another. His father once went to a gas station only to be told he could have to wait for the white people to get their gas first. He waited and waited, and, when his turn never seemed to come, he started to pull off. The owner came up, put a shotgun to his head and told him he was not to leave until all the white people had been served. "Boy, don't you ever do what you just started to do," the station owner said. As for Russell's mother, a policeman once grabbed her on the street and ordered her to go and take off the suit she was wearing. He said that she had no business dressing like a white woman and that he'd arrest her if he ever saw her like that again. Bill Russell watched his mother sit at the kitchen table in tears over the straits they were in."[7]

Joy DeGruy Leary remembers when her father, who was dying, wanted to have a talk with her. Though he could barely talk, it was important that she listen to what he had to say. She recounts the very painful conversation, the last she was to have with her father:

> "There are some things I need you to know. The road of life is long and hard and you should not try to walk it alone. You need people to help you along the way."
>
> The next thing my father said to me seemed strange and disconnected at the time; however, years later its relevance became clear. He began to tell me about his life, first as a young boy growing up in Louisiana, He recounted a story where he was walking along a dirt road down in the Bayou when some white men approached him and said, "Boy, you get over here and you load these boxes, y' hear me, boy?"

> I noticed that my father was now becoming visibly upset as he spoke. He was quiet for a while, then he turned to me and said, "And I did what they told me to do, but I did it for you, Joy." . . .
>
> He began to speak again. He said, "When I was a young man in the Navy . . . I was a man! Joy . . . when some white officers walked up to me and they said, 'Boy, get over here and peel these shrimp. . . .'" I could clearly see the tears beginning to well up in my father's eyes, a rare sight for a man whom I'd always known to be a pillar of strength. . . . And for a second time, he repeated, "But I did it for you, Joy."[8]

These experiences were not isolated. Almost every African American had a story or two to tell of an experience or experiences that had greatly impacted his or her life. Racism was kneaded into the very "freedom documents" of this nation, and even in the nation's capital, racism and slavery lived inside the city and hovered over it. In 1846, residents of the District of Columbia who lived south of the Potomac petitioned Virginia, asking to rejoin the Commonwealth, in order to keep free African Americans out of the District. The Emancipation Act of 1862 abolished slavery in the District, but that did not mean blacks were freed or that, if or once they were freed, they realized a life of dignity. Slavery had been legal there, after all, for some time; it had existed there since 1790! Slave dealers housed future slaves in the nation's capital in prisons or crowded, dirty pens. Records tell of "slave coffles," long lines of shackled blacks marching from one site to another."[9] It hadn't been all that long ago and many people living in Chicago and other Northern cities had had relatives who had experienced the indignities.

Those experiences might be talked about in private, and some preachers made a point of trying to bring those experiences to the fore, but the trend tended to be not to talk about them, and certainly not in church!

The fact was and is, however, that those experiences had settled in the souls of black people. Their pain was held in; they learned to cope with the indignity and lack of respect they dealt with on so many levels on a daily basis. Wright knew that there had to be a way and a safe place for those experiences to be exposed, put on the table, looked at, dissected, and understood, in order for black people to *want* to know who they were! There had to not only be an opening up about their experiences, but a connection made between what they had lived and what the biblical peoples had lived as well. Oppression was not new; they had to know that. There are at least six different oppressive regimes in the Bible: Egyptian, Assyrian, Babylonian, Persian, Roman, and Greek.

Black people knew the story of the Red Sea (or Sea of Reeds) but what would their lives look like if they could see how God had acted throughout history for "the least of these" as they lived under oppression? Feeling oppressed in America was lonely and isolating; one could easily feel like nobody had been through what African Americans had been through, and truly, nobody had, but many people, many groups, had been through oppression, even and especially people in the Bible. Many people had lost sight of Yahweh and of their religion in an attempt to be accepted into an oppressive society that would never accept them . . . and they had made it through. Wright had to deliver the message to these who were living oppression, even as he had had to internalize the message himself as he experienced racial oppression. There had to be a way to connect a good God to a bad situation, and Wright's ministry would do that. He would tell the biblical stories as well as the stories out of American history, making a protective cloth that had no seams for a people who needed a special kind of covering and a blessed assurance that God was there for them like God was there for everyone else.

∞

In the Afterword of Wright's book *A Sankofa Moment* are these words: "The focus of the ministry at Trinity United Church of Christ was to introduce Christ to a people and a community who had known the horrors and ugliness of slavery, the Transatlantic Slave Trade, white supremacy, segregation, Jim Crow, and who now experience what Tim Wise calls 'Racism 201.'"[10]

This being the case, the prophetic yoke placed on Wright's neck was going to be no more popular than was the yoke placed on any of the biblical or other modern-day prophets. Heschel said, "the prophets see the world from the point of view of God as transcendent, not immanent truth," and he defines truth as "the "reality reflected in a mind." Heschel goes on to say that "prophetic truth" is "reality reflected in God's mind, the world *sub specie dei*."[11] Heschel explains his perspective in accordance with his understanding of the biblical Israelites, with which this work agrees, as a people who were supposed to show the majesty and fairness of God. The "chosen ones" were to give a new spirit and a new understanding to those who were "not chosen," per se, of this God who had created all. They were to be models of goodness, such that the rest of the world would not only follow, but would *want* to follow Yahweh. Instead, the people consistently disappointed Yahweh; Heschel notes that "the countries of the world were full of abominations, violence, (and) falsehood.[12] God's people, according to the Hebrew Scriptures, *had failed!* They had rejected God and disrespected God understanding that God required God's people to love each other as they loved God. Their lack of ability to love God in the full prevented them from caring for each other, and the world, as a result of that shortcoming, was not even close to being as God had envisioned it."

Gomes said, "In the absence of a visible God, the temptation is always near to make a god of whatever is visible and related in some proximate way to the real thing."[16] Perhaps the "divine absence" was too much for God's people; because God could not be seen, it was easy for many to most people to give lip service to the presence of God, but not get too uptight about perhaps not walking in the "way" of God. The people God had created, it seems, needed a visible God in order to feel compelled to do God's work and will, at least consistently. God's apparent absence gave the people a sense of free will and a rather flippant way of regarding God's directives. There might be consequences of disobedience, but when? Also, the very mercy of God—that is, God's tendency to punish but then to mete out inordinate mercy and forgiveness, seemed to give the biblical peoples the sense that they could pretty much do what they wanted; in the end, God would love them anyway.

It was the prophet's task to try to create a more authentic relationship between God and God's people; the prophet was to present God's pleading and God's will to a wayward people. The prophet Hosea offered some of the most heartfelt words in the Bible, on God's behalf, as he spoke God's sentiment to Israel, who was consistently disobeying him, and, actually, disrespecting him:

> When Israel was a child, I loved him, and out of Egypt I called my son. The more I called them, the more they went from me. They kept sacrificing to the Baals, and offering incense to idols. Yet it was I who taught Ephraim to walk, I took them up in my arms; but they did not know that I healed them. I led them with cords of human kindness, with bands of love; I was to them like those who lift infants to their cheeks. I bent down to them and fed them. They shall return to Egypt and Assyria shall be their king, because they have refused to return to me. The sword rages in their cities, it consumes their oracle-priests, and devours because of their schemes. My people are bent on turning away from me; to the Most High, even if he does not raise them up at all. (Hos. 11:1–7)

God's sadness and frustration presents the role and the need for the prophet, who, as we've said, speaks the truth as understood by God to the people. Heschel says that "to a person endowed with prophetic sight, everyone else appears blind; to a person whose ear perceives God's voice, everyone else appears deaf. No one is just; no knowing is strong enough, no trust complete enough. The prophet hates the approximate; he shuns the middle of the road. . . . There is an interaction between man and God which to disregard is an act of insolence."[14] The prophet not only hears God's voice; the prophet also hears God's yearning, God's pain, God's frustration and anger, and he or she cannot keep quiet, for it is, as Jeremiah the prophet says, "like a fire shut up in my bones": "So the word of the Lord has brought me insult and reproach all day long. But if I say, 'I will not mention him or speak any more in his name,' his word is in my heart like a fire, a fire shut up in my bones. I am weary of holding it in; indeed, I cannot" (Jer. 20:9).

So the prophet finds him or herself in a not-so-envious position of being damned if he does and damned if he doesn't. For the sake of comfortable human relationships, he or she would rather be silent, but the connection between the spirit of the prophet and God is so strong that the prophet cannot keep silent about the very things he or she would rather be silent about! The prophet feels pushed by God to speak to the people and say what God wants them to hear, whether they want to hear it or not, and most often, they really do not want to hear it at all. People have been willing to revise and adapt what appears to be God's will to their own likes and situations, a practice that leads them further and further away from the perfect will of God. The prophet Ezekiel likens the prophet's duty to that of a watchman: "If the sentinel sees the sword coming and does not blow the trumpet, so that the people are not warned, and the sword comes, and takes any of them, they are taken away in their iniquity, but their blood I will require at the sentinel's hands. So you, mortal, I have made a sentinel for the house of Israel; whenever you hear a word from my mouth, you shall give them warning from me"(Ezek. 36:6–7). Thus, the prophet really has no choice than but to speak what words God gives. The prophet's role is to bring the world into, as Heschel says, "divine focus."

But what is this divine focus, and why does the job of bringing the world into divine focus produce such ire among the very people God is attempting to reach? God's people appear to have been confused from the start. They were convinced that elaborate worship services, lavish fasts, and periodic sacrifices would be enough to appease God, but over and over in the Hebrew Scriptures it is as though God is yelling, screaming at the people, saying, "No!" The prophet Isaiah says, on God's behalf:

> Hear the word of the LORD, you rulers of Sodom; listen to the teaching of our God, you people of Gomorrah! What to me is the multitude of your sacrifices? says the Lord; I have had enough of burnt offerings of rams and the fat of fed beasts; I do not take delight in the blood of bulls, or of lambs, or of goats. When you come to appear before me, who asked this from your hand? Trample my courts no more; bringing offerings is futile; incense is an abomination to me.Your new moons and your appointed festivals my soul hates;. they have become a burden to me, I am weary of bearing them. When you stretch out your hands, I will hide my eyes from you; even though you make many prayers, I will not listen . . . cease to do evil, learn to do

> good; seek justice, rescue the oppressed, defend the orphan, plead for the widow. (Isa. 1:10–17)

If, as Philip Yancey says, it is true that many Christians do not read the Hebrew scriptures, there is a fair chance that many people do not know this sentiment of God is even in the Bible, but for the prophet, biblical and modern-day, these words of God were piercing and were not intended to make people comfortable, but were, instead, meant to stir up the passions of the people to "do right," and God defined "right" as seeking "justice." God apparently is serious about prophets communicating this thought to God's people, for it is seen more than once; the prophet Amos says, again on behalf of God, "Even though you offer me your burnt offerings and grain offerings, I will not accept them; and the offerings of well-being of your fatted animals I will not look upon. Take away from me the noise of your songs; I will not listen to the melody of your harps. But let justice roll down like waters, and righteousness like an ever-flowing stream" (Amos 5:22–24).

And so, according to Heschel, justice for God is a divine concern, and the job of the prophet is to communicate that concern, hopefully in a way that will inspire people to action. God wants the people to know that, yes, God created them, and, yes, God is good . . . but God requires something of God's creation—and that is, least of all, that they care for each other and seek justice for each other. One is reminded of Mother Teresa, who understood the justice mandate of God in a unique way; the justice of God meant that "the least of these" were worthy of material comforts, but also of the hand of God through the touch offered to those who were despised and sick from those who were apparently well. As God would touch the infirm, so should God's people touch the infirm; justice for Mother Teresa included compassion. In other words, for her and the prophets, the relationship between God and humans·was *quid pro quo*: God gives life, but God expects us to give back to God by helping give life to God's people. Justice, sprinkled with compassion, is part of the ultimate will of God. At least that's how Jeremiah Wright understood it.

Jeremiah Wright's understanding of the Bible was that God meted out justice and mercy to us, and that we, God's people, were to give the same to each other. Because of America's enslavement to racism, however, the people in power, primarily white males, had not given much of either to America's most unique underclass—African Americans. The adjective "unique" is used because although African Americans are not the only ethnic group in America's underclass, they are the only group that did not come to this country voluntarily, and although it was the labor of African Americans that most certainly built the economy and resultant wealth of America, their work is almost completely ignored and understated. So, while America professes an appreciation for a strong "work ethic," the work ethic of African Americans has been nearly totally disregarded.

America was not only dismissive of the contributions of African Americans, but, as time progressed, its citizens seemed less and less able and willing to acknowledge the evil of racism and its child, slavery. In spite of government and religion-sanctioned discrimination against blacks, and overt oppression, those in power began to fall into a pattern of denial about the evils perpetuated by America's contradictory practice of economic and social oppression in light of its ethos of freedom and liberty. There simply was not a problem, they would begin to say. This was America, the land of the free and home of the brave. Anybody could make it, if only he or she wanted to. America's illness of racism was exacerbated and complicated by its denial that there was an illness at all. Blacks who talked about racism and its effects were simply acting as victims, seeking attention and pity—and a hand-out. So venomous were the accusations of overreacting to what the dominant culture refused to acknowledge as a real problem that many African Americans began to internalize the everyday hellish experiences they went through because of racism and opted not to talk about it; it was easier to buy into the denial of the dominant culture than to deal with their own pain.

The problem was, as it is with any pain, that if it is not acknowledged and dealt with in a healthy way, it will come out in other, sometimes unhealthy ways. What Jeremiah Wright knew—because he had lived it and seen it—was that in spite of coping as best they could in spite of the roadblocks put up in front of them at every turn, African Americans were hurting inside. They needed hope—and they needed to hear someone give a prophetic word—that is, give voice about the injustice that was flooding America and ruining its foundation. Somebody had to stand up and say that what was going on was not only wrong, but was an offense to God. The "least of these," in this case, African Americans, needed a prophet to give them voice, even as they were given courage and the energy to keep on pushing through a system that did everything it could to hold them back.

In so doing, Wright would acknowledge the needs of this people who had been so effectively marginalized, and would "treat their needs as holy," as Obery Hendricks describes in his book *The Politics of Jesus.* Although Wright preached in the tradition of the Old Testament prophets, he was also a devout Christian who believed that Jesus walked in that same tradition. Jesus, after all, quoted the prophet Isaiah when he acknowledged the work that Yahweh had called him to do: "The Spirit of the Lord is upon me, because he has anointed me to bring good news to the poor. He has sent me to proclaim release to the captives and recovery of sight to the blind, to let the oppressed go free, to proclaim the year of the Lord's favor" (Luke 4:18–19).

While those who heard him quote Isaiah were "amazed," the powers that be were not. For some reason, what he said was immediately threatening. It was not Jesus' job to worry about the poor and the oppressed; things were "okay" as they were. In Jesus' day, as in our own, there was a society clearly composed of the "haves" and "have-nots." Caring for the poor and oppressed would upset the balance of power, which left the powerful in control and the powerless at their behest. The people *in the synagogue* were angry at Jesus for his audacity and boldness, not unlike that of the prophets whom he knew so well. They drove him out of Nazareth and tried to kill him.

What Wright would say to his members would not be threatening; conversely, his sermons would be empowering. But he would eventually draw harsh criticism from the powers that be . . . at the very moment one whom he had empowered was about to make history. What should have been a moment of glory for the pastor/prophet would end up being a moment of excruciating pain and betrayal, not only from those from whom he expected the opposition, but from some who had themselves been empowered by his work.

8

THE PECULIAR ROLE OF WRIGHT AS PROPHET/PREACHER

How, then, can they call on the one they have not believed in? And how can they believe in the one of whom they have not heard? And how can they hear without someone preaching to them? And how can they preach unless they are sent?

—ROMANS 10:14–15 NIV

Black people needed a peculiar and unique prophet and preacher, one who could help them make sense out of hundreds of years of nonsensical treatment from fellow Christians, based almost entirely on the color of their skin.

Martin Luther King had been one type of prophet, leading people to the streets to fight the overt discriminatory treatment that black (and later, poor) people received at the hands of government. What King did was an absolutely necessary first step in moving black people from being on the sidelines of American life to being full, participating citizens.

But Jeremiah Wright's ministry would take what Dr. King did a step further; it would get black people to understand why, politically and historically, they were where they were. His ministry would give their anger and frustration a voice, allow them to know that what they had gone through was not in their imaginations and was worth understanding in order to fight it. The tentacles of racism were deep, and Wright's ministry gave voice to that fact.

The world knew of America's bipolar spirit when it came to freedom and black people. Though the words penned in the Declaration of Independence were glorious and hope-filled, they represented little more than a myth, as many people would learn in time. There it was written, plain as day, the *ideal* of this democracy, an ideal that contributed to the myth that America was a place where the ideal was respected and even agreed upon: "We hold these truths to be self-evident, that all men were created equal, that they are endowed by their Creator with certain inalienable Rights (sic) that among these are life, Life, Liberty and the pursuit of Happiness."[1]

Even as they wrote those words, the signers of the Declaration knew that was not what they really meant. America had a cultural reality—slavery—that was by now an ingrained American institution. The talk of "freedom" was troubling for some of our country's founding fathers; they did not know how to connect slavery with the ideal of freedom, and yet, it was clear that neither the idea/ideal of freedom nor the institution of slavery would be done away with. We have already seen how some of the signers owned slaves, and those who did not own them were conflicted about how to treat the Negro among them. Some, like George Mason of Virginia, argued against slavery: "Every master is born a petty tyrant. They bring the judgments of heaven on a country. As nations cannot be rewarded or punished in the next world, they must be in this. By an inevitable chain of causes and effects, providence punishes national sins by national calamities."[2]

Mason owned more slaves than any other of the signers of the Declaration, except for George Washington, who also appeared conflicted. Wrote Washington: "I hope it will not be conceived from these observations, that it is my wish to hold the unhappy people, who are the subject of this letter, in slavery. I can only say that there is not a man living who wished more sincerely than I do, to see a plan adopted for the abolition of it; but there is only one proper and effectual mode by which it can be accomplished, and that is by Legislative authority."[3]

Neither Mason nor Washington was moved to free his slaves even as both wrestled with the ideals of democracy and the reality of the state. Mason reportedly never freed his, and Washington only did so posthumously, writing his desire for their freedom in his will.

With the Civil War and the white backlash that came following the issuance of the Emancipation Proclamation, many believed that the "problem" of slavery and racism was over, but in fact, its roots were about to dig even deeper into the American psyche. The South was infuriated that former slaves would now be free to compete for jobs that whites might want, and some were afraid that blacks would retaliate for poor treatment endured during their enslavement. After a brief period of time where blacks in the South enjoyed some freedom and the ability to participate fully in American society, the backlash began. According to Douglas Blackmon in his book *Slavery by Another Name: The Re-Enslavement of Black Americans from the Civil War to World War II*, whites in the South began finding ways to again be able to use the labor of black people while not paying them, and concurrently strip them of newly realized privileges and denigrate them and characterize them as being unworthy of being free. There were businessmen in the South who were angry that the slaves had been freed, based on their belief in the inherent inferiority of black people, but perhaps even more important, they were bothered by the loss of slave labor because they would no longer be able to build their fortunes with little cost to themselves. Real effort thus went into creating a system that would allow blacks to be used as they had been used during the time when slavery was legal, circumventing not only the Thirteenth, Fourteenth, and Fifteenth Amendments to the Constitution, but the Emancipation Proclamation itself. The Convict Leasing system allowed companies and corporations to use blacks as they desired. Supporters of the system would argue if confronted that technically they were doing nothing wrong, because the Thirteenth Amendment stated that a person could be held "in neither slavery nor involuntary servitude except as punishment for crime whereof the party shall have been duly convicted."[4] In other words, if a black person were convicted of a crime, he or she could be enslaved; *slavery was totally legal if a crime had been committed.*

That meant that the powers that be merely had to insure that blacks were regularly convicted of crimes in order to support or rebuild the economy that had produced the Southern aristocracy, which had been decimated by the War between the States. To do that, they created laws, including vagrancy laws, that made it illegal for a person to be without a job, to be "caught" looking for a job (because if one was looking, one presumably did not have a job). African Americans began to be systematically criminalized, feeding into the dominant culture's position that they were not capable of being free in the first place. Under these vagrancy laws, one could be arrested for walking alongside a railroad track, for selling products grown off one's own farm after dark, for drinking or spitting or being loud. If one could not prove one's place of residency, one could be arrested; if one stole a pig, again, one was apt to be arrested. These trumped-up arrests were upheld most often in court. The accused were sentenced to "time" working for a plantation or a corporation, and were assessed fees, which many of the arrested could not pay. The result was the Convict-Leasing system, which allowed white capitalists in the South to rebuild their fortunes on the backs of black people, and which contributed to an overall opinion that black people, who were disproportionately arrested and jailed, were inherently criminals. This entire system of re-enslaving black people started in the midst of what historians call "Radical Reconstruction." The white resistance to biracial governments, possible because blacks now had the right to vote and were gaining political and economic power, grew slowly yet steadily.

After the 1870s, there wasn't any sustained federal presence in the South, so the Southern noblemen had pretty much free reign to do what they wanted with "their" Negroes. The argument against having free blacks in the South was racial, to be sure, but the economic incentive cannot be overstated. Just as Lincoln's desire to free the slaves was more because he wanted to save the Union than it was because he believed in the right of blacks to be equal with whites (which he did not support at all), so did this Convict Leasing system have an economic component that drove it. It was racially and economically motivated; both factors seemed to figure equally.

Once a company acquired a "convict," that company could do whatever it wanted with him or her. Blackmon argues that while domestic, agrarian slavery was bad, at least slaves were something like extended family members and were apt to be somewhat cared for by their captors. In the industrial world, however, there was no incentive to take care of the convicts. They were "bad" people, working off their sentences for having been an affront to society. They were due no consideration, no care, no touch of humanity. These convicts, who were primarily men, worked in coal mines, in turpentine camps, building roads, and laying railroad tracks. They worked from the wee hours of the morning until late at night, in any kind of weather. They endured the treatment because some honestly believed in the Emancipation Proclamation. In their minds, the good President Lincoln had freed them . . . and they would be free! But many of them never got out of the "system." Sometimes they would finish their sentences and be resentenced on another trumped-up charge. They were always assessed fees that they could not pay, and if one could not pay, the only choice was to "work the debt off." These debts could not be worked off.

Blackmon writes that this Convict Leasing system, along with peonage, went on largely unspoken about until World War II. The federal government, as previously stated, was not a protector of black people. By the 1890s, the federal government had legalized segregation; President Woodrow Wilson actually mandated segregation throughout the federal government. The courts were not sympathetic to blacks, local, state, or federal. The country, it seemed, had shut its ears to the cries of injustice that came from these who were supposed to have been freed. In World War I, it is estimated that in excess of four hundred thousand black men had fought for the United States, but once home, the reality of racism and slavery, including the Convict Leasing system and peonage, greeted them.

The federal government lent a deaf ear and a blind eye to the situations endured by black people until December of 1941, the year Jeremiah Wright was born. Pearl Harbor had been bombed and it was a sure thing that the United States would be at war with Japan. President Franklin Delano Roosevelt called a meeting of his cabinet. He was worried. African Americans would surely be called upon to fight in this war, yet the world knew of America's treatment of them. The president was afraid that Japan and Germany would use America's ideals of "freedom" against her, saying to the world that a country that treated some of its own citizens so poorly could not be expected to fight for the freedom of others. At least some cabinet members agreed. "America's treatment of the Negro" would definitely be an issue.

Thus, to validate America's fight for *everyone's* freedom, FDR ordered Attorney General Francis Biddle to issue Circular 3591.[5] Up until this time, the federal government had adopted and followed a "hands-off" policy when it came to how states legislated what happened to their black citizens. Now, however, the very life of the nation was at stake—not unlike it had been during the Civil War. In spite of the Emancipation Proclamation and the Thirteenth, Fourteenth, and Fifteenth Amendments, slavery had persisted—legally. Now, the federal government had to take the blinders off its eyes. Peonage (where people were restrained in order pay off debts) had been illegal for years, but had never been enforced, and most of the "peons" were black people. Biddle wrote, in Circular 3591:

> It is the purpose of these instructions to direct the attention of the United States Attorneys to the possibilities of successful prosecutions stemming from alleged peonage complaints which have heretofore been considered inadequate to invoke federal prosecution . . . In the United States, one cannot sell himself as a peon or slave—the law is fixed and established to protect the weak-minded, the poor, the miserable. . . . Any such sale or contract is positively null and void and the procuring and causing of such contract to be made violates the statutes.[6]

The year was 1941, remember. Blacks had been living under the spirit of slavery, supported by state and federal government, as well as the courts. What did that sort of existence do to the minds of black people, their worldview, and even their conception of God? Was God good? Was God present? Was God not all good and all powerful? Couldn't God see what was going on? Did God really care about all people? Were black people a mistake, as many in the dominant culture sometimes suggested?

Were black people supposed to just "be content with their situation" as catechism lessons on plantations had taught them? What was wrong with a country that claimed to be the land of the free, but which so blithely and carelessly enslaved so many? Jon Meacham wrote in *American Gospel: God, the Founding Fathers, and the Making of a Nation* that "all of the Founders were devoted to liberty, but most kept slaves."[7] For the African American, many must have asked, "Where is God in all of this?" It was a question Jeremiah Wright would seek to answer in his preaching and teaching, the spirit of slavery notwithstanding. His job as prophet/preacher was to make good sense out of horrid nonsense.

Christianity had been a source of disappointment to African Americans since the time of slavery. Meacham recalls an experience of Frederick Douglass, who, at least up to a point, believed in the power of Christianity. Douglass, according to Meacham's book, had great hope that his master might be "converted" to a more humane way of living after going to church and "experiencing religion." At least, Douglass mused, perhaps his master might become more gentle and humane in dealing with his slaves. To his horror, however, his master became worse: "I was disappointed in both these respects . . . Christianity neither made him to be humane to his slaves nor to emancipate them. If it had any effect on his character, it made him more cruel and hateful in all his ways; for I believe him to have been a much worse man after his conversion than before."[8]

Douglass said that religion seemed to have given his master "religious sanction and support" for his slaveholding cruelty. . . . The master became a model of public piety, hosting traveling ministers and conspicuously holding household prayers, especially when there were guests."[9]

Here Wright was, then, in the midst of a new ministry that was devoted and committed to helping black people know who they were and whose they were . . . but there were nagging questions about God and God's goodness that he would have to address. He knew and believed that being a Christian was and is "about relationship, not scholarship," but he was going to have to weave scholarship between the words of hope that he gave his people. God *was* good, Wright would preach, and we know that because in spite of a country in which black people have not been safe, or felt safe, and in spite of horrible discrimination sanctioned by law, black people have not only survived, but thrived! He preached:

> What makes you so strong, black man? How is it that 370 years of slavery, segregation, racism, Jim Crow laws and second-class citizenship cannot wipe out the memory of Imhotep, Aesop, Akhenaton and Thutmose II? What makes you so strong, black man?
>
> This country has tried castration and lynching, miseducation and brainwashing. They have taught you to hate yourself and to look at yourself through the awfully tainted eyeglasses of white Eurocentric lies, and yet you keep breaking out of the prisons they put you in. You break out in a W. E. B. DuBois, and a Booker T. Washington; you break out in a Louis Farrakhan and a Mickey Leland; you break out in a Judge Thurgood Marshall and a Pops Staples; you break out in a Luther Vandross, Magic Johnson, Michael Jordan, Harold Washington or a Doug Wilder. What makes you so strong, black man?[10]

In that sermon, Wright mixed scholarship with religion; he quoted a poem by Sterling Brown, whom, by the time Wright preached this sermon at Trinity, some may have known, but whom many in the African American community would still *not* have known. Wright's overarching message, his prophetic message, was that "you don't have to be ashamed! You are, we are, a great people!" He wanted and needed all black people, but especially black males, young and old, to see black men who had "made it" in spite of racism.

One of the things Wright often preached was that a black youth "couldn't be what he hadn't seen." Little black boys who grew to be young men often saw nothing but despair and hopelessness in the eyes and lives of the black men in their lives. They were labeled early on in school, when they acted as little boys will act; instead of being corrected and encouraged, they were often made to feel like they were bad. Many attended poor schools and operated below grade level, receiving little encouragement and/or help from loved ones. These little boys couldn't see nor could they understand the racism that their fathers met on a daily basis. Wright knew, from his own upbringing, that many black parents sought to shield their children from the realities of racism, and yet, it was there, an invisible wall against which these young men pushed. Black poets wrote about the struggle and the pain; Langston Hughes wrote that much of what he created was done with the thought in mind that there was and should be pride, and not shame, in the "Negro identity." His main concern was to uplift black people, to make them know their worth, and for those who read his poetry, his words were powerful.

But the little black boys too often didn't read poetry. They needed to see black men succeeding in the classic American definition of success; they needed to see black doctors, attorneys, engineers . . . but too often, they saw black men falling through the cracks, unable to get a job or make a living wage. Nobody had talked to black people about their greatness in school, and few had talked about it in church.

Wright went to the heart of this situation, expressed through a historical recitation, through a poem, and now, through the Bible. Wright used the story of Samson and Delilah. He talked about how Samson's people were under oppression. (The message for black people: "Good! We are not the only ones!") He talked about how Samson's people were continually under attack, hounded by "the twin demons of assimilation and segregation."[11] (You mean *that's* in the Bible?) Wright was getting his people, beaten down by oppression, to relate to God's biblical people. We are not so different. . . . Wright's message in that sermon was that we can be fooled by those who purport to care for us. We can trust the wrong people and, in so doing, do the wrong things, to our detriment. Wright reminded his people in that sermon to remember that, just as God had a plan for Samson's life, so did God have a plan for each of their lives. They were strong, like Samson. They were blessed, like Samson. What Wright didn't want them to do was to make Samson's mistakes:

"You see, God has a work that God wants to do through African Americans—a people who have known hatred yet who still have the strength to love; a people who have known degradation yet who still have the strength to stand tall and produce giant after giant in field after field; a people who have known belittlement and humiliation yet you have maintained their integrity and kept their souls intact, a people who have been lied to, lied on, and lied about, yet who still have the strength to forgive and to build strong families, regardless of those families' configuration."[12]

Wright then had to get to the truth about what slavery and racism had done to the minds of black people. In this same sermon, he said,

"You give them your heart; they chain your body and then your mind. As Carter G. Woodson and Dr. Bobby Wright would both say: "They can take the chains off your bodies and have absolutely nothing to fear from your mind."[13] Wright reminded them that Carter G. Woodson said, "If you tell a person to go to the back door over and over again, and then one day you say, 'You no longer have to go to the back door,' do you know what that person will do? He will not only go to the back door but if there is not one back there, he'll cut one in."[14] Wright drew vivid pictures of experiences many of his members had been through: being told they weren't good enough, that they were not college material, that they were second-class citizens . . .

Using the scripture, and telling the story of how Samson was blinded after he had told "Delilah his whole heart," Wright said that trusting those who do not have your best interests at heart will result not only in you being chained, but being blinded as well. He preached: "Do you know what happens when you can't see? You, the victims, become the staunchest supporters of a sick system of perpetual slavery because you can't see what the enemy has done and keeps on doing to you."[15]

Finally in this sermon Wright says if people give their "whole heart" to those who seek to destroy them, their enemies will "parade them" in front of the world in order to cement a false impression of who they are, reminiscent of how blacks were criminalized after the Civil War in the concerted effort to support Convict Leasing. In Wright's words, "They'll parade you as the primary example of pathology in America. They'll parade you as the user and the victim of the drugs that they brought into the country in the first place. Why is it that with a drug czar and the millions of dollars that we spend to fight drugs, we can't stop drugs from coming into the country? But they'll parade you as the primary victims. They shout, 'Bring him out! Let him entertain us. You know his kind always make the best entertainers.'"[16]

Wright winds down the sermon by answering the question "What makes you so strong?"—none other than God. God's spirit, God's *ruah,* is what makes us strong and is what has kept us. Samson used God's strength at the end of his life, not his own strength, and that's what we must use, Wright preached. What makes us so strong is God's strength, God's constant presence with us. This spirit of God does not bow to racism or oppression or discrimination or lies. This spirit of God rests within all of us. Wright preached it as a prophetic word, perhaps *the* prophetic word, that brought oppressed people out of dungeons of despair, believing in themselves and in their God because Wright had reminded them that in spite of the "nonsense" of oppression, God was above it all. It was his peculiar and unique prophetic task, and he did it well.

9

TEACHING A THEOLOGY OF FREEDOM

The courage to be is the ethical act in which man affirms his own being in spite of those elements of his existence which conflict with his essential self-affirmation.

—PAUL TILLICH[1]

Jeremiah Wright's his mission, or at least a big part of it, as evidenced in his sermons and teachings, was to teach African Americans to have the courage to *be*.

Because of the ever-present spirit of racism, African Americans lived persistently under a peculiar pressure placed upon them by American society. African Americans were forced to "prove" themselves, to show themselves worthy to be in the midst of America, trying to enjoy its freedoms and privileges. There was always a cloud overhead, questioning their intelligence, their aptness to do certain things or have certain jobs. One couldn't just be an American if one were black; one had to fight for the privileges that white Americans took for granted. Even though America's laws and policies, as well as its history toward African Americans, had been fraught with injustice, blacks were not really "allowed" to be angry. African Americans were supposed to be grateful for the progress that had been made and were really expected not to talk about the history that had so abused them. They were supposed to swallow the discrimination in housing, in employment, in education . . . and just "get on" with their lives.

It was hard to live that way.

African American men, so effectively criminalized during the period of time after Reconstruction and continuing through to the present day, seemed to have had it particularly hard. Qualified African American men were up against white men for jobs, and despite the image that America had put out that African American men were lazy and shiftless, the truth of the matter was that many employers would not hire them for jobs, no matter their education and qualification. If America had a cold, the African American community had pneumonia. In *The Worst Hard Time*, a book that describes the dust bowl that hit America's high plains during the depression, author Timothy Egan writes:

> More than two million people had found government public works jobs, which paid a minimum of twelve dollars a week, putting bandages on the wounds of American life. But nearly twenty-five million were still without regular income, relying on part-time jobs, private charities, or black-market income. For African Americans, the unemployment rate was 50 percent. Throughout the South, and in some places in the North, notes were posted on job sites that read, "No jobs for niggers until every white man has a job." It took an executive order from Roosevelt in May 1935 to open up the public works ranks to all races.[2]

All over the country, Great Depression or Dust Bowl notwithstanding, the message was the same: African Americans were different and, therefore, deficient. Wright understood it and knew what it would and did do to a person's psyche. In order for African Americans to embrace who they were, they would have to first face the fact that they were battling self-hatred on a daily basis. Once they recognized it, they would be able to become empowered to live and to prosper in spite of the oppression that embraced their lives and the spirit of racism that forever hovered over them. Wright wanted African Americans to have the *courage* to push through the veil that was ever before them, making them believe that which had for too long been said to them and about them.

Paul Tillich called this pushing through to find one's courage, given to us all by God, the "courage to be." Tillich and other white theologians, however, could not embrace the very lives of African Americans. Their notion of God and God's workings were shaped by their own experiences, which were far from those of African Americans. Indeed, theologian James Cone said, "when the master and slave spoke of God, they could not possibly be referring to the same reality. When slaves spoke of Jesus Christ, they spoke out of the depths of suffering and despair and the pain of "rolling through an unfriendly world."[3] Cone rightly says that theology is both universal and particular, and anyone's ultimate theology is framed and shaped by his or her own experiences. The experiences of a privileged person or group will be far different from those of an oppressed or despised group. Tillich said that God was "being" itself, but clearly, the experience of "being" is different for different groups of people. According to Cone: "What could Karl Barth possibly mean for black students who had come from the cotton fields of Arkansas, Louisiana, and Mississippi, seeking to change the structure of their lives in a society which had defined *black* as nonbeing? What is the significance of Nicea and Chalcedon for those who knew Jesus *not* as a thought in their heads to be analyzed in relations to a similar thought called God? They knew Jesus as savior and a friend, as the 'lily of the valley and the bright and morning star.'"[4]

Black people had been kind of holding onto God by their fingertips. Surely this God would see the evil in oppression and discrimination and rescue them! Surely this God would hear their cries and deliver them from their enemies! African Americans had to hold onto that hope, because without it, they could not *be*. The message given them, written even in the United States Constitution and inferred as the correct view in the Bible, was that they did not deserve to be because they were not even full-fledged humans. So, in order to know "who" they were, there were layers of spiritual ruination to be worked through. They were pretty convinced that they would not find freedom on earth, for the most part, and so adopted a more eschatological way of looking at and looking for God. If they didn't get justice here on earth, they would get it when they died. If that's what it was, that's what it was; many blacks held onto the promise of freedom and justice in the afterlife.

But for Wright, that premise, that supposition that so many blacks carried with them was wrong. God would not have created black people just to suffer on earth. God was an entity who loved all whom God created. Because of Jesus, who preached the Great Commandment, that we should love the Lord our God with all our heart and with all our mind and with all our soul, and our neighbors as ourselves (Matt. 22:37–39). And because of the promise that Jesus would not only forgive believers' sins but give them the things they had been denied on earth, owing to the nondiscriminatory love of God, blacks held on. But some surely had doubts, not unlike some had held doubts about God back in the day of the Apostle Paul, who waited eagerly for the "Second Coming." Jesus didn't come as quickly as the early Christians had thought he would, and by the time Jeremiah Wright was preaching and teaching, Jesus still hadn't come. Still, the coming of Jesus, the love of Jesus, and the justice and love of Jesus the son and God the parent was all black people had to hold onto. And so the job of the preacher/theologian/teacher/exegete was to bring hope and meaning to a life on this earth, which for black people had had a muddied meaning. Cone says that the preacher/teacher had to explain what the gospel had to do with the oppressed of the land in their struggle for liberation.[5]

Because of this hunger for an "ear" to hear their cries, the African American perception and conception of God was much more than a thought. Jesus was one who "walks with me and talks with me and tells me I am His own," as the words of the hymn expressed.[6] Blacks didn't care all that much about *homoousia*, that is, God and Jesus being one and the same, a theological concept framed by Athanasius. Black people wanted and needed a companion here on earth who heard their cries and who was so personal as to be felt with one personally on a daily basis. If they hadn't had Jesus to talk to, with the understanding, because of the dual nature of Jesus, that in Jesus' humanity he understood their pain and empathized with them, it really is not clear how they could or would have survived. Feeling like *nobody* on earth, at least in the dominant culture, heard them or cared about them, God was all they had. What they needed, however, was a different perception of God, a more immanent God who wanted them not to live life in the future but in the now.

Wright understood that and began the process of peeling back the layers of pain, self-loathing, and maybe even doubt to get his listeners to see God differently and to see themselves differently. No matter how destitute their lives seemed, no matter how hopeless their lives seemed, no matter how many doors were being slammed in their faces, there was always hope because there was always God. In one sermon, Wright describes a painting called "Hope":

> It shows a woman who is playing a harp, sitting on top of the world. Now that by itself would be all right, for what more enviable position could any of us ever hope to be in than being on top of the world with everything and everybody dancing to our music. But when you look closer at the painting, when the illusion of power starts giving way to the reality of pain, the world on which this woman sits—our world—is one torn by war, destroyed by hate, decimated by despair and devastated by distrust. The world, in fact, is on the very brink of destruction, and Watt depicted that in what he put on the canvas, thereby contradicting what is evoked by the title Hope.[7]

Wright's description of that picture would resonate with many African Americans fighting under the spirit of racism and trying to push through the veil of discrimination. He then wove stories of the types of experiences African Americans had on a daily basis, showing them that he understood their situations—the pain with which his listeners coped on a daily basis. It was easy, perhaps, to fall into thinking eschatologically, thinking that their situations were hopeless and that if they just held on, they would get their reward in heaven. But they couldn't think that way; if they did, they would never know who they were and what great things God had in store for them, in spite of their predicaments.

He had to get them to look not only at what or where they were, but also at what or where they could be. He recalled how, when he had heard another preacher preach about this picture, he was going through his own quiet hell. "Sampson was preaching about hope," he said, but Wright was thinking about a young boy with whom his then-teen daughter was in love with, a boy who was five years her senior. He wanted to let the people in the pews know how difficult it could be to believe in hope when one's life was a private, quiet hell. But then, Wright says, he heard something from the preacher:

> But then Dr. Sampson said he noticed he had only been checking out the horizontal dimensions and relationships in that picture—how the woman was hooked up with that world on which she sat. He had failed to take into the account her vertical relationships. He had looked down on the painting and had seen the war, the hunger, the distrust and the hatred, but he had not looked above her head. He said when he looked over her head, he saw some small notes of music, moving playfully and joyfully toward heaven. And it was then he understood why Watt had called that painting "Hope."
>
> See, in spite of being in a world torn by war, in spite of being on a world destroyed by hate . . . in spite of being on a world where apartheid and apathy fed the fires of racism, in spite of being on a world where nuclear nightmare draws closer with every second, in spite of being on a ticking time bomb with her clothes in rags, her body scarred, bruised and bleeding and her harp all but destroyed except for that one string that was left—in spite of all these things, the woman had the audacity to hope.[8]

There was a not-so-subtle thrill that went through the congregation when Wright got to that part of the sermon; indeed, it is the sermon that got to Barack Obama's very soul and compelled him to turn to God in a serious way, long before he was president, and served as the title of one of his books.[9] *Of course* there was hope! Because there was God there was always hope. Wright taught his listeners not to look at their predicaments—their horizontal dimension—but to look at their God—their vertical dimension. As long as there was God above, there was hope on earth. It was a theology of liberation, sorely needed by a people who had been enslaved for too long despite the Emancipation Proclamation in 1863 and the formal disavowal of slavery as practiced in the convict leasing system in 1941.

Cone says that "Christian theology is language about the liberating character of God's presence in Jesus Christ as he calls his people into being for freedom in the world."[10] Wright understood that, and took on the task, head-on.

Theology for black people, then, had to be different, which Wright well understood. Theology for black people could not present an abstract entity, a transcendent description of "Other" that was too far away to be accessible. Theology for black people had to make God and God's son, Jesus, very personal, so that the lowliest, most hopeless soul could touch him/her. Black people needed a theology that put them in close contact with God and gave them permission to have very personal conversations, conversations they could trust. Their society could not be trusted; they had seen that, but the God who was over everybody, including themselves, could be trusted. And so theology as presented to black people had to meet that need for them to have a trusted, close friend, who also happened to be their God and redeemer.

James Cone gives an account of a sermon given by a white preacher where he said that "in heaven, there must be some Jim Crow partition, with the white saints on one side and the black saints on the other."[11] Black people were sitting in church that day and heard that sermon . . . but didn't buy the theology that would make God do something like that. After the service, the black people gathered and one of the black deacons prayed, "And, O Lord, we thank thee fer the brother preacher who has spoke to us—we thank thee for heaven—we thank thee that we kin all go to heaven—but as to that partition, O Lord, we thank thee that we'se a shoutin' people—we thank thee that we kin shout so hard in heaven that we will break down that partition an' spread all over heaven—an' we thank thee that if the white fokes can't stand it, they can git on out of heaven an' go to elsewhere!"[12]

The black experience, in other words, began to shape black theology . . . and that theology had to present a God that truly despised slavery and oppression and wanted all people to be free.

It was not necessary for white people, especially white men, to have such a theology. It seems that all people need freedom within their religious beliefs, but all people do not need the same kind of freedom. White people, undoubtedly, did have and do have issues that their religious experience needs to address in order for them to be free enough to experience the presence of God. From the perspective of many, there seemed to be no need, however, for the same type of liberating God that blacks needed, because the whites already had freedom and lived in the protection and under the umbrella of white privilege. Peggy McIntosh, a professor at Wellesley College, says that she has "come to see white privilege as an invisible package of unearned assets which I can count on cashing in each day, but about which I was meant to remain oblivious."[13] She is insistent that her observations on white privilege are hers and hers alone, not meant to give an opinion on the phenomenon for all white people, but for her, what she realized in working with African American colleagues, was significant. It would not be surprising for someone who, like McIntosh, had realized the far-reaching fingers of white privilege, touching even religion and the Bible. For white people, the Bible was on "their side." God, they believed and taught, had created the world for white people. (The definition of "white" would evolve over time.)

Indeed, from America's earliest beginnings, there existed among white Christians what Forrest G. Wood calls "typical cultural myopia," where the belief prevailed that other races, including blacks and Native Americans, were beneath whites; such beliefs, says Wood, came directly from Christianity.[14] White people believed themselves to be the "new chosen people" and seemed to believe that because they were so "chosen" God had discriminated, allowed "in effect, discrimination against everyone else."[15] Wood goes on: "The Chosen People mandate was ultimately enlarged by the principles of the Revolution, in which it was made clear that the destiny of the American people was not duty to a single monarch, but, in William R. Brock's words, 'to God and mankind. . . . God's selection (of them as the New Chosen People) had meant power and conquest for Anglo Americans. . . .'"[16]

Wood further writes that Samuel Harris, who was a professor of systematic theology at Yale University, "argued in his *Kingdom of God on Earth* God has always acted by chosen people, and to the Anglo-Saxon, more than to any other the world is now indebted for the propagation of Christian ideas and Christian civilization."[17] Wood says, "Thirteen years later, James M. King, a prominent Methodist clergyman in New York, declared that God had chosen the Anglo-Saxon 'to conquer the world for Christ by dispossessing feeble races and molding others.'"[18]

Clearly, then, the theology of white people would be different from that of black people. White theology did not work, not in the folds of the souls of black people, because white theology seemed to support the racism that was oppressing black people. Cone said that the master speaking of God wasn't referring to the same reality, the same God, as that of the black man. Jeremiah Wright shaped his sermons and teachings within the context of a people "desperately seeking God," but not the God that had been presented to them historically by white people. Black people needed God, but they also needed freedom from believing they were inferior just because they had been born black.

In his sermon "What Makes You So Strong?" Wright tapped into that troubling and burdensome thought that black people carried. "Those who are inferior can't stand those who are superior, especially when those who are superior are of a despised race, a race that everybody has been taught does not have the mental equipment to be superior."[19] There it was: the nagging, ever-present thought that had been ingrained into blacks and whites alike, only here, in Wright's church, the reality and the emotion behind that reality was being expressed. Wright was talking about the Israelites being under the thumb of the Babylonians, but the comparison and the similarity between the situation of the Israelites and African Americans was clear. The Israelites were in a strange land, under oppression from the Babylonians; African Americans were also in a foreign land, brought here under duress, and under oppression from a dominant culture. Wright went back to his theme of hope— the Babylonians tried to take away the hope of the Israelites, but "their efforts were in vain."[20]

Thus, theology from the African American perspective was not "a reflection upon an eternal being" for black people. Theology, said Cone, and shown to be so by Wright, "was anthropology."[21] Cone said that "what theologians mistake for God is nothing but the 'latent nature' of humanity," and later said that "what people think about God cannot be divorced from their place and time in a definite history and culture."[22] Because race was and is such a tender topic in America, shunned by blacks and whites, this anthropological and cultural connection to God was not often heard in churches, black or white. What preachers often taught that God was the creator of everyone and that Jesus died for the sins of all. That was good, but not enough for the souls of an oppressed people. They needed to know where God was for *them*. Traditional theology wanted to make God an idea, an objective idea, but liberation, or black theology sought to make God real; Cone says that theology is "subjective speech about God, a speech that tells us far more about the hopes and dreams of certain God-talkers than about the Maker and Creator of heaven and earth."[23]

The reality was that the ruling class, in America, yes, but throughout history, promotes its ideology and often passes it off as theology. The traditional ideology of America was that whites were supreme and superior to all other races, but it was passed off, or passed into, the speech of religion and thus became theological by substitution. Cone says that "the ruling class promotes religion because it justifies the present material relations and also because it serves as a sedative for the oppressed, making them remain content with humiliation and suffering."[24] That was counter-productive, keeping African Americans, in this case, from becoming or even wanting to know who they were. Cone said that "as long as the oppressed believe that their future is found in a heavenly world, they will not focus on the revolutionary praxis needed to change this world."[25]

So Wright knew that it was not going to be enough, not according to the vision and mission he had been given by God, to merely shape his sermons in the context of the traditional theological discourses. Surely, there were elements of Tillich, Barth, Fuerbach, and others that informed Wright's theology, but they were not the only informants. Wright had to create a broader theological context for his congregation, so that they would know a God who was all-loving and who had a place for them, in spite of what the world had taught them.

Jeremiah Wright identified a condition of African Americans that he knew he had to address. Because of racism, blacks had historically had trouble accepting themselves, liking themselves. It was almost foolhardy to teach and preach them to know who they were if, in the knowing, their sense of self-loathing would increase. The message blacks had received in America was that they were deficient because they were different. In the process of assimilating, or trying to assimilate into the majority culture, black people were eager to deny who they were. Lighter skinned blacks decided they were better than darker-skinned blacks. Nobody wanted to be "too black." In fact, one of the first things people would look for upon the birth of an African American baby was the quality of his or her hair, and the color of his or her ear lobes; a darker ear lobe meant the child would be darker skinned—and nobody wanted that. It was as if they wanted to be anything other than "who they were."

Wright related the experience of African Americans to that of the Israelites who survived the Babylonian exile. In "Faith in a Foreign Land," Wright explained that people in power often downgrade those over whom they have power. "If you downgrade where the exiles came from and what they were once called, the grandchildren and great-grandchildren don't want to have anything to do with their history. And they embrace the culture of the 'Babylonians'"[26] Wright explained how African Americans had been subsumed by the dominant culture, relating their experience to that of the biblical Israelites.

So, yes, he had a "black theology," a theology that came out of the experience of black people, but that does not mean he ignored traditional theology. He had studied traditional theology as well and, in fact, seemed very aware that black people were in a place of being, or needing to be, as Paul Tillich described, "struck by grace." According to Tillich, "Grace strikes us when we are in great pain and restlessness. It strikes us when we walk through the dark valley of a meaningless and empty life. It strikes us when we feel that our separation is deeper than usual, because we have violated another life, a life which we loved, or from which we were estranged."[27]

Blacks had been walking through, pushing through a veil that was ever before them: the bane of having been born black in a world that wanted to be white. As a group, blacks knew they were not accepted; the theological message had to be that they were in fact accepted. In his sermon "You Are Accepted," Tillich eloquently stated this: "You are accepted. You are accepted, accepted by that which is greater than you, and the name of which you do not know. Do not ask for the name now; perhaps you will find it later. Do not try to do anything now; perhaps later you will do much. Do not seek for anything; do not perform anything; do not intend anything. Simply accept the fact that you are accepted! If that happens to us, we experience grace."[28]

Wright, then, used traditional theology and melded into the message about God that black people needed to hear. Wright believed that Jesus came to "set at liberty those who are oppressed" (Isa. 61:1; Luke 4:18). Jesus, after all, lived during a time where people suffered under Roman oppression. They had to be set free in order to experience the fullness of God. They could not remain submerged under a theology that sanctioned oppression and racism.

Not surprisingly, some people of the dominant culture have dismissed the need and the importance of liberation theology. As James Cone said, "The Bible was written from the perspective of the dominant class in Israel."[29] He says that he is black first, and "everything else comes after that,"[30] a fact that Jeremiah Wright and African Americans in general knew all too well. In everything in America, it seemed, race was involved, and African Americans could never forget—were never allowed to forget—who they were according to the American ethos. It was a yoke around their necks, but more than that, a yoke around the spirit of America. Blacks were not the only ones in this nation needing liberation; women, Asians, gays—pretty much anyone who was not a white, Protestant male—needed liberation from a theology and from ideologies that declared them "less than."

Blacks could not get away from the tell-tale sign of their deficiency—their color. Those who had not tasted the oppression would not and could not understand this need to be liberated because they had not felt the chains of oppression around their spirits. Some viewed the cry for liberation, especially from African Americans, to be another way of inviting big government—interference, they would say, in the way people were treated by local, state, and federal government. Said conservative radio host Glenn Beck:

> I have taken a lot of hits from people like Rev. Jim Wallis on "social justice." But I needed you to know there is a poison in some

of our churches. Social justice—the way Jim Wallis and Jeremiah Wright understand it—isn't in the gospel, neither is the redistribution of wealth. Jesus never said, "Take from the rich and let the government redistribute it." Take the parable of the Good Samaritan. The Samaritan chose to take it upon himself to help; he took on the bills himself. The government never told him to do it. Anything else is a perversion of Christianity and a perversion of the principles of God."[31]

Wallis had criticized the religious right, saying that it "gets the public meaning of religion mostly wrong—preferring to focus only on sexual and cultural issues while ignoring the weightier matters of justice." Wallis further states, "It's time to reassert and reclaim the gospel faith—especially in our public life. When we do, we discover that faith challenges the powers that be to do justice for the poor, instead of preaching a 'prosperity gospel' and supporting politicians who further enrich the wealthy. We remember that faith hates violence and tried to reduce it and exerts a fundamental presumption against war, instead of justifying it in God's name."[32]

Cone would not be surprised at Beck's dismissal of the importance of liberation theology, for, he says, "the problem of faith . . . as defined by white theologians, is limited to their social interests."[33] American theologians, says Cone, "from Cotton Mather and Jonathan Edwards to Reinhold Niebuhr and Schubert Ogden, including radicals and conservatives, have interpreted the gospel according to the cultural and political interests of white people. . . . They have rarely attempted to transcend the social interests of their group by seeking an analysis of the gospel in the light of the consciousness of black people struggling for liberation. White theologians, because of their own identity with the dominant power structure, are largely boxed within their own cultural history."[34]

Black people intuitively knew what the scholars were writing about; they lived it and felt it on a daily basis. Jeremiah Wright sought to give shape and substance to what they felt, theologically, creating an image of a God whose love extended to them as well. God knew. God cared. It was a liberating message.

African Americans were a group of people in a country that really did not want them, trying to hold on, mouthing the principles written in this nation's founding documents and in the Bible. Jeremiah Wright wanted them to stop struggling to hold on, and to instead hold on and push through with a sense of power. He reminded them that they were a strong people who had endured much:

> What makes you so strong? This country has tried negation and degradation. They have taught you to look down on your broad hips and thick lips. They've taught you to hate your hair and to keep it at all costs from going back. Going back to what? Africa? Going back to the way God made it? To what? They have taught you that the less you look like "Miss Ann" the worse off you are. And yet, you keep breaking out of the prisons they put you in. You break out in a Nannie Burroughs, a Fannie Lou Hamer, and a Jessie "Ma" Houston. You break out in a Roberta Flack, an Anita Baker, a Jackie Joyner-Kersee, and a Nina Simone. I don't care what field we pick, you black women keep turning out giants in the field, even those fields they told you were reserved for men only. What makes you so strong, black woman?[35]

There was a need for liberation. There was a need for African Americans to love themselves and, as Tillich wrote, to accept themselves. There was a need for African Americans to realize they had been "struck by grace." And there was a need for them to know that they were loved and accepted . . . and needed . . . by God.

It was Wright's mission to let them know just that.

10

ANGER IS NOT HATE

We confuse God and government.

—Jeremiah Wright[1]

From the moment the infamous sound bites of sermons by Jeremiah Wright hit the airwaves during the 2008 presidential election, commentators labeled him "angry" and said that his sermons were hateful. But anger is not hate.

Jeremiah Wright spoke in the tradition of the jeremiad, which both black and white preachers have done over time. A jeremiad, according to author David Howard-Pitney, is "a rhetoric of indignation, expressing deep dissatisfaction and urgently challenging the nation to reform."[2] The American jeremiad, according to Sacvan Bercovitch, originated with the Puritans. They saw themselves as the "new Chosen People," and they developed a religion based on belief that they were to act in a certain way to please God. Bercovitch defines a jeremiad as a protest, a lament, that "uses scriptures to present communal norms, then follows a series of condemnations that detail the actual state of the community."[3] The jeremiad presents a "prophetic vision" that, according to Bercovitch, "unveils the promises, announces good things to come, and explains the gap between the real and the ideal."[4]

The jeremiad, as begun by the Puritans, expressed the belief that Americans, specifically the Pilgrims, were the "new chosen people," charged with, or called to, bring about a new world order. The Pilgrims believed they had been called of God and from God to "flee a hopelessly corrupt European religious and social establishment and found a holy wilderness in the American wilderness."[5] This term, "jeremiad," is borrowed or based on the laments of the biblical prophet Jeremiah, who lamented the fact that, though he tried as hard as he could to get wayward Israelites to follow the way and will of God, they would not. He warned that their disrespect of God and God's will would lead to their destruction; the people's refusal to honor the Mosaic covenant was working to their destruction. Yet, no matter how much he tried, Jeremiah failed to get the Israelites to heed his warnings, and as a result, the society and the culture of the "Chosen People" were in danger. The prophet also, however, looked forward to the mercy of God that would be shown, in spite of the fact that many of God's own people would fall by their own refusal to listen to and heed to God's will.

The American jeremiad had three distinct components, according to Howard-Pitney: a promise, a criticism of the present declension, and a resolving prophecy.[6] Preachers denouncing the ways of people as being out of the will of God would do so with passion, sometimes with anger and frustration, but they were also sure to announce the promise of God's mercy. Howard-Pitney says that the jeremiad, specifically the American jeremiad, "never questioned America's promise and destiny"; according to Berkovitch, it did so by "ritualistically inverting 'the doctrine of vengeance into a promise of ultimate success.'"[7]

As the Puritans began life in the New World, they saw themselves as a chosen people with a special task. When they pulled away from the aristocracy and the repressive government and religion of England, they saw themselves as called to present a new reality, and those who did not help that new reality come to be were, frankly, out of line with what the Puritans believed to be "God's will" for them. Bercovitch says that the Puritans believed in an "American mission," that is, to bring this new world order into fruition.

The Puritan definition and understanding of America's mission, its jeremiad, identified a tension or anxiety in America; there was the possibility of success for everyone and there was an anxiety that existed as people tried to attain that success. Contrary to the culture of England, which supported an aristocracy, this new world would allow all people, or more people, to have economic success. This was the beginning of the formation of a "middle class." The new world order began to open up the possibility not only of economic success, but political, educational, and commercial success to a relatively large number of Americans.[8] The anxiety that existed in the new world was both an ends and a means; nobody ever quite "arrived" at a place of success, but everyone had the opportunity to do so.

This wide-scale broadness, however, began to change over time. First came the American Revolution, which produced a "civil religion" having as its core belief that Americans were sent to save and remake the world."[9] With the revolution, however, came a more constrained and constricted notion of who were actually the "chosen people." According to Howard-Pitney, the revolution was a "religious experience." Those who had fought in the war understood that they had "saved the liberty founded by their fathers by changing and expanding it for themselves and were now creating and actualizing themselves in a time and arena of their own making."[10] This apparently was, according to Catherine Albanese, an "intoxicating experience," a "religious experience."[11] Thus was born the spirit of American patriotism. Any jeremiad, preached by any preacher, would be allowed to warn people to stay in the will of God, but they would also have to show a deep love for America and its mission, despite the fact that America's mission did not line up with what America practiced. Soldiers in the Revolutionary War fought for freedom, to be sure, but it was for the freedom of *some*. America began to live on and within a myth of democracy, which the founding fathers described as something that was offered to all in this new country. That was not the fact, but to say so, or to criticize the government and not come back to optimism based on written words that were never intended to apply to everyone, was not tolerated, not then and not now.

America struggled with race from the very beginning. According to Howard-Pitney, the struggle wasn't quite as severe before the nineteenth century as it would become later. He notes that "all Americans were heir to the national promise" before the country came to the eve of the Civil

War.[12] But in the mid-nineteenth century, the promise of "liberty to all" underwent a transformative understanding; white Americans began "equating the national promise and identity with the special traits of Anglo-Americans."[13] Howard-Pitney writes:

> By the mid-nineteenth century . . . it was customary to ascribe American national greatness and success to the unique racial gifts of the Anglo-Saxon, who one scholar has written, "was represented as carrying in his blood a love of liberty, a spirit of individual enterprise and resourcefulness, and a capacity for practical and reasonable behavior, none of which his rivals possessed."[21] America's missionary genius thus was narrowed from a sphere of universal beliefs and principles to a matter of blood with physical qualifications for membership. . . . Western intellectual orthodoxy came to stress the primacy of race and heredity in human affairs, and polygenesis, the theory of human origins as distinct and separate species, was ascendant.[14]

The Civil War brought race front and center. Though many will and do argue that the war was not about slavery, it is a fact that the South fought to keep its slaves because of the boon their labor was for the Southern economy. Indeed, after the War, many Southerners grew worried because they could not get their economy jump-started and flourishing without slave labor. That accounted for the South's backlash against Reconstruction, so that by the late nineteenth century, the political rights blacks enjoyed after the war began to be systematically whittled away, and the Convict Leasing System was instituted to get the benefits of slave labor without having to take care of the workers.

The War Between the States was about slavery because it was about economics; in the final analysis, it was the labor of the slaves that made the South's economy what it grew to be. Clearly capitalistic mind-sets prevailed, understanding that the way to make money was to spend as little money as possible to get one's product produced. Slaves were needed for that. Nobody cared about the liberty and or freedom of blacks. In fact, it was understood that the founding fathers did not even think about blacks when the words of this country's charter documents were written up. The Convict Leasing System helped criminalize blacks, as we have mentioned before, so that one of the prevailing thoughts was that black people were not *worthy or capable* of being free and having the same rights as white people. By the mid- to late nineteenth century, it was a foregone conclusion in both the South *and* the North that whites, were "innately superior to non-Caucasians, and that Anglo-Saxons were the elect branch of the favored race."[15]

Some people struggled against this trending train of thought, both white and black, while many people—again, both white and black—simply bought into it. The buying into it by blacks was enough to enrage some abolitionists and black activists, who often blamed black preachers for the apathy shown among black people. Frederick Douglass, one of the great activists working for the freedom and dignity of black people, absolutely abhorred black preachers who would not or could not inspire their congregants to fight against slavery and oppression. But the self-hatred was settling in, and blacks were beginning to believe the hype—that they were inferior and were made that way by God.

The blatant racism and exclusion of black people from the dignity of an American existence was rampant after Reconstruction. Those who fought for the inclusion of black people into the American mainstream, to be treated as equals to whites, found it hard to survive. In 1891, a preacher by the name of Francis Bellamy was forced to leave his church because his sermons highlighted his belief in the equality of all people. His sermons were dubbed "socialist" and were not appreciated.

Bellamy was also the chairman of a committee of state superintendents of education in the National Education Association, and as its chairperson he prepared a program celebrating the birthday of Christopher Columbus. The year was 1892 , and in this program, Bellamy had a ceremony celebrating the American flag. He had hated the way blacks were treated and was said to have stopped attending church when he moved to Florida from Boston because he could not stand the bigotry he found within the church. In 1892, however, he wrote what we now know as the Pledge of Allegiance, keeping in mind what this country was supposed to stand for, but was falling short. The original pledge, written by Bellamy, said: "I pledge allegiance to my flag and to the Republic, for which it stands, one nation, indivisible, with liberty and justice for all."[16]

John Baer notes in his book *The Pledge of Allegiance: A Revised History and Analysis, 1892–2007* that Bellamy wanted to include the word "equality" in this pledge, but knew he would be struck down by members of state boards of education who were both racist and sexist; he not only abhorred the discrimination practiced against blacks, but against women as well.[17] Those who saw the division between America's doctrine and its praxis, and who were not afraid to speak against it, did so, but they were relatively small in number. America was building a nation based in large part on a belief in the superiority of the white race.

America loved its founding documents and prided itself on being "the land of the free and the home of the brave." White Americans seemed unable, unwilling, or both, to see the contradiction between what America purported to be and what America was. But those who were forced to live as second-class citizens could see it because they lived it . . . and it made them angry.

White preachers, including John Winthrop, who came with the Pilgrims to the New World in 1692, preached that democracy was "God's special blessing to America." Howard-Pitney said that "no belief has been more central to America's civil religion than the idea that Americans . . . are a chosen people sent to save and remake the world."[18] Early white American preachers preached what is known as the "American jeremiad," which Howard-Pitney defines as "a rhetoric of indignation, expressing deep dissatisfaction and urgently challenging the nation to reform."[19]

African Americans preached a jeremiad as well, but one that was not accepted or appreciated by the white ruling class. While it was all right for whites to preach for reform, it was as though they had a special right and privilege to do so, as they were talking to "their own," and admonishing "their own" to get right with God. In the end, God would show them mercy. . . . But African Americans, preaching an African American jeremiad, denounced the country, for its travesties of justice, for its treatment of black people, and for falling away from the will of God, which black preachers would contend was the equality and dignity of all human beings. Both preachers, the white and the black, were preaching a jeremiad, but one was acceptable and one was not. Both were angry, but the anger of the white preacher was not seen as threatening, while the anger of the black preacher was. The white preacher was delivering a sermon of self-reproach, but the African American preacher was delivering a set of criticisms about the country and its policies. The African American jeremiad questioned America's "promise and destiny; these preachers turned a doctrine of vengeance into a promise of ultimate success."[20] The American jeremiad contained an admonition to white people to "get right with God," but it really left the core, the essence, of America alone.

It was as though the American government, for all its faults and contradictions, was too holy to be touched. The African American jeremiad, however, was used to preach against the American government. Some viewed the African American jeremiad not as an admonition to blacks to get right with God, but rather as a warning from blacks to whites about what would happen to them and to the nation if they did not "fix" the problem of racism. The African American jeremiad was, according to Howard-Pitney, "a primary tool of black protest against all forms of racial injustice."[21] That was offensive to whites, who held their nation above being criticized. It was almost as if one could not criticize the country and be considered loyal and/or patriotic. That was not acceptable, because blood had been shed for this new country to be free.

Frederick Douglass was an early preacher of an African American jeremiad. He loathed the apathy of some black people, those who chose to live in and under oppression and not protest and fight for their freedom and dignity; he called them "oppressed cowards."[22] He believed that America had not lived up to its principles. He believed that America could be as great as it claimed to be, but that the country had work to do. He believed that America had to deal with racism and slavery in order to "get right with God." He believed that "prejudice against color [was] rebellion against God."[23] He had no time to buy into America's belief, by the time he began to speak, in its "purity" and "supremacy." He believed that America could be neither pure nor supreme as long as Americans continued to ignore the words of the founding documents and continued to treat black people as second-class citizens, if that. He believed that racism could be overcome, but not by ignoring it. America had to face its demon, racism, so that it could see it for what it was and then fight to eliminate it . . . and he truly believed that racism could and would be overcome. He believed that the Civil War was a godsend and at its end there would be liberty and justice for all. His speeches were fearless in his criticism, then, of America and her government, but they also contained that necessary element of a jeremiad: hope. He believed a new day was dawning for black people and for America.

He was deeply disturbed when, by the 1890s, the move was on with a vengeance to put blacks back in their place. He struggled with a country that was supposed to honor the freedom and dignity of all, yet whose Constitution had "authorized the national government to return fugitive slaves to their masters and forbade Congress, for twenty years, to abolish the African slave trade."[24] He rejoiced when Abraham Lincoln issued the Emancipation Proclamation, believing it to be "a sign that America was living up to her founding principles,"[25] only to realize, as time went on, that America had no intention of living up to those principles when it came to black people.

And so he delivered fiery, angry jeremiads, both before and after the Civil War, usually with the fleeting hope that things would be better for blacks in time. He delivered what is a classic African American jeremiad in 1852, denouncing America for not living up to its principles; it seemed not to contain a note of hope for America and her broken government as concerned slaves and black people:

> Fellow citizens, pardon me, allow me to ask, why am I called upon to speak here today? What have I, or those I represent, to do with your national independence? Are the great principles of political freedom and of natural justice, embodied in that Declaration of Independence, extended to us?
>
> What, to the American slave, is your 4th of July? I answer: a day that reveals to him, more than all other days in the year, the gross injustice and cruelty to which he is the constant victim. To him, your celebration is a sham; your boasted liberty, an unholy license; your national greatness, swelling vanity; your sounds of rejoicing are empty and heartless; your denunciations of tyrants, brass fronted impudence; your shouts of liberty and equality, hollow mockery; your prayers and hymns, your sermons and thanks-

> givings, with all your religious parade, and solemnity, are, to him, mere bombast, fraud, deception, impiety, and hypocrisy—a thin veil to cover up crimes which would disgrace a nation of savages. There is not a nation on earth guilty of practices more shocking and bloody, than are the people of these United States, at this very hour. . . .
>
> Fellow-citizens! I will not enlarge further on your national inconsistencies. The existence of slavery in this country brands your republicanism as a sham, your humanity as a base pretense, and your Christianity as a lie.[26]

Black and white preachers, over time, have presented jeremiads, using words that show anger. . . . Anger is an integral part of any jeremiad. But it isn't hate. If we keep in mind that the goal, or one of the goals, of a jeremiad is to get people or a nation to turn toward God, to repent, if you will, then we can see the urgency behind the words, even as the anger is expressed. The American jeremiad didn't express anger toward the government; to those who preached these jeremiads, the government was sacrosanct, untouchable, but those preachers did express anger toward people who were not living up to what the preachers interpreted as the word and will of God. Those who preached African American jeremiads did not concentrate on individuals, but on a government that was violating the rights of people . . . and in so doing, violating the word and will of God. Both types of jeremiads point to a pulling away from the word and will of God, but while the African American jeremiad criticizes the government, the American jeremiad leaves the government pretty much alone, as it tackles the problem of individuals losing their way.

Martin Luther King preached jeremiads; he decried what he called the "tragic duality" in white American culture.[27] His anger and frustration with the American government was palpable in some of his sermons, writings, and speeches, especially as he neared the end of his life. There could be no real freedom for black people (and later, poor people) without attention to "the least of these," and a necessary part of that attention had to be a difference or change in America as concerned wealth distribution. There had to be economic reform in America in order to create "genuine equal opportunity in America," he believed. But America was not interested in his opinion on how to create genuine equal opportunity for black people, nor was America willing to give up its perception of black people being prone to crime and disorder, a perception spurred on by the media. King was angry as he noticed what was and what was not happening in America. He preached forgiveness . . . but the desired goal of forgiveness did not eliminate the anger.

America, he believed, was not committed to equality for black people, any more than Abraham Lincoln had believed in equality for blacks, the Emancipation Proclamation notwithstanding. He realized that America had never gotten over its tendency to talk about the equality of all people without really meaning it. America was still caught in that place where people said that slavery was wrong but did nothing to get rid of it. Economic disparity might not be right, but America did little to nothing to correct the problem, King believed, and his recognition of this made him angry.

He realized that racism received its power to continue to oppress people because of the economic imbalance in America. Improved life for black people could not happen in a vacuum; blacks were American citizens and, therefore, their transformation and betterment "could only come within the larger transformation of America's political and economic structures."[28] His position on this issue led him to call for a national "Bill of Rights for the Disadvantaged."[29] America was not interested.

America's lack of interest did not dissuade King from speaking against the policies and spirit of America as concerned black people. In "Letter from a Birmingham Jail," King voiced his displeasure with white clergy who urged him to stop, to slow down, that change would come for black people in time. That was not acceptable to King. He wrote:

> I have traveled the length and breadth of Alabama, Mississippi, and all the other southern states. On sweltering summer days and crisp autumn mornings I have looked at [the South's] beautiful churches with their lofty spires pointing heavenward. I have beheld the impressive outlay of her massive religious education buildings. Over and over again I have found myself asking, "What kind of people worship here? Who is their God? Where were their voices when the lips of Governor Barnett dripped with words of

interposition and nullification? Where were they when Governor Wallace gave the clarion call for defiance and hatred? Where were their voices of support when tired, bruised and weary Negro men and women decided to rise from the dark dungeons of complacency to the bright hills of creative protest?"[30]

King expressed his anger over the fact that there was such distance between what America purported itself to be and what it actually was for black people. He spoke of the "spirit of dissent" that pervaded American life, saying,

> Thus was born—particularly in the young generation—a spirit of dissent that ranged from superficial disavowal of the old values to total commitment to wholesale, drastic, and immediate social reform. Yet all of it was dissent. Their voice is still a minority; but united with millions of black protesting voices, it has become a sound of distant thunder increasing in volume with the gathering of storm clouds. This dissent is America's hope. . . .
>
> America has not yet changed because so many think it need not change, but this is the illusion of the damned. America must change because twenty-three million black citizens will no longer live supinely in a wretched past. They have left the valley of despair; they have found strength in struggle; and whether they live or die, they shall never crawl or retreat again. Joined by white allies, they will shake the prison walls until they fall. America must change."[31]

King saw glaring issues within America's governmental structure, not least of which was its capitalistic system, which left far too many people on the fringes. He felt that America must be totally restructured:

> There are forty million poor people here. And one day, we must ask the question, "Why are there forty million poor people in America," and when you begin to ask that question, you are raising questions about the economic system, about a broader distribution of wealth. When you ask that question, you begin to question the capitalistic economy. And I'm simply saying that more and more, we've got to begin to ask questions about the whole

> society. We are called upon to help the discouraged beggars in life's marketplace. But one day we must come to see that an edifice which produces beggars needs restructuring. . . .[32]

The anger at the inequality and inequity in America owing to capitalism is evident. Dr. King was not promoting communism, but he had serious misgivings about capitalism. He recognized that America had damaged many people by its social ethos, which seemed to be supported by capitalism. He said, "Your whole structure must be changed. A nation that will keep people in slavery for 244 years will 'thingify' them—make them things. Therefore, they will exploit them and poor people generally, economically. And a nation that will exploit economically will have to have foreign investments and everything else, and will have to use its military might to protect them. All of these problems are tied together. What I am saying today is that we must go from this convention and say, 'America, you must be born again.'"[33]

Perhaps one of the most brilliant examples of an American *and* African American jeremiad can be found in the sermon "Beyond Vietnam: A Time to Break Silence," which King preached at Riverside Church on April 4, 1967. King's sphere or focus of ministry and work had widened; not only was he working for the rights for black people but for poor people in general, and he came to believe that America was unable to help its poor not because it didn't have the money, but because it was spending its money on what he believed was an unjust war. "A time comes when silence is betrayal," he said in the sermon, referring to a statement issued by the Clergy and Laymen Concerned about Vietnam. "That time has come for us in relation to Vietnam."[34]

The Vietnam War, he said, had "broken and eviscerated" the poverty program "as if it were some idle political plaything of a society gone mad on war."[35] The diversion of funds from helping poor people in America to this war bothered King; he said that "I knew that America would never invest the necessary funds or energies in the rehabilitation of its poor so long as adventures like Vietnam continued to draw men and skills and money like some demonic destructive suction tube."[36] He saw war not only as an enemy of the poor but also as a sign of America's failure to honor its stated covenanted principled to be a government, "of the people, by the people, and for the people." The war also allowed a falling away from Jesus' mandate to his followers to take care of "the least of these." Not only were "the least of these" being exploited on a daily basis in American society, now they were being exploited by war. The war, he said, was not only devastating hope for the poor at home, but it was also "taking the black young men who had been crippled by our society and sending them eight thousand miles away to guarantee liberties in Southeast Asia which they had not found in Southwest Georgia and East Harlem."[37]

King delved into classic jeremiad protest in that sermon as he criticized the United States for its duplicity in values. On the one hand, America was shaped by the principles and tenets of the Declaration of Independence and the Bill of Rights, but on the other hand, America seemed hopelessly unable to break loose from the curse of racism. America was the "city on the hill," for goodness' sake. America was to be the example of godly behavior for the rest of the world. And yet, King decried, America was seriously falling short of its ideals:

> They watch as we poison their water, as we kill a million acres of their crops. They must weep as the bulldozers roar through their areas preparing to destroy the precious trees. They wander into the hospital, with at least twenty casualties from American firepower for one "Vietcong"-inflicted injury. So far, we may have killed a million of them—mostly children. They wander into the towns and see thousands of the children, homeless, without clothes, running in packs on the streets like wild animals. They see the children, degraded by our soldiers as they beg for food. They see the children selling their sisters to our soldiers, soliciting for their mothers.[38]

Dr, King was speaking with the heart and passion of the biblical Jeremiah, who saw the Israelites leading themselves to destruction as they fell further and further away from God's will. The biblical Jeremiah could not keep his peace; what he saw the people doing, in direct opposition to God's will, was like a "fire shut up in his bones," (Jer. 20:9) and he must have felt it would have been a betrayal not to speak. He was angry at what he saw, and what he said made the people angry who heard him.

Yahweh had had great hopes for the people whom Yahweh had created, but as time passed, Abraham Heschel writes, "God's hope was dashed. The people deserted their Redeemer and worshipped instead the 'works of their own hands.'"[39] God has great wrath, because God's people have fallen away from God's will, but God is also anguished. Importantly, Jeremiah the prophet is anguished himself, as he becomes the voice and spirit of God, speaking to a people who will not listen. Heschel writes, "Israel's distress was more than a human tragedy. With Israel's distress came the affliction of God."[40] Heschel explains the spirit and purpose of the prophet:

> The ultimate purpose of a prophet is not to be inspired, but to inspire the people; not to be filled with a passion but to impassion the people with understanding for God. . . .The call to be a prophet is more than an invitation. It is first of all a feeling of being enticed, of acquiescence or willing surrender. But this winsome feeling is only one aspect of the experience. The other aspect is a sense of being ravished or carried away by violence or yielding to overpowering force against one's will. The prophet feels both the attraction and the coercion of God, the appeal and the pressure, the charm and the stress. He is conscious of both voluntary identification and forced capitulation.[41]

Thus, the prophet feels anger from two sources: that ingested from God, and that which one feels on one's own as when sometimes reflecting on the futility of the preached message. Heschel writes, "In spite of public rejection, in spite of inner misery, he felt unable to discard the divine burden, unable to disengage himself from the divine pathos. He knew why he had to yield; he knew how to explain his inability to resist the terrible errand."[42]

King was rejected; it is said that he felt deep despair as he delivered what he felt God was telling him to deliver, and yet, he could not extricate himself from the divine and "terrible errand." He spoke about Vietnam and the "wrongness" of America being there with the same passion with which he had decried segregation and racism. It was all right for him to talk about those things; after all, segregation and racism affected only a specific group of people, was the sentiment. But once he started talking about the Vietnam War, and its wrongness, he crossed a line which all prophets inevitably cross, earning the ire of the ruling class. His message was like a "fire shut up in his bones," and he was angry that America seemed not to understand. He sharply criticized America for ignoring the divine directive to be "righteous," that is, to be in right relationship with God, but he ended his sermon on a note of hope and inspiration, typical of the American jeremiad:

> We must move past indecision to action. We must find new ways to speak for peace in Vietnam and justice throughout the developing world—a world that borders our doors. If we do not act, we shall surely be dragged down the long dark and shameful corridors of time reserved for those who possess power without compassion, might without morality, and strength without sight. Now let us begin. Now let us rededicate ourselves to the long and bitter—but beautiful—struggle for a new world. This is the calling of the sons of God, and our brothers wait eagerly for our response. Shall we say that the odds are too great? Shall we tell them that the struggle is too hard? Will our message be that the forces of American life militate against their arrival as full men and we send our deepest regrets? Or will there be another message, of longing, of hope, of solidarity with their yearnings, of commitment to their cause, whatever the cost? The choice is ours, and though we might prefer it otherwise we must choose in this crucial moment of human history.[43]

Jeremiah Wright preached in the tradition of the prophets and preachers gone before him, from the biblical Jeremiah to Frederick Douglass to Martin Luther King and, like those prophets, suffered the angst of having to say what was "shut up in his bones," being rejected by some because of it.

By the time Wright began preaching, he had been personally stung by racism, most notably when he was in the Marines. He had seen neighborhoods change after one black family would move into a previously all-white neighborhood. He had seen the overt racism in the South and experienced the not-so-obvious racism in the North.

He was thirteen years old when the *Brown vs. Board of Education* decision was rendered and no doubt had seen the ugliness that accompanied black students in the South when they tried to integrate into public schools. He had seen "Bull" Connor terrorize young people in Birmingham, turning fire hoses and dogs on young people who had decided they were tired of being treated as second-class citizens.[44] He had experienced the horror of learning that the Sixteenth Street Baptist Church in Birmingham, Alabama, had been bombed, killing four little girls.

He knew about Rosa Parks; he heard Dr. King give his "I Have a Dream" speech in 1963; he knew about the sit-ins and the violence perpetrated against young people who began to belligerently confront segregation. He was at Howard University when students decided they were tired of singing "white" music in a black school, and were tired of hearing that black music was inferior to white music and started a gospel choir He knew about police brutality and how black males seemed to be treated worse by law enforcement. He had read W. E. B. DuBois, Carter G. Woodson, had read *Native Son* and *The Invisible Man*; he had read James Baldwin and Zora Neale Hurston. He knew the poems of Countee Cullen and Paul Laurence Dunbar, and he also knew that white educators did not consider it important that students read any works by African Americans. He no doubt knew blacks who had been passed up or passed over for good jobs because of the color of their skin.

So, if one were to ask if he was angry, the answer would be "yes," but he was not alone. Most blacks who had experienced discrimination and shoddy treatment were angry. Because many whites were unaware of or refused to acknowledge the depth and breadth of racism, many thought that any anger of blacks was unfounded; because there had been some progress in ostensible, tangible areas, like the end of racial discrimination in public places, or blacks being able to be treated in white hospitals, many whites naively believed that things were better. In fact, many whites resented it if any anger on the parts of blacks was expressed because their denial was so deep that they believed that—as opposed to really needing the government to help end discrimination—blacks were merely complaining and begging for assistance.

Whites could not understand the pressure that blacks lived with on a daily basis; blacks wondered, as Howard Thurman wrote in *Jesus and the Disinherited*, "under what circumstances was survival possible?"[45] Blacks were like strangers in a strange land; one is reminded of Psalm 137, where the psalmist wrote, "How can we sing the Lord's song in a strange land?" This country was not a "safe space" for black people. Blacks could not expect justice or fairness from the justice system, not even from the United States Supreme Court. Blacks were always hearing how inferior they were, how bad they were, and there was no place to turn for comfort and strengthening and an installation of hope, except from the black church. Thurman wrote that in ancient history Jews who lived in Rome suffered oppression; Rome, he said, was "the great barrier to peace of mind." Jews had to deal with their position in society—which was not high—and had to see their status for what it was and adjust so that they could succeed as much as possible.

Thurman said—and Wright understood this innately—that what the Jews went through was what the "Negro" in America was experiencing and had experienced for a long time. Thurman wrote: "This is the position of the disinherited in every age. What must be the attitude toward the rulers, the controllers of political, social, and economic life? This is the question of the Negro in American life. Until he has faced and settled that question, he cannot inform his environment with reference to his own life, whatever may be his preparation of his pretensions."[46]

Wright knew what Thurman was talking about because he lived it. And he knew that the people to whom he preached had lived it as well. Some of them had suffered so much under racism that they could not or would not speak of it. Others had anger that would rise to the surface at any time. Some of the people to whom he preached suffered mental trauma because of the pressure of being black in America. Wright knew it. He had lived it. He had tasted it.

What, then, should he say and how should he say it? It would be wrong and disingenuous to pretend that racism did not exist, in spite of there being a God, and it would be wrong to pretend that racism and discrimination, in addition to being painful, did not make people angry. It was almost a taboo to express anger and be labeled as an "angry black" man or woman, but it was necessary, Wright knew, to express the anger, to pull the top off of spirits that were nearly exploding with anger over the way they had been treated. Many black people didn't know who they were and didn't want to know. Wright knew that they *needed* to know who they were, but before they would want to do that, some of the pressure would have to be released. Their feelings would have to be affirmed. No, they were not crazy. Yes, they had reason to be angry.

Wright helped them to release their anger, but, using Jesus and Jesus' life as the role model, taught them that they could not hate and still call themselves Christian.

The travesty of the what happened in 2008 with sound bites played from primarily two of Wright's sermons is that the media reporting revealed and verified that white America did not have a clue about what it was to be black in America, that they could not distinguish between anger and hate because of their unfamiliarity with the black preaching style, and that they were poor journalists who did not remember that a journalist is supposed to be objective and get all the facts before reporting an event. Had journalists taken the time, it is possible, but not guaranteed, that the reporting of Wright's statements would have been different. Journalists failed Wright and failed America. Had journalists taken the time to read or listen to the entire sermons from which they lifted the sound bites, they might not have reported the sound bites at all, because Wright's jeremiad in these sermons criticized the American government and offered hope not for a better government but to a people who for too long had been marginalized by that same government.

The sermon from which the words "God damn America" were lifted was entitled "Confusing God and Government." Wright's sermons were always carefully and impeccably prepared. He was and is a scholar, both biblical and historical, and he wove the two disciplines together masterfully so that his congregation of "the disinherited" would be able to connect the scriptures and their lessons to their own lives.

In "Confusing God and Government," Wright began by explaining that Jesus wept (John 11:35) . . . but then he began to break down the reasons Jesus wept. He said:

> He cried for his people because they were blinded by their culture, they were blinded by their condition, they were blinded by their circumstance, they were blinded by their oppression, they were blinded by being in a spot where they desired—deeply de-

> sired—revenge, and they could not see the things that make for peace. We keep forgetting . . . and we need to remember; Jerome Ross wrote about it like he reminded you of it, write it down so you don't forget it. These people had, in Luke 19, an occupying army living in their country. Jesus in verse 43 calls them their enemies . . . their enemies had all the political power. Remember, they had to send Jesus to a court presided over by their enemy; a provisional governor appointed by their enemies ran the civic and the political affairs of the capital. He had backing him up an occupying army with superior soldiers—they were commandos trained in urban combat and trained to kill on command.[47]

As Wright laid out the biblical landscape of the scripture he was using, it was hard for anyone listening, black or white, to miss the parallels to current day life. Blacks knew firsthand what it was like to have courts "presided over by their enemy," they knew about government officials in high places being their enemy; not even the nation's highest court had protected them or their interests. Here was Wright's brilliance, sewing together past and present with masterful language and imagery, bringing his listeners from their own places of frustration into the time of Jesus where, perhaps, Jesus had felt the same way.

Wright continued explaining the situation of the Jews back in Jesus' day, further drawing in people who knew all too well what he was describing. These people, he said, were tired of their oppression; "they wanted the enemy up out of their land (some of them did, some of them didn't; not the businessmen, not those in bed with the enemy, let's be clear . . .)."[48] Wright continued to paint the picture, to set up the scene.

Then he began to get into the gist of his message. He talked about the "Italian" (Roman) army leading Jesus out to Calvary. They looked strong and mighty as military regiments frequently do. There is something seductive and inspiring about seeing men (and women) in uniform, "going to war." Their appearance signifies or suggests strength, and the image is appealing. But Wright jolted people out of thinking that way, understanding it all too well and saying, "Let me help you with something . . . let me help you. The military does not make for peace. The military only keeps the lid on for a little while. The military doesn't make for peace, and the absence of armed resistance doesn't make for genuine peace. . . . War doesn't make for peace, war only makes for escalating violence, and a mindset to pay the enemy back by any means necessary."[49]

The people wanted a new king but they were blinded by their circumstances, Wright preached. They were confused; they were confusing "external appearances with external power." Wright said we as humans look at signs and miss what the signs are pointing to: "The deeds of power point to a God who is greater than any physical limitation and a God who can overcome any limiting situation. The things that make for peace, only God can give. Y'all looking to the government for that which only God can give. No wonder he wept. He had good cause to cry. The people under oppression were confusing God and Government."[50]

Wright goes on to explain how people confuse what the government says with what God says:

> We confuse Government and God. We believe God sanctioned the rape and robbery of an entire continent. We believe God ordained African slavery. We believe God makes Europeans superior to Africans and to everybody else too. We confuse God and Government. We said in our founding document as a Government, "We hold these truths to be self-evident, that all men are created equal"—created, that means God—"and endowed with certain inalienable rights"—that means given by God, and then we define Africans in those same documents as three-fifths of a person. We believe God approved of African slavery.[51]

He goes on and explains how people have bought into the message of the government instead of into the message of God. God, Wright says, is loving, stands for equality and equity, loves all of his/her children equally, with no preference for rich or poor, gay or straight, white or black . . . but people have become confused and believe the government over God. He preaches with intensity and passion, wanting, like the biblical Jeremiah, for the people in his pews to "get it," and lose what has helped keep them oppressed. Believing in government over God is one of those things.

Wright then makes three points: governments lie, governments change, and governments fail. He's in trouble, now, with those who preach an American jeremiad. If one preaches an American jeremiad, one preaches about the *people* who make up the government, not the government itself. The American government is deemed sacred, and anyone who criticizes it is out of line. Wright, like Douglass before him, ignores the taboo against speaking or preaching against the government and hits what he sees as the ways the government has helped keep the minds of oppressed people in chains. Though historical evidence points to the fact that America has been racist, imperialistic, and militaristic to the detriment of many, those subjects are left virtually alone, especially in pulpits. Wright, however, addressed them frequently, speaking to a people who had tasted the afterbirth of such practices and beliefs. African Americans had been used, many times, to help support America's imperialist drives, and African Americans had likewise been used in numbers disproportionate to their percentage in America's general population, but had often come home from serving their country only to find constraints and restraints due to racism. What Wright talked about his listeners knew about full well; they had lived it.

So they understood Wright when he said, in this sermon, that the government lied about the belief in all men being equal. That it meant only white men were created equal; neither blacks nor women were included in the proclamation. He says that America knew that the Japanese were going to attack Pearl Harbor. Governments lie, he repeats. He mentions the Tuskegee Experiment, where African American men were purposely infected with syphilis and were told, falsely, that they were being treated. The government lied, he preached, about there being weapons of mass destruction in order to justify the starting of the Iraq War, and more. Governments lie, he preached, *but God does not lie.* There is the reality that we have all seen, but there is God . . . and therefore, there is the hope. He paints a picture and uses current events and current history in much the same way that Jesus preached in parables using images and situations with which the people were very familiar. Don't hold onto governments, he preached. They lie. Hold onto God; God does not lie.

Wright's second point in this sermon was that governments change. In this section of the sermon he took his listeners back to biblical times, when the government of Egypt was colonizing much of the ancient Mediterranean and African world. (He noted that those who colonized back then were not white, and made the people in the pews repeat, "All colonizers ain't white.") After the Egyptians, there were the Babylonians, and then there were the Assyrians and then there were the Persians. . . . His point was, using the Bible as illustration, that governments change.

Then he jumped to American history:

> Prior to the Civil Rights and Equal Accommodations laws of the government in this country, there was Black segregation by the country, legal discrimination by the government prohibited Blacks from voting by the government; (the government said) you had to eat in separate places; you had to sit in different places from White folk because the government (said) so, and you had to be buried in a separate cemetery. It was apartheid American-style from the cradle to the grave, all because the government backed it up. But guess what? Governments change!
>
> Under President Bill Clinton, we got (the) messed up Welfare to Work Bill, but under Clinton, blacks had an intelligent friend in the White House. Oh, but governments change! . . .
>
> Where governments change—write this down—Malachi 3:6 –"thus sayeth the Lord"—repeat after me—"for I am the Lord and I change not." That's the King James Version. The New Revised (Standard Version) says, "For I the Lord do not change." In other words, where governments change, God does not change. God is the same yesterday, today and forevermore.[52]

For a community that had been treated as second-class, thrown about, and used at will, yet denied full respect and citizenship, the fact or even mere suggestion that God did not change was a word of "blessed assurance." If nothing else, Wright had to teach the people that no matter how badly they had been thrown about or taken advantage of by the government, they could rest assured that they could always count on God, who was "the same yesterday, today and forevermore."

Then, finally, Wright got to his third point: Governments fail. This is not an unusual theme from those who preach jeremiads, but the focus of some modern-day preachers who criticize the government is a bit different from that of Wright. The late Jerry Falwell, speaking in the aftermath of the destruction of the twin towers of the World Trade Center on September 11, 2001, criticized the government . . . but his criticism suggested that the government was awry because of decadent *people* within it. If America (and therefore its government) is not the best it can be, it is because the morals of individuals have caused the government to diminish and be less than it was created to be:

> [T]he Lord has protected us so wonderfully these 225 years. . . . [But] what we saw on Tuesday, as terrible as it is, could be miniscule if, in fact, God continues to lift the curtain and allow the enemies of America to give us probably what we deserve. . . . The ACLU's got to take a lot of the blame for this . . . throwing God out successfully with the help of the federal court system, throwing God out of the public square, out of the schools. The abortionists have got to bear some burden for this because God will not be mocked. And when we destroy 40 million little innocent babies, we make God mad. I really believe that the pagans, and the abortionists, and the feminists, and the gays and the lesbians who are actively trying to make that an alternative lifestyle, the ACLU, People for the American Way—all of them who tried to secularize America—I point the finger in their face and say, "you helped make this happen."[53]

Because Falwell's statements blamed the government's shortcomings on what the Religious Right deemed the "undesirables" in America, he was not demonized. He was preaching an American jeremiad. But Wright boldly and forcefully criticized the government, and in his third point of this sermon, said that "governments fail":

> Governments fail. The government in this text comprised of Caesar, Cornelius, . . . Pontius Pilate—the Roman government, failed. The British government used to rule from east to west. The British government had a Union Jack. She colonized Kenya, Guyana, Nigeria, Jamaica, Barbados, Trinidad, and Hong Kong. Her navies rule the Seven Seas, all the way down to the tip of Argentina in the Falklands, but the British failed. The Russian

> government failed. The Japanese government failed. The German government failed. And the United States of America, when it came to treating her citizens of Indian descent fairly, she failed. She put them on reservations. When it came to treating her citizens of Japanese descent fairly, she failed. She put them in internment camps. When it came to treating her citizens of African descent fairly, America failed.
>
> She put them in chains. The government put them in slave quarters, put them on auction blocks, put them in cotton fields, put them in inferior schools, put them in substandard housing, put them in scientific experiments, put them in the lowest paying jobs, put them outside equal protection of the law, kept them out of their racist bastions of higher education and locked them into positions of hopelessness and helplessness. The government gives them the drugs, builds bigger prisons, passes a three-strike law, and then wants us to sing, 'God bless America?' No, no, no. Not "God bless America"; "God damn America!" That's in the Bible. For killing innocent people. God damn America for treating her citizens as less than human. God damn America as long as she keeps trying to act like she is God and she is supreme.'"[54]

Wright, in that sermon, asks people to forgive him for saying, "God damn." Preached Wright: "That's in the Bible. Blessings and cursing is in the Bible. . . ."[55] He finishes the sermon with the proclamation, the word of hope present in jeremiads; this word of encouragement is "God never fails!"

It is and was impossible to understand what Wright was preaching, because his sermon was reduced to a thirty-second sound bite. Interestingly, because America was uneasy with the thought of a black man headed to the White House, it was easy for the media to jump on and demonize Wright for his words. Whatever else is going on in America, there is always racism. And there is fear and distrust of black people; pulling up a tiny portion of Wright's sermon was calculated and did what it was intended to do: bother and scare white people and make black people nervous that Wright's words would keep Barack Obama out of the White House.

It is also worth noting that whites who preach and have preached jeremiads and who have said controversial things have not been, for the most part, demonized like Wright has been. Frank Schaeffer, who with his father was among the founders of the Religious Right, noted this very point. In an article that appeared on the *The Huffington Post* Schaeffer said, "When Senator Obama's preacher thundered about racism and injustice, Obama suffered smear-by-association. But when my late father—Religious Right leader Francis Schaeffer—denounced America and even called for the violent overthrow of the U.S. government, he was invited to lunch with Presidents Ford, Reagan and Bush, Sr."[56] Continued Schaeffer:

> Every Sunday thousands of right wing white preachers (following in my father's footsteps) rail against America's sins from tens of thousands of pulpits. They tell us that America is complicit in the "murder of the unborn," has become "Sodom" by coddling gays, and that our public schools are sinful places full of evolutionists and sex educators hell-bent on corrupting children. They say, as my dad often did, that we are "under the judgment of God." They call America evil and warn of immanent destruction. By comparison Obama's minister's shouted "controversial" comments were mild. All he said was that God should damn America for our racism and violence and that no one had ever used the "N-word" about Hillary Clinton.[57]

Wright was criticized for being "angry," while Schaeffer and other members of the religious right were never called such. Wright was also accused of being "hate-filled." But his sermons had no hate. Anger, yes, but all who preach jeremiads, whether white or black, liberal or conservative, express anger. The biblical Jeremiah expressed anger because the people would not listen. The biblical Jeremiah was filled with the spirit of God; it was like a "fire shut up in his bones," and he was angry, yes, but hopeful. Jeremiah Wright was angry because in spite of God, America refused to listen, just as the Israelites had refused to listen to their prophets. Dr. Martin Luther King was angry. Frederick Douglass was angry. But their messages contained anger supported by hope . . . because in the end, there was a God, who had no favorites, who would, surely, correct the wrongs that caused his prophets to weep.

11

THE OPPRESSOR AND THE OPPRESSED, UNITED

I'm not mad at this country anymore.
I'm worried. This country has no idea
of what it has done to Negroes
or what it has done to itself.

—James Baldwin[1]

Jeremiah Wright spoke to a disinherited people, but perhaps what is surprising was that many white people who heard him understood exactly what he was talking about; it was as though he was speaking to their souls as well. The rancid stench of racism did not touch and affect just black people; white people, including those white people who perpetrated racism, were just as damaged as well, and the sermons Wright preached reached those injured and perhaps ashamed in parts of their spirits as well.

The connectedness between blacks and whites in America was always there; from the beginning, the subjugation of blacks by whites was a part of Americana, part of the legacy of being "an American" that was being developed. But it was never a healthy connection, and it produced a social system that circulated ill will, suspicion, hatred, and anger between the two races. One race believed it was superior; the other was thrown into a never-ending quest to find its worth. Baldwin said that white people were trapped in a history that they didn't understand, but so were blacks. Said Baldwin: "I didn't want to be white, but I didn't know what being black meant. I couldn't accept what I had been told—that blacks were inferior. You have to decide who you are and force the world to deal with you."[2] Baldwin went even further, saying, "Blacks represent a level of experience that Americans deny. It's hazardous to really hate white people because we're too involved with them. It's easy for an African to hate a white, but not an African American. White people see what they've invested you with. . . . One of the great psychological hazards of being an African American is that all the standards, all of the images . . . none of it applies to you . . . are not you. It becomes a great psychological collision."[3]

That way of forced existence created a false—yet intimate—relationship between blacks and whites, but it seemed that blacks were and are more aware of the chasm that existed and exists still to this day between the two races. Knowing who one was as a white person in America did not seem all that difficult. One could and would claim one's whiteness and distance him- or herself from the blacks over whom he or she was supposed to be superior. Blacks, however, were caught; they were African, yet American. Blacks knew and would not, in fact could not, deny the historical intimacy that existed between the two races. Wright himself said on many occasions that some of his African-centered friends wanted him to deny his *American-ness* and just claim his African-ness, to "check" his American-ness, but that is not possible. The two—African and American—are inextricably linked. Said Wright:

> There are some things that are not African. The spirituals are not African. They are American, African American, and every now and then, I have to reach down into my "carry on" luggage and pull out the words of a spiritual that ministers to my soul. Sometimes people want me to "check" all of my American baggage . . . when I get to the airport with my bags, there's some baggage that I keep with me. Some baggage is too precious to check.

> Some things are African American. Collard greens and Southern fried chicken—that's not African. That's American. One of my seminarians . . . said while you were in Cote d'Ivoire, did you see any fried chicken? No, we didn't, because that's American, African American. I've got some precious baggage. . . . I've got Miles Davis and Byron Cage . . . that's not African, that's African American. Sometimes, I feel discouraged, and feel my work's in vain, but then, the Holy Spirit revives my soul again. . . . There is a balm in Gilead . . . ."[4]

Wright expressed what others before him had expressed and showed he understood the inextricable relationship between whites and blacks, a relationship that many whites either do not realize or will not admit. Frederick Douglass also recognized the connectedness between whites and blacks and said, "More than simply surviving white society, we adopt it and will follow it and will follow you in your civilization."[5] Douglass might be said to have felt the intimacy and closeness between the two races, in spite of racial enmity, because he was the son of a slave; he saw firsthand how the races intermingled and borrowed from each other. Howard-Pitney noted that "Douglass thought that white racism was isolated and he believed it would fade; he thought it would be 'swept away by the providential tide of history,' and based his continued hope for blacks in a mystic faith in American destiny." Howard-Pitney concluded that Douglass was "an Anglophile and occasionally referred to whites as 'Anglo-American.'"[6]

The complex and intimate relationship between whites and blacks was described vividly by James Baldwin, again in the interview he did with Studs Terkel. Baldwin said:

> No matter who says what, in fact, Negroes and whites in this country are related to each other. Half of the black families in the South are related, you know, to the judges and the lawyers and the white families of the South. They are cousins, and kissing cousins at that—at least kissing cousins. Now, this is the terrible depth of involvement.
>
> It is easy for an African to hate the invader and drive him out of Africa, but it is very difficult for an American Negro to do this.

> He obviously can't do this to white people; there's no place to drive them. This is a country that belongs equally to us both. One has got to live together here or there won't be any country.[7]

Maybe that belief—that America belonged equally to both races, fueled Douglass's optimism. That optimism for collegiality and harmony between the races faded, however, even before he died, and by the time Wright preached, most optimism on the parts of those so inclined had diminished or disappeared, replaced with apathy, anger, or both. Those emotions notwithstanding, the connectedness between the two sparring races could not be ignored. People of African descent will proclaim that they are American. The origin of ancestral birth does not negate the fact that Africans, brought to this country, became American, and most African Americans will own that fact and defend it.

Despite being American, however, blacks in this country were the stepchildren, so to speak; Howard Thurman calls blacks "the disinherited," and compares them to none other than Jesus. In his lifetime, Jesus felt the unique pressure and angst of being one considered "less than" in a dominant, oppressive society. Thurman points out that Jesus could be considered "disinherited" because he was first of all a Jew in a Roman society; he was, number two, a poor Jew, meaning he understood and bore the oppression which comes from economic inequality; and finally that he was a member of a minority group "in the midst of a larger dominant and controlling group."[8] And what Thurman notes is that "there is one overmastering problem that the socially and politically disinherited always face: Under what terms is survival possible?"[9] The disinherited, says Thurman, have two alternatives as they consider their survival: whether to resist or not resist:

> In essence, Rome was the enemy; Rome symbolized total frustration; Rome was the great barrier to peace of mind. And Rome was everywhere. No Jewish person of the period could deal with the question of his practical life, his vocation, his place in society, until first he had settled deep within himself this critical issue.
>
> This is the position of the disinherited in every age. What must be the attitude toward the rulers, the controllers of political, social, and economic life? This is the question of the Negro in

> American life. Until he has faced and settled that question, he cannot inform his environment with reference to his own life, whatever may be his preparation of his pretensions.[10]

The disinherited, ensconced as they are within a dominant and oppressive society, have to be able to recognize who they are and then fight to hold onto that identity. That is difficult when it is easier to survive by imitating or assimilating into the dominant culture. Jesus and the Jews in Jesus' day had that struggle, as African Americans have had the same struggle historically. Thurman says that Christianity "as it was born in the mind of this thinker and teacher (Jesus) appears as a technique of survival for the oppressed . . . he announced the good news that fear, hypocrisy, and hatred, the three hounds of hell that track the trail of the disinherited, need have no dominion over them."[11]

In spite of hearing words of encouragement, words designed and constructed to strengthen their faith, many African Americans found life on earth miserable. Although the Africans were taught the Christian God, many found it hard to relate to this God who apparently had no trouble, no issue, with the evils of racism and slavery. During the period of peonage, many African Americans, trapped in a new slavery that must have seemed interminable, found it impossible to go to church.

They had lost their faith.

Elie Wiesel writes of how the very religious can lose their faith when evil seems to run its course through the hearts and lives of human beings. As a child, he watched adults who had seemed to have great faith wither under the evil of the Holocaust. He records in *Night* that one of the Jews he noticed had finally come up missing; he had been the victim of selection. Wiesel remembered this.

> Lately, he had been wandering among us, his eyes glazed, telling everyone how weak he was: "I can't go on. . . . It's over. . . ." We tried to raise his spirits but he wouldn't listen to anything we said. He just kept repeating that it was all over for him, that he could no longer fight; he had no more strength, no more faith. His eyes would suddenly go blank, leaving two gaping wounds, two wells of terror.

He was not alone in having lost his faith during those days of selection. I knew a rabbi, from a small town in Poland. He was old and bent, his lips constantly trembling. He was always praying, in the block, at work, in the ranks. He recited entire pages from the Talmud, arguing with himself, asking and answering himself endless questions. One day, he said to me:

"It's over. God is no longer with us."[12]

African Americans certainly had to strain to look for a God whom, they believed, was a proponent for the oppressed. They adopted the story of the Exodus as their own (although whites adopted that same story as their sign from God that they had been led to the United States), and they believed that as God had delivered the Jews from Pharaoh, a ruthless ruler who had demanded that they make "bricks with no straw," that this same God would deliver them.

> So the taskmasters and the supervisors of the people went out and said to the people, "Thus says Pharaoh, 'I will not give you straw. Go and get straw yourselves, wherever you can find it; but your work will not be lessened in the least.'" So the people scattered throughout the land of Egypt, to gather stubble for straw. The taskmasters were urgent, saying, "Complete your work, the same daily assignment as when you were given straw." And the supervisors of the Israelites, whom Pharaoh's taskmasters had set over them, were beaten, and were asked, "Why did you not finish the required quantity of bricks yesterday and today, as you did before?"
>
> Then the Israelite supervisors came to Pharaoh and cried, "Why do you treat your servants like this?" (Exod. 5:10–15)

Clearly, the slaves, though they were forbidden to learn to read, did learn enough about this story even before they could read to ascertain that there was a great parallel between their situation and that of the unfortunate Israelites. (Ironically, in the biblical narrative, it is the Egyptians, who lived in North Africa, who oppressed the Israelites.) What the African American preacher had to do was convince and convict the slaves that God was good . . . because the Bible said so . . . and he had to do it even as many African Americans were becoming convinced that God was "no longer with" them. Here we had, then, a group of people, whites, who believed the Exodus story was their story; they had been delivered by God from England to America to found a new society . . . and another group of people, African Americans, who claimed the same story; this same God was in the process of delivering them out of their oppression. It is not certain that the African Americans could ever have believed that blacks and whites were looking at the same God as their own; the God that African Americans pulled out of the Exodus story was a good God who hated oppression, while that same God, for the whites, seemed to be one who *condoned* oppression. The two groups would not have spent much time debating or even thinking of such an irony, and yet, it is ironic that both races were again tied together by a deity who had seemingly worked different purposes for different racial groups.

It was not the job of the African American preacher, however, to concern himself with the God of white people; he had the job of gluing African Americans to God in such a way that they would not fall into despair. John Jasper, who founded the Sixth Baptist Church in Richmond, Virginia, after the Civil War, preached a stirring sermon, "De Sun Do Move," artfully and skillfully reminding African Americans that *their* God was capable of doing the impossible. Jasper admonished his listeners to believe in the goodness of God over the evil of human beings. It was "all there" in the Bible, Jasper would teach. The sun was something the African Americans would be able to relate to in a very personal way. Many, even most, of his listeners were ex-slaves; they had toiled in the hot sun. The power of a story in the Bible about the sun moving in order to effect God's purposes—which were good—would not be lost on them:

> But I kin read de Bible and git de things whar lay on do top uv de soil. Out'n de Bible I knows nuthin' extry 'bout de sun. I sees 'is courses as he rides up dar so gran' an' mighty in de sky, but dar is heaps 'bout dat flamin' orb dat is too much fer me.
>
> I know dat de sun shines powerfly an' po's down its light in floods, an' yet dat is nuthin' compared wid de light dat flashes in

> my min' frum de pages of Gord's book. But you knows all dat. I knows dat de sun burns oh, how it did burn in dem July days. I tell yer he cooked de skin on my back many er day when I wuz hoen' in de corn fiel'. But you knows all dat, an' yet dat is nuthin' der to de divine fire dat burns in der souls uv Gord's chil'n. Can't yer feel it, bruthrin?[13]

Though Jasper said his text for this sermon was Exodus 15:3, which reads, "The LORD is a warrior; the LORD is his name," the power of the sermon revolves around the story found in Joshua 10, where Joshua, one of God's anointed, had defeated Ai, an important city, "totally destroying it." The king of Jerusalem, Adoni-Zedek, grows worried, because Ai was an important city. He asks for assistance to attack Gibeon, which had been a part of Zedek's kingdom, but which had made peace with Israel. He called for many soldiers to attack Joshua's significantly smaller army. It was a war, but God was a warrior for the oppressed. Jasper picks up the story of this war as he illustrates that God was in fact a warrior for justice. Jasper preached:

> And Joshua was sent for. He war at Gilgal, and they sent for him to come immediately, and saw the array of battle, Joshua found that the sun war advancing rapidly to go down and that he could not avenge himself on the enemies before the sun did went down. He beseech-ed (sic) God that the sun should stop. The Lord commanded him to stand in the sight of Israel and speak to the sun, and say unto the sun, "Sun, stand thou still upon Gibeon, and thou, moon, in the Valley of Ajalon, and the sun stood still, and the moon stayed, and hasted not to go down for a whole day. . . ."
>
> Now, then, I have proved to you all these things as they are laid down in the Bible, chapter and verse. According to the text, Joshua showed in the sight of all Israel that the Sun Do Move, because he stopped it, by God's command, for a whole day, as the text states. If he stopped it, that proves that the sun war moving over Joshua and the Amorites, and of course they war nowhar else than on this here earth, and consequently, it war moving

> around the earth, and after the battle war over, it begun moving again in its regular course. Therefore it is proved that the Sun Do Move around the earth . . . Notice Malachi, Chapter 1, verse ii (sic) and that come from God's own mouth, and thar can be no properer authority that God's authority. With His own lips he said, "For from the rising of the sun unto the going down of the same, my name shall be great among the Gentiles." What strikes us here is that the Sun Do Move![14]

This sermon stirred the souls of a people looking for hope because Jasper made sure that they understood that *their* God was powerful enough to make the sun stand still so that the oppressed could score a victory. That type of spiritual feeding was necessary in order to give his listeners hope and to dilute some of the anger and frustration they undoubtedly felt.

At the same time, however, white preachers were preaching about *their* God, a God who sanctioned white supremacy, slavery and the mistreatment of blacks by whites. Ebenezer Warren, who was the pastor of First Baptist Church of Macon, Georgia, delivered a sermon entitled "Scriptural Vindication of Slavery." To a standing-room only crowd, he preached:

> Slavery forms a vital element of the Divine Revelation to man. Its institution, regulation, and perpetuity constitute a part of many of the books of the Bible. . . . The public mind needs enlightening from the sacred teachings of inspiration on this subject. . . . We of the South have been passive, hoping the storm would subside. . . . Our passiveness has been our sin. We have not come to the vindication of God and of truth, as duty demanded . . . it is necessary for ministers of the gospel . . . to teach slavery from the pulpit as it was taught by the holy men of old, who spake as moved by the holy Spirit. . . . Both Christianity and Slavery are from heaven; both are blessings to humanity; both are to be perpetuated to the end of time. . . . Because Slavery is right; and because the condition of the slaves affords them all those privileges which would prove substantial blessings to them; and, too, because their Maker has decreed their bondage, and has

given them, as a race, capacities and aspirations suited alone to this condition of life. . . .[15]

So there was one set of Christians who derived their hope from a notion of a God who not only stood up for, but performed miracles for, the oppressed, and another set of Christians who were hearing at the same time about a God who sanctioned that very system of oppression. The races were groomed to be dialectically opposed to each other, and with each sermon—on both sides—a spirit, the spirit of slavery, was being deepened. Though these two groups of people were so intimately connected because of their relationships, spawned by slavery, they were at the same time so deeply divided that that the chasm would only grow wider, especially because God was being used as the savior for both groups, but for diametrically opposed purposes. How could one God be so differently conceived? Some African Americans would wonder, just as some Jews did during the Holocaust. Surely, many African Americans, perhaps more than dared admit it, wondered, like the poor soul remembered by Elie Wiesel: "I'm neither a sage nor a just man. I am not a saint. I'm a simple creature of flesh and bone. I suffer hell in my soul and my flesh. I also have eyes and I see what is being done here. Where is God's mercy: Where's God? How can I believe, how can anyone believe in this God of Mercy?"[16]

Wiesel says if this man "had kept his faith in God, if only he could have considered this suffering a divine test, he would not have been swept away by the selection. But as soon as he felt the first chinks in his faith, he lost all incentive to fight and opened the door to death."[17]

It was the job of African American preachers to make sure that there would be little loss of faith. Slavery was ongoing; first de facto, and then de jure, during the long years of the convict leasing system. Frederick Douglass wrongly thought that the human spirit yearned to rise above slavery; maybe it was that he wished that to be the case. But history would tell the story of a people who felt justified by their God to suppress and oppress a people who had a very different notion of God. It was the job of preachers like Jeremiah Wright to keep that vision of a just God before a people whose spirits were dried and warped by the persistent, dry winds of racism, which did nothing but suck life out of souls that yearned to live.

ꝏ

So many atrocities happened to African Americans in this, the land of their citizenship, that they suffered from what Joy Degruy Leary called "post traumatic slave syndrome." African Americans suffered from what Leary calls "vacant" esteem, which she describes as being worse than having low self-esteem. Vacant esteem, says Leary, is "the state of believing oneself to have little or no worth, exacerbated by the group and societal pronouncement of inferiority."[18] People with vacant esteem, she continues, "believe themselves to have little worth, little power, little self-efficacy, will often do whatever they can do to don the trappings of power, even if it means acting out the demeaning roles society considers appropriate for them."[19] That produces a very unbalanced relationship between any two entities that are closely or intimately related; it lends itself to one entity, the one with "normal" or high self-esteem, bullying the other entity suffering from vacant esteem.

It seems to be the same dynamic that exists between two people in an abusive relationship; the abused person tends to take whatever the abuser gives out, believing that somehow he or she deserves it. The abuse continues and gets worse as the abused person cowers and tries, unsuccessfully, to please the bully. Often an abused child or woman will exhaust him- or herself, changing behavior so that the other person will accept them, but it is a losing proposition, because a bully cannot or will not be pleased; it is in the abuser's best interest to continue the abusive behavior because it keeps him or her in power. The abuser knows how to do just enough to placate the bullied person, or reach that part of the bullied person that wants to please and fit into the bully's world, and manipulates the bullied person with acumen. The bullied person keeps going back, believing he or she can do something to make the bully stop the abuse, but it never happens.

This has been the relationship between whites and blacks in America. It has been as though the two races are and have been in a sorely misguided marriage. There hasn't been anything that African Americans have been able to do to stop the bullying—because the relationship was tainted and was wrong from the beginning. Blacks yearned to be accepted and tried to "act white" in order to fit into a group that was never going to bend. The dysfunction was there from the beginning. Whites could say they loved their "nigras" and perhaps they did, in a weird way, like an abusive spouse "loves" the one he or she abuses, even unto death, but whites, in general, could never accept blacks as equal, as human beings equal to whites, deserving of liberty and freedom. Black women nursed white babies, only to have those children grow up to debase and abuse them. Black soldiers volunteered to fight in the Civil War, earnestly wanting to show their white fellow soldiers that they were worthy of dignity and respect. But nothing blacks did worked. The dysfunctional, abusive relationship remained.

Gary D. Schmidt's novel, *Lizzie Bright and the Buckminster Boy,* shows this dysfunctional relationship between the two races brilliantly, though through the telling of a tragic story. The novel traces the story of Malaga Island, Maine, where black people lived for about a century. They lived on the island, though they went off the island daily to work in a town called Phippsburg, because the white people didn't want them to live in their town. So they would work in Phippsburg, many in the homes of white people, and then head back to their island where they lived.

According to Schmidt, "the island had galled the people of Phippsburg for a long time before the settlement was finally destroyed."[20] The island was destroyed by the government of Phippsburg (a decision supported by churches in the town and by the government of the state of Maine), because the state wanted to make the area more attractive for tourists. According to Schmidt's story, the governor of Maine, Frederick Plaistead, concerned because Phippsburg and another whites-only city, Harpswell, were arguing over who should "get rid of Malaga Island," went to the island himself in 1911 and said, "We ought not to have such things near our front door." And he suggested burning down the homes (which he called "shacks") that the people of Malaga Island called their homes.[21] The order and opinion of the governor received little push-back; indeed, it was widely supported—and this in the North, where racism was not supposed to be so evil or prevalent. The next year, the residents of Malaga Island were told by the sheriff that they would have to be off the island by July of that year. The state of Maine got all the people off the island and burned their homes. One family uprooted their home off the island before the fires were set and floated it downriver to another location.

Residents who refused to leave the island, says Schmidt, were taken to Pownal, Maine, to the Home for the Feeble Minded. All graves on the island were dug up and buried next to the asylum.[22]

Schmidt's novel about the relationship of a little black girl who lived on Malaga Island and a little white boy who lived in Phippsburg and who was the son of the pastor of the local Congregational Church at the time was based on a true story.

Who knows how many people, now in other parts of the country, had relatives who were affected by what happened in Maine, or by, perhaps, what happened in Rosewood, Florida, or in Tulsa, Oklahoma, both places where whole towns or communities of blacks were decimated? What is known is that many blacks had those experiences and would not talk about them. That they would not, or could not talk about their or their family's experiences because of racism, however, did not mean that they were not affected, and deeply so. Many African Americans, sitting in churches in the North, West, and Midwest, were tormented, wondering, like Wiesel, where God had been for them. Their faith had to be stoked, and it was the job of preachers to do the stoking.

African Americans were linked to whites, and whites to African Americans, and neither group was happy about it. James Baldwin, in a 1970 interview with David Frost, talked about the interconnectedness of blacks and whites: "No one really knows who's white or black, and when the chips are down, it doesn't really matter. Who knows how many black people got pale enough to pass across the color line? It's a buried part of American history. So, it makes the American estimate of twenty-two million black people extremely shaky. Nobody in this country really knows who his grandfather is. No one can examine his history, which is the trouble."[23]

Wright dealt with that reality—the fact that we are connected, yet separated. White people, he said, gave blacks new names, stripping them of their names and of their African identity, putting them down for being black, urging them to act "in a white way," yet letting them know that no matter how "white" they would act, they would never be white and, therefore, never be graced with full dignity. Some people in America, after slavery, rejected their American names given to them by white slave-owners. Members of the Nation of Islam recognized the damage done to the African psyche as they were stripped of their names and identity, and so asked people who joined the Nation to discard their American last names and use "X" instead. African Americans were connected to white people by white people yet rejected by white people. It caused a sort of cultural schizophrenia, and Wright's sermons dealt with this schizophrenia, the results of which many African Americans felt but could not describe or verbalize:

> No African would just willy-nilly change his or her name because each name has a history to it. The Africans in North American chattel slavery sang, "I told Jesus it would be all right if he changed my name," but they didn't change their names, because wrapped up in their names was their history. They sang, "written down my name," they sang "Hush, somebody's calling my name," they sang "I've got a new name over in Glory and it's mine, all mine." But no African ever willingly changed his or her own name, because that would be like telling their mamas, their daddies and their ancestors to go to hell, and that's most uncharacteristic of Africans.[24]

Blacks were "in" the white world, pulled in against their will, but not "of" the white world. Religious African Americans understood the biblical passage where Christians are advised to be "in" the world but not "of" the world: "Do not conform any longer to the pattern of this world, but be transformed by the renewing of your mind" (Rom. 12:2 NIV). The Bible also quotes Jesus as saying that those who believe in him are to be "in" but not "of" the world: "If the world hates you, keep in mind that it hated me before it hated you. If you belonged to the world, the world would love you as its own. Because you do not belong to the world, but I have chosen you out of the world" (John 15:18–19).

The sentiment to be "in" but not "of" the world is repeated in 1 John, one of the pastoral epistles: "Little children, you are from God, and have conquered them; for the one who is in you is greater than the one who is in the world. They are from the world; therefore what they say if from the world, and the world listens to them. We are from God. Whoever knows God listens to us, and whoever is not from God does not listen to us" (1 John 4:4–6a).

Finally, in that same pastoral epistle, we see that believers are not to love the world more than they love the God who made the world: "Do not love the world or the things in the world. The love of the Father is not in those who love the world; for all that is in the world—the desire of the flesh, the desire of the eyes, the pride in riches—comes not from the Father but from the world. And the world and its desire are passing away, but those who do the will of God live forever." (1 John2:15, 17).

This eschatological theology was helpful for preachers before and after the Civil War, and indeed seemed to feed many sermons of black preachers trying to give slaves and former slaves hope. One had to close ones eyes and push away one's feelings of anger due to the injustice of racism, and look for, pant for, and reach for heaven. That type of preaching drew the ire of people like Carter G. Woodson and Frederick Douglass, and many others, but it seems that what these preachers were trying to do was to reconcile this connectedness yet division between blacks and whites, and make God look good in spite of the mess that God apparently had created.

Later preachers, especially those who preached immediately before and during the civil rights movement, would have none of this eschatology. If God was good, then God meant for all people, regardless of color, to have good things, including dignity, while they were yet alive. They didn't have to wait until death and thereafter to be treated well. The message of the newer preachers jostled against the sentiments expressed in favorite hymns of the black church, including "We'll Understand It Better By and By":

We are often tossed and driv'n on the restless sea of time,
Sombre skies and howling tempest oft succeed a bright sunshine,
In that land of perfect day, when the mists have rolled away,
We will understand it better by and by
Trials dark on ev'ry hand, and we cannot understand
All the way that God will lead us to that blessed promised land;
But He'll guide us with His eye, and we'll follow till we die,
We will understand it better by and by
We are often destitute of the things that life demands,
Want of shelter and of good, thirsty hill and barren land;

But we're trusting in the Lord, and according to His word,
We will understand it better by and by.
Temptations, hidden snares, often take us unawares,
And our hearts are made to bleed, for each thoughtless word or deed;
And we wonder why the test, when we try to do out best,
But we'll understand it better, by and by

Chorus:

By and by, when the morning come,
All the saints of God are gathering home.
We will tell the story how we've overcome
We will understand it better by and by.[25]

"By and by" was not understood to be a chronological event, but rather a "kairos" event, something that would happen in God's time, which was apparently in the afterworld. Black people were to keep their faith and wait until death and afterward.

This understanding of faith was helpful in one sense; to a group of people who could not see how their situation was going to change while they were yet alive, the hope of something better "up there with God" was like an elixir to dry souls, but it was also damaging, because it kept African Americans in general from fighting for their rights and for their dignity. To do so would mean that they were "of" the world, which the Bible clearly frowned upon. They realized they were "in" the world, not of their own choosing, but because of God's will, and they believed that if they followed the Bible and didn't make waves, giving into their desire for freedom and dignity and all of the economic and political and social advantages that white people had, that they would surely get into heaven, where God would separate the good from the evil, the wheat from the chaff. So they internalized the need to be like white people but not "of" white people; they believed God would deliver them . . . after they died. Black people were in exile in America, not unlike the Israelites were in exile in Babylonia. Wright needed African Americans to understand what and how they were thinking, and why:

> The North American slave owners, those "Babylonians," prototypes of the empire and the imperialistic mind-set that disregards

> anything everybody else has ever done, did away with the natives' names in an attempt to take away their history. . . . What happened to them? . . . As Dr. Ofori Atta Thomas of the Interdenominational Theological Center puts it, "They forgot their story." They lost their history, so they died. Our children don't know our story. Any people who lose their story are a dead people. And the established authority, the empire, knows that, so it makes every deliberate attempt to take away the exiles' history. The empire tells them they have no history prior to the Babylonians introducing them to civilization; the empire tells them outright lies and blatant distortions so that they will disown any linkage that they once had with Africa, and they become more Babylonian than the Babylonians.'[26]

Wright's words spoke life into a people who really had distanced themselves from themselves and moved closer to the so-called "Babylonians," the white culture that seemingly despised them. Hearing the breakdown of the history, the saving history, of the Israelites, was like hearing their own stories in a new way, or maybe for the first time. Their disconnection with the culture in which they were "in" but not allowed, really, to be "of" was finally being verbalized. They could now whisper what they had felt for so long and not be deemed crazy. The culture almost demanded that nobody speak of racism or even mention it. It was as though by not mentioning it, it would go away.

Whites and blacks seemed to adhere to that point of view. Michele Norris, an NPR commentator, wrote in her book *The Grace of Silence: A Memoir* that there were events that had happened in her parents' lives, solely because they were black, that the family simply never talked about. Black people learned how to act in a white world; Norris writes that "black children were advised to lower their eyes and their voices when speaking to white adults, and white children learned that certain courtesies were never offered to a Negro."[27] There were secrets based on experiences that came from being black that many families just did not talk about. Norris recounts a painful story given by one of her relatives, who had been one to "keep quiet," about her experiences in America:

> "What do you remember about life in Birmingham?" There was a long pause, then sniffles. She said she needed a moment; I heard her set the phone down. Soon she returned to the line and asked me if I had time to hear her out. "Let me tell you one of my strongest memories," she said. "I remember your grandparents, walking home, all in white. They were coming home from church. Probably a revival, because they had white on head to toe. And I remember some kids. Some white kids came zoomin' down the street, hanging out of car windows, and they pelted them with rotten tomatoes. They threw tomatoes at churchgoing folks and they laughed and they called them names I am not going to say out loud. Their clothes were ruined and they were so upset. Those kids in that car were just evil. . . . I have never forgotten that. People do what they can get away with, and in Birmingham, they could get away with anything."[28]

Norris's relatives, including her own father, kept to themselves many of the experiences they had "growing up black." In her book, she talks about the incident her father never talked about, never brought up, really, about being shot by a white police officer in Birmingham when that officer and others accosted him and a group of friends—ostensibly for no reason.

> During the second week of February the bad weather ceased and, as Morris Beaton tells it, Belvin, Woody, and Morris' brother John headed downtown to an event at a public park near the Smith and Gaston Funeral Home, before deciding to go to the Pythian Temple. . . . "It was a get-together that they was having upstairs and they were standing in the lobby there trying to wait for the elevator to come down before the police walked up," Morris explained.
>
> "And when the police come up, they were behind them, but when the elevator door opened, a policeman stuck his stick out there where he wouldn't let them get on the elevator, and this is where your father knocked the stick down and stepped on the elevator, and this is where everything got started, the beating and the cursing and all that stuff. They got a good whupping that night."[29]

In the confusion, Norris' father was shot by one of the officers—grazed, actually, but it was critical moment in his young life. Surely it must have stoked anger; he was, after all, a war veteran. He had worn the uniform and gone into battle for his country, and still he got no respect. It had to have wounded him to his core, yet he never talked about it, never shared it with his daughter, or, for that matter, with his wife. Michelle asked the storyteller, Morris, who had been there the night her father had been shot, why he thought her father never talked about it, and Morris answered, "I have no idea, honey. I guess some things like that, I mean . . . people misuse you, abuse you . . . I mean, it's better forgotten than to keep talking about it."[30] There were other experiences America's African American soldiers had; Norris says she listened to Attorney General Eric Holder tell the story of how his father, an immigrant from Barbados, "had to stand for hours on end during the train ride, while German prisoners of war, all white men, sat comfortably in cushioned seats."[31]

It just wasn't pretty, being black in America. Too many blacks wanted to be white—to talk white, to look white, to have anything that was white, because white was all that was honored and respected. Blacks did as much as they could to deny who they were . . . from using bleaching cream to lighten their skin to putting harmful chemicals on their hair to make it straight, like white hair, as opposed to kinky. Anything that was white was more preferred than anything that was black or African. James Baldwin said, "The Western world, which has always stood on very shaky foundations, is coalescing according to principle under which it was organized, and that principle is white supremacy."[32] It was that reality to which the late Rev. Fred Shuttlesworth was referring in President Obama's inauguration in 2009; blacks and whites had grown up thinking, had been taught to think, that "if it's white it's right." The Babylonians, aka white Americans, were dictating to the new Israelites, African Americans, and setting standards for these oppressed to meet yet simultaneously making it nearly impossible for them to meet them.

And so, when Jeremiah Wright preached, the oppressed heard him and were lifted. He urged African Americans to see the weird relationship between whites and blacks and not to ignore it, but to recognize it for what it was and realize that they had the power to disconnect and be people of African descent and not be ashamed. He taught that blacks were skilled at living in this, a bifurcated society. He lifted up the strengths of black people as legitimate people of God, given much by God and therefore required, racism notwithstanding, to give a lot back, and the first thing they had to "give back" was the love of and for themselves that they had given up so long ago. They belonged to God, just like everyone else God had created. It was a reason to celebrate, not to mourn.

12

PREACHING AND REACHING FOR LIBERATION

The Spirit of the LORD God is on me, because the LORD has anointed me, he has sent me to bring good news to the oppressed, to bind up the brokenhearted, to proclaim liberty to the captives, and release to the prisoners; to proclaim the year of the LORD's favor, and the day of vengeance of our God; to comfort all who mourn; to provide for those who grieve in Zion—to give them a garland instead of ashes, the oil of gladness instead of mourning, the mantle of praise instead of a faint spirit. They will be called oaks of righteousness, the planting of the LORD, to display his splendor.

—ISAIAH 61:1–3

It was Jeremiah Wright's call, or a part of his call, to preach a message that would free his people from the reality of racism and the spirit of racism. Both pervaded their lives; both were relentless in their attacks on the sense of personal dignity and worth of African American people, and both were stubbornly held in place by American culture. In spite of the claim of "American exceptionalism," African Americans found the reach of exceptionalism to fall short of many of America's own citizens, a group to which they rightly belonged. The realization of being fringe members, so to speak, forced to the sidelines on nearly every American court of privilege, produced a rage that had to be contained in order to survive, but which existed anyway. Dr. Robert Franklin, former president of predominantly black Morehouse College, spoke of the rage of not only African Americans, but of Wright in particular:

"Dr. Wright lives with a constant rage. Rage is a better term than anger . . . its intent is always redemptive. [Wright] is trying to save lives, not destroy them. He is using this language to try to stop the baby from going over the cliff. It was the same rage we heard from Dr. King."[1]

This "redemptive rage" was translated and described, in the 2008 presidential election, as "black anger" by the media. Wright's criticisms of American culture as it pertained to protecting the rights of the oppressed were interpreted almost as political treason, showing a lack of respect and patriotism for this "land of the free and home of the brave," but Franklin said the interpretation came from a "disbelief" by many in white America that "there was still this measure of black anger and black rage."

"The majority of Americans," said Franklin, "thought there had been so much progress in terms of racism. When you look through the window, look into human nature, it was that disbelief that there was still this measure of anger alongside the march toward freedom. There was an impatience with him for exposing it. Wright was opening the bag and exposing the hypocrisy and he wouldn't shut up. They worked to annihilate him. He violated the civil contract that if you are doing well (in America), you will keep your mouth shut."[2]

Wright was speaking the language and the emotions of the oppressed, the "brokenhearted," proclaiming that there would be, that there must be, according to the prophet Isaiah, "freedom for the captives." He was preaching a message of liberation, not just for African Americans, but for people who were oppressed anywhere and by anyone. In his speech given at the National Press Club in April of 2008, Wright spoke of the importance and historical commitment of the black church to the cause of liberation, saying:

> It is our hope that this must might mean that the reality of the African American church will no longer be invisible. Maybe now, as an honest dialogue about race in this country begins, a dialogue called for by Senator Obama and a dialogue to begin in the United Church of Christ among 5,700 congregations in just a few weeks, maybe now, as that dialogue begins, the religious tradition that has kept hope alive for people struggling to survive in countless hopeless situations, maybe that religious tradition will be understood, celebrated, and even embraced by a nation that seems not to have noticed that 11 o'clock on Sunday morning has been called the most segregated hour in America. . . .[3]

Liberation was something called for by God; that was plain to see in Isaiah 61 and in other parts of the Bible. This God was not a God who ordained or even approved of the oppression and suppression of one race over another. It was present, and had always been present, not just in America, but in all civilizations, but just because it had always been a part of the human experience did not make it right. God demanded that all God's people be free! The idea, he posited in the National Press Club speech, was first heard in the 1960s, not in America, but in Latin America:

> In the 1960s, the term "liberation theology" began to gain currency with the writings of preachers, pastors, priests, and professors from Latin America. Their theology was done from the underside. Their viewpoint was not from the top down or from a set of teachings which undergirded imperialism. Their viewpoints, rather, were from the bottom up, the thoughts and understandings of God, the faith, religion, and the Bible from those whose lives were ground under, mangled, and destroyed by the ruling classes or the oppressors. Liberation theology started in and started from a different place. It started from the vantage point of the oppressed.[4]

Wright said the theology of the black church was liberation theology, to be sure, but that it could be "traced back to the prophets in the Hebrew Bible and to its last prophet, in my tradition, the one we call Jesus of Nazareth." He continued:

> The prophetic tradition of the black church has its roots in Isaiah, the 61st chapter, where God says the prophet is to preach the gospel to the poor and to set at liberty those who are held captive. Liberating the captives *also liberates those who are holding them captive* (italics mine). It frees the captives and it frees the captors. It frees the oppressed and it frees the oppressors. The prophetic theology of the black church, during the days of chattel slavery, was a theology of liberation. It was preached to set free those who were held in bondage spiritually, psychologically, and sometimes, physically. And it was practiced to set the slaveholders free from the notion that they could define other human beings or confine a soul set free by the power of the gospel.[5]

Even though a theology of liberation had largely (not totally) been a staple of black preaching, African Americans still found themselves oppressed, which caused the ever-present rage. According to Franklin: "Blacks still live with a constant, seething rage. It lives under the surface and is easily exposed and it is raw. We saw it as concerns Trayvon Martin. It is the sleeping giant of the black community. The effort to drive a cultural, generational wedge between those in the black community and those who were doing well failed. Wright was capable of bridging the gap between the two sides of black culture. Malcolm was the last person to do it with authority. Wright is able to effect class reconciliation in the black community."[6]

Wright's preaching helped bridge the breach between classes in the black community, and was able to also reach across gender lines and generational lines. His messages resonated with a large group of people because his messages were incredibly able to voice the concerns of a wide range of people. Wright's messages also appealed to white people who heard the messages in their entirety. They heard the messages in their contexts. They were led to understand that the gospel, the "good news" was good for everyone, not just white Protestant males. Wright said in his National Press Club presentation, "When you read the entire passage from Isaiah 61 or Luke 4 and do not try to understand the passage or the content in the context of a sound bite, what you see is God's desire for a radical change in a social order that has gone sour."[7]

The use of the sound bites in the 2008 election not only did damage to Wright, but damage to people who genuinely needed to hear a message of liberation and inclusion in this country, which has been damaged, in turn, by its refusal to let go of its mythical belief in American exceptionalism, its refusal to see what America is and has been for countless individuals. It was Ronald Reagan who used the phrase "the city on the hill" to describe America, a phrase he borrowed from John Winthrop's sermon, "A Model of Christian Charity," preached to Puritans either as they crossed the Atlantic from England to America, or once they landed.

According to Stephen Prothero, in his book *The American Bible*, Winthrop wanted to purify religion from every vestige of Roman Catholicism and wanted this new land to be a "biblical commonwealth." He didn't want this new community to have practices based on tradition, says Prothero, but rather on "biblical principles." The settlers in the New World, were to recognize the total sovereignty of God and the depravity of human beings.[8] America was to be, according to Peter Gomes, on reading and studying Winthrop's work, "an exemplary nation called to virtue and mutual support."[9]

But Winthrop's ideas and his "ideal America" may very well have laid the basis for the problems that America would encounter as she grew. Inherent in Winthrop's message was a theology of confinement, or a theology that sanctioned the "haves" and "have nots." He exhorted Americans to "work to create a model Christian commonwealth, "knit together" not by freedom or equality, but by the "bond of love."[10] The "beloved community," was to be hierarchical! Edmund Burke, says Prothero, wrote that "God in His wisdom has ordained for some to be rich and some poor," some "high and eminent in power and dignity" and some "mean and in submission."[11] Winthrop (and apparently Reagan) took Burke at his word and wrote that it was biblical for there to be two unequal classes! Social inequalities, Prothero writes of Winthrop's beliefs, "provide opportunities for all to nurture Christian virtues."[12]

Prothero says that the United States has "strayed far and wide from Winthrop's model of a community made harmonious by inequality," but that may not be the case. It may be, and indeed it probably feels like, the norm for many people of color. While Prothero and others say that the American value of "rugged individualism" has moved this nation far from Winthrop's ideal, it may be that Winthrop's idea of a nation made "beloved" by the very fact of its different classes has not slipped into nothingness. The chasm between rich and poor in the United States has widened, not shrunk, accounting for the protests of the 99 percent against the 1 percent who are said to hold at least 35 percent of the wealth in the nation, causing some to call America not a democracy, but an oligarchy or a plutocracy.

In an article written for *The Huffington Post* on September 12, 2012, Bonnie Kavoussi reported that "households in the wealthiest one percent were 288 times richer than the median American household in 2010."[13] Winthrop's "city upon a hill" was to be a model city, one that all nations would look to and look at and attempt to emulate, but the reality, as opposed to the ideal, makes one wonder how this idea of "American exceptionalism" has withstood the test of time. Prothero asks, "Of what is America a model: Freedom? Equality? Capitalism? Christianity?"[14] Oppressed people would give a different answer to the question, but to be sure, there is a divide between Winthrop's vision and ideal, and America's reality. It is to that chasm that Wright directed his attention. Too many people lived within that chasm. Speaking about it, bringing it up, exposing it, has wrought trouble for anyone who dared do it—from Jesus to Martin Luther King to William Sloan Coffin and others . . . but operating under the directive of Isaiah 61, Wright could do little else.

Wright was criticized and in fact, pummeled, by people who resented his criticism of the chasm he had not only seen but had lived and experienced. Winthrop believed and preached that Americans were chosen people, "God's new Israel," entrusted by providence with a "unique mission to the world."[15] If, he preached, the new people in the new world would love God and follow God's commandments, this new world would be blessed—complete in its policy of inequality, the biblical directive of the need for the "haves" and the "have-nots." Prothero calls this concept of a "conditional covenant," a variation, one might say, to the conditional covenant found repeatedly in the Bible, "I will be your God if you will be my people." Winthrop believed he had the understanding of how a people would and could be "God's," a concept that immediately sanctioned inequality, which led to racism and perhaps even to sexism.

Now, however, according to Prothero, the conditional covenant has been replaced by an "unconditional covenant," in which God offered blessing to whatever America did, at home or abroad. That idea has led to Americans feeling all right in oppressing people on its land and in other lands; the policy of manifest destiny was birthed from this idea that America was blessed to do whatever it wanted, to whomever.

Wright protested, as have others over time. Martin Luther King said that his "dream" had become a nightmare, as he looked at what America was doing not only on its own shores, but also in Vietnam. In his sermon "Beyond Vietnam: A Time to Break Silence," he said, "A time comes when silence is betrayal. . . . Some of us who have already begun to break the silence of the night have found that the calling to speak is often a vocation of agony, but we must speak."[16] As America has grown, there have been times when some questioned publicly if what the country was doing or supporting was in line with God's will. That query most certainly came, at least partly, from an awareness of the conditional covenant found in the Bible and verbalized by Winthrop. Jefferson wondered what God would think about America supporting and sanctioning slavery; Lincoln wondered "whether slavery had set God's teeth on edge" in his Second Inaugural Address. Prothero said that Lincoln "did not call God to his side."[17] Theologians and preachers wrestled with the thought of what God thought about what America was doing, but they wrestled, oftentimes, from different places in the same theological context.

Perhaps stemming from Winthrop's planting of the seed that there were to be at least two different classes of people, two different theologies and ideas about where God stood on social issues emerged. Writes Prothero:

> Even in the twenty-first century, some have continued to warn that God was punishing, (or would punish) America for its collective sins. On the right, Jerry Falwell and Pat Robertson said

that 9/11 was a just punishment delivered by a righteous God on a gay and lesbian nation. On the left, Reverend Jeremiah Wright said that God was damning America, and for good reason. The fact that such warnings have been almost universally condemned indicates how firmly the conviction that the nation deserves God's blessing, come what may, has taken hold.[18]

There was a need for all African Americans to feel liberated from the stronghold of racism and all that it wrought in America, but it was especially important and vital for African American *men* to be liberated. If anyone had felt the stinging whips of American racism, black men had, from slavery to the present day. It was black men who had been primarily and permanently criminalized by the Convict Leasing System; it was black men who eagerly joined armed forces in American wars, hoping to prove their worth as human beings and their value as Americans, only to come back home and be treated again as worthless property. It was black men who wanted, as much as does any man of any color, to prove their worth by the work they did, who were often not hired for jobs due only to the color of their skin in a country that allowed blatant discrimination. It was black men who yearned to provide for their families, and who had to do so working two, three, four jobs to the one job of a white man.

To put it bluntly, it was and is hard to be a black man in America. James Baldwin said that black men were "demoralized too soon," only because of their color, and once that demoralization set in, it was hard for a black man, as male as any white man, to "make it" in a country that continued the demoralization process throughout his life. Black men had to fight through indignities, which they, frankly, sometimes dared to challenge. Such challenges could and did lead to death or some other act that essentially paralyzed them in a land that promised freedom to everyone. It made black men angry and resentful—rightfully so—but the country would not acknowledge the validity of their anger. It seemed that many actions taken on the part of individuals sought to both stoke the anger they knew was there while simultaneously criticizing it for being there.

Black men who jumped into the fray, publicly, fighting racism with everything they had, paid a price. Robert Franklin said that blacks who jumped out front paid a price, and commenting on Jeremiah Wright, said that he supposed Wright was lonely: "The cost of his prophetic leadership was that he stood alone for a while . . . he was unfairly blamed for things that were not his. Rush Limbaugh, for example, said that Wright hates white people. That was a foil to get to President Obama. Dr. Wright never conveyed that sentiment."[19]

But what Wright did, lonely or not, was tap into this need for black men to feel connected to a country that had in effect severed them while yet holding onto them, primarily for economic gain. Franklin noted Wright's particular gift for relating to black men in America:

"The way in which he has experienced the world of boys and men of color is significant. He could empathize. He deserves a lot of credit for the current focus on the state of black men and boys. He always did it . . . and held black men accountable. He called black men to be accountable husbands and fathers. He even was an early voice pushing against the patriarchy that he himself was a product of."[20]

His language to the men was not incendiary. It was an acknowledgement of the reality they faced and knew—even if they never talked about it—and it was intergenerational. He could and did talk to and relate to men of all ages, from the very young, who needed inspiration and direction in order to become accountable, to the older men who had lived in the clutches of racism and may have felt that they just could not make their way through the barriers racism constructed. Franklin said that Wright had a unique gift:

> I think that perhaps more than any other preacher I know living today, Dr. Wright has combined the intellectual fervor and the spirit of Malcolm (X) and Martin in very creative ways. He is a key liberation theologian with a global perspective and he understands the church and himself as being interrelated. . . .
>
> He does this with a strong sense of an African American aesthetic. He constantly links black people to their African roots and he frames the case using language that incorporates the urban

> street rap with high poetry, urban lyricism, and the poetry of hip hop artists. All of that is going on in the mind of Jeremiah.[21]

Wright did in his sermons what African American authors did in literature—but the fact that he did it in sermons, where he had a captive audience and where he did what he needed to do to relate to everyone listening—made his genre perhaps more effective in liberating black men than did literature. In fact, it might be said that his sermons, which sewed together the raw experiences of black men along with history and politics, and all under the umbrella of the inclusive love of Jesus the Christ, were more effective in the spiritual, social, and emotional liberation of the men who listened to him. They were made to understand that the anger they felt was justified, the slights they felt were real, and that they had a place in this world. They carried a burden and they knew it, but it seemed that nobody else really knew, or gave credence to it. They knew that their parents struggled to make it in a place where "making it" was supposed to be a lot easier. They knew that they were looked down upon. They knew that, as Baldwin said, "you make do with nothing and you get, if you survive, a kind of authority from that."[22] They might have gotten authority from that, but they didn't get validation as human beings. Wright's sermons offered that validation, and in that came liberation not only from feeling worthless, but also from the anger that accompanied that feeling.

Wright knew that African Americans needed to hear where God was in this world of oppression. Author Richard Wright wrote, in describing how he created the character Bigger Thomas in his novel *Native Son*, that Bigger was a character built out of different necessary personality components that African Americans, notably African American men, must have in America in order to survive:

> Then there was Bigger No. 4. . . . His rebellious spirit made him violate all the taboos and consequently he always oscillated between moods of intense elation and depression. He was never happier than when he had outwitted some foolish custom, and he was never more melancholy than when brooding over the *impossibility of his ever being free* (italics mine). He had no job, for he

> regarded digging ditches for fifty cents a day as slavery. "I can't live on that," he would say. Oftentimes, I'd find him reading a book; he would stop and in a joking, wistful, and cynical matter ape the antics of the white folks. Generally, he'd end his mimicry in a depressed state and say: "The white folks won't let us do nothing." Bigger No. 4 was sent to the asylum for the insane.[23]

Jeremiah Wright knew about the "oscillation" of mood that African Americans, notably men, felt. He felt that the black church had always been about the liberation of the souls and spirits of African Americans; in other words, liberation was not about the physical condition of slavery, but rather about the mental and emotional slavery that African Americans lived with. In his presentation to the National Press Club in 2008, he described what the "prophetic theology" of the black church was: "not only a theology of liberation; it is also a theology of transformation, which is also rooted in Isaiah 61."[24]

African Americans had had to learn a unique way of surviving in a country that had brought them here but did not want them here. He had to tell them that God saw and God cared . . . and that God's purposes were not as the world, or the happenings of the world, would have them believe. At the Press Club on that April day in 2008, Wright offered what might be felt as a balm by those who wondered about the power, presence, and purpose of this God who allowed such wretched oppression: "God's desire is for positive, meaningful, and permanent change. God does not want one people seeing themselves as superior to other people. God does not want the powerless masses, the poor, the widows, the marginalized, and those underserved by the powerful few to stay locked into sick systems which treat some in the society as being more equal than others in that same society."[25]

That being the case, Wright said, the prophetic theology of the black church "is a theology of liberation, it is a theology of transformation, and it is ultimately a theology of reconciliation."[26]

There was a problem, though, in getting to the God behind this three-pronged theology. Because of the racism, not only in the United States but in the world, there were at least two conceptions and perceptions of who God was. "The Christianity of the slaveholder is not the

Christianity of the slave," he said at the Press Club.[27] Reconciliation becomes difficult because of the different perceptions of God by different racial and even gender groups:

> Reconciliation, the years have taught me, is where the hardest work is found for those of us in the Christian faith, however, because it means some critical thinking and some reexamination of faulty assumptions when using the paradigm of Dr. William Augustus Jones.
>
> Dr. Jones, in his book *God in the Ghetto*, argues quite accurately that one's theology, how I see God, determines one's anthropology, how I see humans, and one's anthropology then determines one's sociology, how I order my society. . . .
>
> The implications from the outside are obvious. If I see God as a male, if I see God as a white male, if I see God as superior, as God over us and not Immanuel (sic), which means "God with us," if I see God as mean, vengeful, authoritarian, sexist, or misogynist, then I see humans through that lens.
>
> My theological lens shapes my anthropological lens, As a result, white males are superior; all others are inferior. How we are seeing God, our theology, is not the same. And what we both mean when we say, "I am a Christian," is not the same.[28]

Jeremiah Wright was saying from the pulpit what writers alluded to in their novels and essays. Richard Wright, in explaining or breaking down the character of Bigger Thomas, basically said the same thing as did Jeremiah Wright. The anthropology and sociology of the whites in Bigger's world were ever upon him, ever challenging him, and causing his "oscillation" between two worlds, the one which eluded him yet kept him captive for its own use, and the other in which he was trapped, never, seemingly, to get out, because of his color:

> Then there was Bigger No. 5, who always rode the Jim Crow streetcars without paying and sat wherever he pleased. I remember one morning his getting into a streetcar (all streetcars in Dixie are divided into two sections: one section is for whites and is la-

> beled—FOR WHITES; the other section is for Negroes and is labeled—FOR COLORED) and sitting in the white section. The conductor went to him and said, "Come on, nigger. Move over where you belong. Can't you read?" Bigger answered, "Naw, I can't read." The conductor flared up: "Get out of that seat!" Bigger took out his knife, opened it, held it nonchalantly in his hand and replied, "Make me." The conductor turned red, clenched his fists, and walked away, stammering: "The goddam scum of the earth! . . ."
>
> The Bigger Thomases of the world were the only Negroes I know of who consistently violated the Jim Crow laws of the South and got away with it, at least for a brief spell. Eventually, the whites who restricted their lives made them pay a terrible price. They were shot, hanged, maimed, lynched, and generally hounded until they were either dead or their spirits broken.[29]

Wright then noted the painful reality that African Americans knew too well, and that whites took for granted: "In Dixie, there are two worlds, the white world and the black world, and they are physically separated. There are white schools and black schools, white churches and black churches, white businesses and black businesses, white graveyards and black graveyards, and, for all I know, a white God and a black God."[30]

This very real and felt perception by blacks (and by whites, one would imagine, although it seems highly unlikely that they would admit it) was an issue the black church and, specifically, the black prophetic preacher had to address. The "two worlds within one" accounted for the frustration and "seething anger" felt by so many African Americans. The role of the black prophetic preacher, said Rev. Jeremiah Wright, was to "root out any teaching of superiority, inferiority, hatred, or prejudice."[31]

So, he preached "liberation to the captives." A long-time member of Wright's church, Kevin Tyson, recalls Wright saying that "God will take you as far as you want to go if you truly want to be free." Jeremiah Wright knew the experience of the men in his pews, black men always trying to "prove" themselves to a society that rejected their efforts for the most part. He knew how they "oscillated." He knew their frustration and the seething anger that too often could and did lead them to stop trying to push against the stone in front of them. And yet, he said they could and must keep pushing. Tyson said:

> He never separated faith from *our* experience. So, whenever we talked, he would remind me of why God put me here, and that it was not something that could be separated from my day-to-day life. "Your faith is not in a vacuum; neither is your legacy," he would tell me. "'If it had not been for the Lord on your side' is just as applicable today as it has been in history," he'd say. That helped me to grow as a husband, father, and common brother on the street. It made me understand that any letters that I had made me no different from any other. Still God's child, still flawed and broken, still looking for help.[32]

Wright, said Tyson, wouldn't let them (the men) off the hook. He told them what they needed to do in order to be free. He also gave them unconditional love, something, said Tyson, that was rare for black men. In many churches, there was love given, but it had always been conditional. Wright, he said, "[h]as been the radical, who would really step out of the pulpit if he had to do something that would help someone else. He has made it very clear in the way he has approached subjects that black men wrestle with. I know dozens (and those are only the ones I know) who have come to him, pleaded with him, and cried with him, wanting help."[33]

Unconditional love was what men might need in general, said Tyson, but African Americans, in particular. In spite of "oscillating" between two worlds, white and black, and between hope and depression, it was ultimately hope that Wright sought to make them claim as the dominant emotion in their lives. In order to have hope trump the depression, they would have to leave room for the anger to dissipate, go away, and not constantly throb within their spirits. Wright allowed the anger, he acknowledged the anger, but he preached hope. It was not hatred, said Tyson:

> I think for the most part, there is anger and not hatred. We are angry for a few things. We are angry at the way we have been

> treated in this country. We are angry about the failure of the post–civil rights era of how everything went to pot (sic); we're starting all over again, it feels like, and we are angry at the way society has molded us to be our own worst enemies. I don't think we have hate enough to give up. I see hate in a sense that there can be no reconciliation, whether it's with white folks, ourselves, women . . . but there is hope in anger, if it is channeled correctly, channeling the anger into action. I am angry at our president for a number of reasons, but I don't hate him. Anger is more appropriate because it's in the context of the condition we're in. Anger isn't personal; hatred is personal.[34]

The media, said Tyson, has consistently warped the image of African Americans, molding images and making statements about the words and lives of black people that are not accurate or close to being accurate. The media characterized Jeremiah Wright as spewing hatred, and yet, said Tyson, that was far from the truth. There was nothing personal in what Wright said, not even in those now-notorious sound bites; there was anger at the government and what it has done to people over the years. There was no attack on any person; it was not personal. Asked about the difference between what Wright had said and what other preachers have said, Tyson mentioned Pat Robertson and said,

> The difference between a Jeremiah Wright and a Pat Robertson is that he (Robertson) can't put what he says in the context of his own personal experience. What is the origin of Robertson's condemning government? I go back to his idea of tradition. For us, tradition, from the dominant culture lens, is slavery and oppression. When I think about it, that scene in *In the Heat of the Night* when the plantation owner said, "There was a time when I could have had you shot," is the perspective of people in the dominant culture. That's what Pat Robertson would say: "There was a time when this country was great. Now this country has changed as a result of protest and anger." So, I look at it and ask, "What is your personal experience that leads you to your conclusions?"[35]

Robertson and others who have spoken out on social issues like abortion or homosexuality are speaking their personal prejudices, their ideology, which they pass off as theological in content and origin. It is the lack of personal experience in and about which they speak that helps to characterize their words as hatred, as opposed to what Wright says, speaking in a cultural, historical, and biblical context to a people who have been wrongly treated; this separates Wright's speech from Robertson's and others.

Wright's message, though, apparently could not be heard as the cry for liberation for the oppressed because, as he said in his presentation to the National Press Club, whites and blacks hear differently and have different definitions of who God is. For Wright, the goal to and for his audience was always to preach liberation, which would lead to transformation (getting rid of anger that was counter-productive but encouraging anger that was transformative) and, ultimately, reconciliation—with themselves, with God . . . and with those in society who had kept them down. He had to touch the nuclei of the damaged spiritual cells of black people who carried the message within them that they were different and therefore unworthy of the American dream and all things good while they were yet on this earth.

Wright strove to make them understand intellectually, spiritually, and emotionally the forces at work in their world, forces that made them hold in their spirits a hunch that they could never be free of the forces of racism. They longed for a better life in the here and now, not after they died, and Wright had to make them know it was not only possible, but biblical, to think that way. Black people had a desire to taste the dignity that had for too long eluded them. Wrote Richard Wright:

> I've even heard Negroes say that maybe Hitler and Mussolini are all right; that maybe Stalin is all right. They did not say this out of any intellectual comprehension of the forces at work in the world, but because they felt that these men "did things," a phrase which is charged with more meaning than the mere words imply. There was in the back of their minds, when they said this, a wild and intense longing (wild and intense because it was suppressed!) to belong, to be identified, to feel that they were alive as other people were, to be caught up forgetfully and exultingly

in the swing of events, to feel the clean, deep organic satisfaction of doing a job in common with others.[36]

Richard Wright created in his character Bigger Thomas the feeling that Jeremiah Wright addressed in his sermons—the "deep hunger" for dignity. Richard Wright wrote about, and Jeremiah Wright preached about, the feeling that Richard Wright said made one "feel more than ever estranged from the civilization in which I lived, and more than ever resolved toward the task of creating with words a scheme of images and symbols whose direction could enlist the sympathies, loyalties, and yearnings of the millions of Bigger Thomases in every land and race. . . ."[37]

Both Wright the author and Wright the preacher reached for black people who were "products of a dislocated society." Bigger Thomas, and by extension, the black man, was "dispossessed and disinherited man; he is all of this and he lives amid the greatest possible plenty on earth and he is looking and feeling for a way out."[38] Jeremiah Wright didn't want the man, or the men, to feel for a way out; he worked to make them understand that they needed to "stay in" and be accountable to God and not to racism, to let God and not racism define them and encourage and empower them. To be liberated, he preached, meant that they would not only understand that point, but in fact, do it.

Jeremiah Wright knew, however, that his job of encouraging and empowering black people but most especially black men was never going to be easy. The system had been intentional from its beginning, to keep black men "in their place." That was part of the reason, some conclude, that the Convict Leasing system was so successful and lasted for so long. Black men had forgotten, if they ever knew, that they had not always been oppressed. They did not know, many of them, their own rich legacy. That's why Wright's words in "What Makes You So Strong?" hit places in all who heard that had perhaps been covered with the pain of oppression and of feeling inferior. Wright was bound and determined to let his listeners know that God, and not racism and its attendant oppression, were in control, and had always been.

Wright had to go "there," to the place within black people who had perhaps ingested and digested the language and perceptions of racial oppression. Though slavery had been dealt with by the Emancipation Proclamation and the Thirteenth Amendment to the Constitution, it had never really gone away and black people knew it; they had lived it. Almost everyone over the age of thirty-five in Wright's congregation had tasted the vestiges of a lingering racism and the ever-present spirit of racism. There were sons and daughters in his congregation whose parents had tasted that racism even more. There were people in his congregation who had heard stories of how racism had affected one beloved relative of theirs, if only one. Almost all of them had tasted and experienced racism on their jobs, subjected to treatment that was purposely, if surreptitiously, on purpose. Too many of them had had to swallow pride and keep their mouths shut, just so they could keep their jobs.

So this sermon lifting up their strength was water to parched souls.

These were people who had worked hard for "the American dream." Some had attained more of it than had others, but none of them had attained any of it without the struggle caused by racism. Wright knew that when one is in a cesspool of suffering he or she feels alone; it was his job to reveal the commonality of their experiences—even in the twentieth and twenty-first centuries.

Some of them probably had relatives who were still tasting the sting of racism. Almost everyone who came from the South (many of Chicago's African American residents migrated to the Windy City from the Deep South during the Great Migration) knew of or had heard of the infamous chain gangs, part of what was used during the years of the Convict Leasing program. That had been injustice sanctioned by "the law," and everyone knew it. The thought was that chain gangs were a thing of the past . . . but they were not and are not. A 1995 *New York Times* article described the resurgence of chain gangs in the South, a system, wrote author Rick Bragg, that made the inmates feel humiliated. "You are telling him that he is an animal," Bragg wrote, quoting Alvin Bronstein, who at that time was the director of the National Prison Project of the American Civil Liberties Union. "People lose touch with humanity when you put them in chains."[39]

The article described how chain gangs would also be returning to Mississippi, with convicts wearing striped uniforms "to humiliate them." They would wear leg irons. They would work for twelve hours a day, chained together like animals. They would live in cells after their day's work, with "no radio, no TV, no visitation." Dignity denied, yet again. Those types of things, the going backward in spite of strides forward, had always weighed on and challenged the faith and hope of African Americans. Bronstein said in the article, "You tell a person he's an animal, you get a self-fulfilling prophecy."[40] Wright knew that. He had to address it and fight it until his listeners understood that they had the power to fight it themselves.

He recounted their experiences, culturally and historically:

> What makes you so strong, black people? No other race was brought to this country in chains. No other race had laws passed making it a crime to teach them to read. No other race had skin color as the determining factor of their servitude and their employability. No other race was hounded and haunted when they wanted to be free. No other race was physically mutilated to identify them as property, not people. No other race was lied to and lied on like the African race. No other race had its names taken away in addition to its language and music. No other race was denied more and deprived of more, treated as badly and less than human. No other race was treated like the Africans were treated, and yet no other race has done so much after starting out with so little, defying all of the odds the breaking all of the records. What makes you so strong, black people? How were you able to do that? Jimmy the Greek wants to know. Ted Koppel wants to know. Geraldo wants to know. I have a feeling that Oprah Winfrey already knows. What makes you so strong, black people?[41]

It was God, he said, who accounted for the strength of African Americans. They were never to forget that. This might not be the same God that white people were taught, but that could not be Wright's concern. This God was a God who understood and appreciated black people. God, he said in that sermon, had a work to do in and through African

Americans. "God has a work of redemption and healing to do through African Americans," he said in that sermon. "Don't you know that God only made one of you and that God pulled off a miracle when he put you together and then threw away the pattern?"[42] The message was one of recognizing and acknowledging that there was a "they" who did not have their best interests in mind, but in spite of "they" there was always God. Through the telling of the story of Samson and Delilah in that sermon, Wright reminded the people who needed liberation that liberation was theirs because of God.

13

WRIGHT AND THE WOULD-BE PRESIDENT

I was drawn to the power of the African American religious tradition to spur social change. Out of necessity, the black church had to minister to the whole person. Out of necessity, the black church rarely had the luxury of separating individual salvation from collective salvation. It had to serve as the center of the community's political, economic, and social as well as spiritual life; it understood in an intimate way the biblical call to feed the hungry, clothe the naked, and challenge powers and principalities.

—PRESIDENT BARACK OBAMA[1]

When one looks at the words Barack Obama has written and at some of the policies he has championed, it is not surprising that, as a young organizer in Chicago, he would be drawn to Trinity United Church of Christ. Obama worked to reach "the least of these," and Wright's ministry did the same. Obama urged people to step out of the box and believe in the work that could be done by and through effective organizing; caught in a box caused by poverty and racism, as well as other factors, they could, by risking stepping out of that box and effect change for themselves and for the communities in which they lived. Obama was to lead them to a higher place; he was, in effect, a community "Moses," leading people through a wilderness they were in not of their own choosing, to the place where they could take part in what was called "the American dream." They didn't have to accept their lot in life, but in order to get something different, they would have to do something different. They were not going to get out of their boxes being comfortable.

By Wright's own admission, his ministry was "out of the box." He never intended to have a "comfortable" church. People who believed in Jesus the Christ had to understand that the work of the Christian was to reach "the least of these," and those were not often found sitting in the pews, not initially. People who professed the Christ were to imitate the Christ. They were to "go and make disciples of all nations" (Matt. 28:19), seeking the lost, the confused, the distressed. While he was committed to pulling African Americans out of oppression caused by white supremacy, they were not going to be pulled out just to sit down. The work of the church was beyond its walls, he taught, and members of Trinity grew to understand that, as did people in Chicago, Illinois, as well as across the nation and eventually, across the world.

Wright says that the challenge to him to have a ministry "outside of the box" was presented to him by Dr. Martin Marty, who was his primary professor in church history at Chicago Theological Seminary. While Marty's words to Wright concerned what was normally found in church bulletins, they also stimulated the call within Wright to have a church that really "reached out," teaching and empowering people, instead of being more like a private social club that met once a week. Said Wright:

> When the average person thinks of a church and the work of that church, the average person thinks of the Sunday Morning Services, the choir, the ushers, the deacons and those who host the social hour after the worship services. For the person who has grown up in or around a church, moreover, that concept of

> "church" would expand to cover the Church School, the Sunday school, the youth programs, and the "outreach" ministry. That "outreach" ministry would normally include a feeding program for the hungry, a clothes closet for the homeless and some benevolence monies given to the work of the church of Jesus Christ in foreign countries. Those are the lines drawn around the "box" when it comes to the concept of church in the minds of most people. At Trinity United Church of Christ, however, dozens of our ministries have been "outside the box."[2]

Wright was already thinking of ministry that would be expansive, reaching "the least of these" wherever they might be, and so Dr. Marty's words to him in 1969 resonated within him. Wright writes in his book *A Sankofa Moment: The History of Trinity United Church of Christ:*

> Dr. Marty said to me (and to all of us in his class) back in 1969 that church publications were really very much like some holy joke. By that he meant that you could walk into any church on any given Sunday and pick up a church publication—either its bulletin or its newsletter—and think you had stepped from the real world into a fantasy world. He challenged us in 1969 to look at the different church bulletins where we worshipped. "See if they talked about anything of substance," he said. He asked us to compare church bulletins with the newspapers to see if they talked about Apartheid in South Africa, to see if they talked about the race problem in America, to see if they talked about what Christians were supposed to do as persons of faith when it came to the issues affecting the poor, the Blacks, the Browns, and those whom Jesus called "the least of these."[3]

Wright took that charge very seriously, and one could not help being struck by the range of work his church was doing. There were Rites of Passage programs for young boys and girls, where caring adults worked with young children, many of whom lived in single-parent homes. "The ministries were started in an attempt to address the needs of parents and children in the African American community where the families were headed by single parents," he wrote.[4] These children not only needed positive role models and mentors, but they also needed to develop a sense of pride to replace the shame too many African Americans carry for being African American, and so in the 1980s, the groups for these young boys and girls, called Building Black Men and Building Black Women, respectively, were changed to *Ishutu* and *Intojane*, South African in origin, to tie the children to their African heritage. While these programs were important for both the males and females, Wright had a special understanding of what young black boys were up against in society, too often feeling like the only thing they could be was a sports figure or an entertainer.

Wright needed them to "think outside of the box," and see that they were able and capable of being anything they put their minds to. He said that a member of his would always say, "You can't be what you can't see," and explained that this member meant that a young black boy "could never be a Black judge, a Black lawyer, a Black preacher, a Black architect, a Black electrical engineer, a Black air traffic controller, a Black ophthalmologist, a Black urologist, or be anything positive if he had never seen that kind of Black man up close and personal in his life or seen that option for his life in his radarscope of possibilities."[5] People who visited Trinity and watched its work understood the foundation of racism in this country upon which most everything had been built, and they could see that Wright was trying to get them to hold onto, or perhaps build, different pillars, different foci from which to launch themselves into American society. Wrote Dr. Marty:

> Yes, while Trinity is "unapologetically Christian," as the second clause in its motto affirms, it is also, as the other clause announces, "unashamedly black." From its beginning, the church has made strenuous efforts to help black Christians overcome the shame they had so long been conditioned to experience. That its members and pastor are, in their own terms, "Africentric" should not be more offensive than that synagogues should be "Judeocentric" or that Chicago's Irish parishes be "Celtic-centric." Wright and colleagues insist that no hierarchy of races is involved. People do not leave Trinity ready to beat up on white people; they are charged to make peace.[6]

There was something electric about being in Trinity or involved in its work. The absence of shame produced an inordinate amount of enthusiasm and empowerment. Wright's members went outside of Trinity to be the church, taking with them a new self-image that was contagious. Young men, in a ministry called "Project Jeremiah" went to young boys in their communities. "Since the boys wouldn't come to church, we would take the church to them," Wright wrote. They did not go to "pray the sinner's prayer" or to "lay out the plan of salvation." Instead, these young men, many of them professional, would show up on playgrounds about one-half hour before classes started and would interact with the boys, then "would go into classrooms and sit with these boys all day long. These men help the youngsters with their Social Studies, their Math, their English, their History, their Music, and their Science projects."[7]

> They patrol the halls when classes are changing and they stay out on the playground until the last child has left the school grounds. Their weekly presence helps the youngsters to know that *there is a Black man who cares about them* (italics mine). They get to see strong Black men who are making an investment in their lives; and those men are not trying to hit on their mamas or get next to the women who gave them birth.
>
> Those men are only helping show them another way of being in the world. Those men are showing them that gangbanging is not the only option.
>
> Those men offer an invaluable gift with the gift of their time and their presence every week. They are in the public schools for the forty weeks that the school is in session every year! They preach Jesus with their lives![8]

Wright's messages and ministries "outside of the box" resonated with young African American men who for the most part had been forgotten in American society. One of Wright's members, Richard Sewell, said that Wright's ministry had a special relevance for him "as a man of African descent whose ancestors were slaves and who has children and grandchildren who have been promised that things were going to get better (because it taught him) that God is on my side when I refuse to oppress anyone and when I struggle against those who would oppress me and my people. . . . In the Kingdom of God, there can be no oppression."[9]

Sewell's thoughts were mirrored by a schoolteacher in Columbus, Ohio (who did not want to be named), who explained why it was so important for African American boys and young men to hear messages of empowerment and hope. "I love my grandson, my little guy, as I call him, so much . . . but my love for him is even greater after I have worked with kids at school.

"These are second graders who cannot read, they cannot spell . . . and they *want* to read and spell, but there isn't anyone to help them or encourage them. Their parents are either too young or too beset with their own problems, and the teachers have given them up as hopeless.

"So we're losing these little boys by the second grade. Nobody cares enough about them to teach them . . . or to even spend quality time with them. My little guy, who's not yet three, asks a ton of questions . . . and I find myself wishing those little boys I teach had enough support so they'd ask questions, or even know it was all right to do it."

Wright knew that situation, and intentionally did ministry out of the box to reach those whom others simply seemed to ignore.

Wright's ministry was compassionately expansive, meaning that while he had a special place in his heart for African American men, his ministry looked to and for all who could be considered "the least of these." God was a God who created and therefore loved women; the Domestic Abuse ministry ministered to them, challenging them to love themselves too much to stay in an abusive relationship and challenging men on their notion of manhood that seemingly made it a badge of honor to beat or abuse women in any way. Before it was popular, Wright had a ministry for individuals who were infected with the HIV/AIDS virus and also had a support group for family members who often felt ostracized in church because one of their relatives had the dreaded disease. Trinity was hit by the disease, and what Wright knew, as he watched their suffering, was nobody should have to die alone. He spoke boldly about how people who followed the Christ were to embrace "the least of these," not turn or run from them. People who had HIV/AIDS were feared; some funeral homes would not take them. There were times when a person who had died of the disease would be put in special caskets, designed to keep even the suggestion of the possibility of the disease from somehow infecting those still alive far away. Wright talked about the disease, he taught how it was contracted, he lifted up gays and lesbians as children of God to be loved and used, not to be shunned and ignored . . . and he did it when most churches, especially black churches, dared not mention the disease at all.

There were ministries for the elders, too often forgotten, where people went to them in nursing homes and to their homes, making sure they were physically all right, that they had enough food to eat, that they weren't in cold houses in the winter or in stiflingly hot houses in the summer. They took young African American kids on black college tours; many of them had been so ensconced and invested in hating themselves and their culture that they hadn't even considered attending a black school. They had a mental health ministry, talking about a subject that is often taboo in churches in general but especially avoided in the black community. Trinity had a hospice ministry, where people were trained to work with the dying. He taught love, which, he reminded all who engaged in any of the work Trinity did, casts out fear. It was fear that had held many up, kept many people trapped in boxed-in ministries. The absence of fear, coupled with the absence of shame, was a winning formula for people who went "outside of the box" to minister to those who most needed God.

Perhaps it was this vast, expansive ministry that allowed people, white people included, to feel not hatred or enmity when they entered Trinity, but rather, a new sense of understanding. Dianna Bass, in a blog on a Trinity member's blogspot in March 2008, says she "came to appreciate the prophetic nature of black preaching. . . . I recognized that these voices emerged from a very distinct historical experience. And I admired the narrative interplay between the Bible and social justice. Over time, they taught me to hear the Gospel from an angular perspective—the angle of slaves, freed blacks, of those who feared lynching, of those who longed for Africa, those who could not attend good schools. From them I learned that liberation through Jesus was a power thing. And that white Americans really did need to repent when it came to race."[10]

It was into this bustling environment, a place where black people loved being black, loved serving God, loved seeking the lost . . . that a young community organizer named Barack Hussein Obama stepped.

Although Barack Obama's mother was white, his father was an African, which made him, in a more pure sense—an *African American.* He wrote in *The Audacity of Hope* that he had experienced some of the indignities that almost every brown-skinned person in America can recite:

> While my own upbringing hardly typifies the African American experience—and although I now occupy a position that insulates me from most of the bumps and bruises that the average black man must endure—I can recite the usual litany of petty slights that during my forty-five years have been directed my way: security guards tailing me as I shop in department stores, white couples who toss me their keys as I stand outside a restaurant waiting for the valet, police cars pulling me over for no apparent reason. I know what it's like to have people tell me I can't do something because of my color, and I know the bitter swill of swallowed-back anger. . . . To think clearly about race, then, requires us to see the world on a split screen—to maintain in our sights the kind of America that we want while looking squarely at America as it is, to acknowledge the sins of our past and the challenges of the present without becoming trapped in cynicism or despair.[11]

The would-be president knew long before he won the presidency in 2008 that being black in America carried its own set of burdens:

> A black teenage boy walking down the street may elicit fear in a white couple, but if he turns out to be their son's friend from school he may be invited over for dinner. A black man may have trouble catching a cab late at night, but if he is a capable software engineer Microsoft will have no qualms about hiring him. I cannot prove these assertions; surveys of racial attitudes are notoriously unreliable. And even if I'm right, it's cold comfort to many minorities. After all, spending one's days refuting stereotypes can be a wearying business. It's the added weight that many minorities, especially African Americans, so often describe in their daily

> round—the feeling that as a group we have no store of goodwill in America's accounts, that as individuals we must prove ourselves anew each day, that we will rarely get the benefit of the doubt and will have little margin for error. Making a way through such a world requires the black child to fight off the additional hesitation that she may feel when she stands at the threshold of a mostly white classroom on the first day of school; it requires the Latina woman to fight off self-doubt as she prepares for a job interview at a mostly white company. Most of all, it requires fighting off the temptation to stop making the effort."[12]

No matter the claims by some that Barack Obama wasn't "black" or "black enough" because he had not had the typical life experience of one who grows up black in America, he had learned quickly enough that the tentacles of racism rarely miss one whose skin belies his or her ancestry. He'd had his own experiences, and he certainly had heard of others' experiences in his work as an organizer. He had seen despair in the eyes of tired single mothers and fatigue in the shoulders of African American fathers who, in spite of how many jobs they worked, never seemed to be quite able to make quite enough money to make ends meet. He had seen the anger in African Americans, anger at the fact that in spite of having built this country, were still denied access to the American dream. He had seen young black boys, seeking affirmation and love, join gangs because that seemed to be the only place where they felt like they were worth someone's time and attention. He had seen the poverty that largely depleted the spirits of men and women in African American communities. So . . . though he had grown up differently than a homespun African American, he had been initiated nonetheless.

Like many African Americans in general, and African American men in particular, this meant he was looking for a faith and a faith message that could help him transcend the challenges of being black in America. He didn't need an easy message, a "pie in the sky" message, but rather a message that, as for Richard Sewell, would empower him to be able to transcend the racism that he confronted and that confronted him on a daily basis. The faith taught at Trinity United Church of Christ presented him with a religion that fed his spirit while it increased his faith.

The faith taught by Jeremiah Wright, as we have discussed, was a faith that empowered those who heard, that would not allow "the oppressed" to sink into the bowels of victimization. The faith he taught required that adherents understand that to be a follower of Jesus the Christ did not make one more privileged or better than a person of another faith, but it did require that one attempt to imitate the very difficult lifestyle and practices of Jesus the Christ. This Christ would not allow or condone revenge, racism notwithstanding. This Christ demanded that followers "love their enemies," a dictate taken straight from the Hebrew Scriptures and interwoven into the New Testament. In the Gospel of Matthew, for example, Jesus instructs his listeners:

> You have heard that it was said, "You shall love your neighbor and hate your enemy." But I say to you, Love your enemies and pray for those who persecute you, that you may be children of your Father in heaven; for he makes his sun rise on the evil and the good, and sends rain on the righteous and the unrighteous. For if you love those who love you, what reward do you have? Do not even the tax collectors do the same? And if you greet only your brothers and sisters, what more are you doing than others? Do not even the Gentiles do the same? Be perfect, therefore, as your heavenly Father is perfect. (Matt. 5:43–48)

Wright taught a *Christian* lesson, meaning he followed the words and directives found in the Sermon on the Mount (Matt. 5–7), which contains not a few very difficult things for humans to do in order to be in "right relationship" with God (righteousness). One of the commands that the Christ commanded was that individuals love each other, no matter the wrong done by one to another. His listeners would be familiar with the words found in the Book of Romans, "If your enemies are hungry, feed them; if they are thirsty, give them something to drink; for by doing this, you will heap burning coals on their heads" (Rom. 12:20). Vengeance belonged to God and must come from God; adherents of or believers in Jesus had a proscription for behavior that they must follow.

It was this very difficult command of Jesus that Martin Luther King used as the glue for his nonviolence movement. The command to love was almost ridiculous, given the virulence of racism against which African Americans fought, and yet, taught King, it was only through a love that transcended the evil that was pushing them back and down that African Americans could hope to prevail and, eventually, to triumph. To practice such love, King wrote, required one to be tough-minded, able to bear and carry on within two dialectically opposed realities:

> A French philosopher said, "No man is strong unless he bears within his character antitheses strongly marked." The strong man holds in a living blend strongly marked opposites. Not ordinarily do men achieve this balance of opposites. The idealists are not usually realistic, and the realists are not usually idealistic. The militant are not generally known to be passive, nor the passive to be militant. Seldom are the humble self-assertive, or the self-assertive humble. But life at its best is a creative synthesis of opposites in fruitful harmony. The philosopher Hegel said that truth is found neither in the thesis nor the antithesis, but in an emergent synthesis which reconciles the two.[13]

In order to survive in America, King taught, those struggling against evil had to be tough-minded, which he said was "sharp and penetrating, breaking through the crusts of legends and myths and sifting the true from the false."[14] To be soft-minded was to be out of the will of God; those who were soft-minded feared change and were prone to embrace "all kinds of superstitions, prone to be invaded by all kinds of irrational fears."[15] Those in the struggle for freedom did not have time to be afraid. They had to be able to withstand the evil of racism and fight against it, no matter what, and they had to know that fear, which was a major component of racism, could only be conquered by love. What was needed was people with courage, and courage and cowardice, a benchmark of fear, were incompatible. "Courage faces fear and masters it; cowardice represses fear and is thereby mastered by it," wrote King. Finally, he said, "fear is mastered through love."[16]

In letting go of fear, one made room for a faith that allowed God to be sovereign. This was a central theme of King's preaching and of

Wright's as well. Neither of them preached that evil as seen not only in racism, but later in sexism and militarism, did not exist. It did in fact exist, and God required co-creators of a new world order, one that supported the creation of a "beloved community" where all of God's children could live with dignity. Both Wright's and King's faith was a faith that empowered people to get out of their comfort zones and align the two parts of their spirits—the human and the divine—so that God's ultimate work, community, could be attained.

For many, this was a message that was at once empowering and liberating. It did not allow people to slide into a spirit of mediocrity or even into a place of apocalyptic hope; one not only did not have to wait to die to experience God's grace, presence, and power in the form of human dignity, one was not *allowed* to wait but was commanded to work for one's own dignity and therefore salvation while yet alive.

Perhaps this was the only kind of faith teaching that Obama, the would-be president, could ingest and digest. He said that for his mother, "organized religion too often dressed up close-mindedness in the garb of piety, cruelty and oppression in the cloak of righteousness."[17] But in spite of her opinion about organized religion, Obama said that her "fundamental faith" made her believe in the "goodness of people and in the ultimate value of this brief life we've each been given."[18]

Obama was looking for a faith and a faith community that fed his mind and spirit, a faith community that understood the concept of "beloved community," a faith community that valued education as well as religion and that empowered people to rise above their circumstances. He understood the historical power and value of the black church in America and knew what the black church had done to fight oppression and help clear the way for African Americans to enjoy full citizenship in the land of their birth. The black church for him was unique, in that it had always played a major role in the American political tradition:

> I was drawn to the power of the African American religious tradition to spur social change. Out of necessity, the black church rarely had the luxury of separating individual salvation from collective salvation. It had to serve as the center of the community's political, economic, social as well as spiritual life; it understood

> in an intimate way the biblical call to feed the hungry and clothe the naked and challenge the powers and principalities. In the history of these struggles, I was able to see faith as more than just a comfort to the weary or a hedge against death; rather, it was an active, palpable, agent in the world.[19]

Wright had a way of preaching the Christian Gospel that his old professor, Martin Marty, admired. Said Marty:

> It would be unfair to gloss over his abrasive—to say the least—edges, so, in the "Nobody's Perfect" column, I'll register some criticisms. To me, Trinity's honoring of Minister Louis Farrakhan was abhorrent and indefensible and Wright's fantasies about the U.S. government's role in spreading AIDS distracting and harmful. He, himself, is also aware of the now-standard charge by some African American clergy who say he is a victim of cultural lag, over influenced by the terrible racial situation when he was formed.
>
> Having said that, and reserving the right to offer more criticisms, I've been too impressed by the way Wright preaches the Christian Gospel to break with him. Those who were part of his ministry for years—the school superintendents, nurses, legislators, teachers, laborers, the unemployed, the previously shunned and shamed, the anxious—are not going to turn their backs on their pastor and prophet.[20]

And neither would have Barack Obama turned his back on his pastor and prophet, at least not in the way it happened, had not Obama decided to run for president. It seemed that this young newcomer, Obama, was too good to be true. He was smart as a whip, personable, able to reach across racial and ethnic lines, effortlessly, it seemed. He was young enough to appeal to young adults and children alike; indeed, commentators often likened the reception he got to that a rock star would get—yet he was old enough to have amassed enough knowledge so that the different pockets of people within the American electorate could trust that he knew what he was talking about. He hadn't been in politics all that long, and while that worried some, for others, it was refreshing and made them believe that the change Obama talked about was really possible. America was bleeding; it was involved in two wars and nobody really knew why. Though few knew how severe the country's economic state was, many knew enough to know that their paychecks were getting smaller and smaller, and that the gap between rich and poor was getting wider and wider. Obama was young enough to connect to the digital generation; he was on Facebook and e-mailed people all over the nation, making a connection between himself and the American populace as no politician before him had done. Barack Obama was a very, very savvy politician.

The Republicans seemed to catch on a little slowly. Perhaps it was because they couldn't believe that this man could and would capture the imagination of America as he did. Perhaps they secretly and privately thought that America was not nearly ready for a black man to be president. Whatever their reasons, they reacted slowly. The Democratic primary was brutal as Obama and Hillary Clinton slugged it out, and again, there was an air of disbelief and incredulity that this young, pretty much unknown could wage as fierce a fight as he did against Washington insider Clinton.

And yet, he did. Obama moved through the primary and then into the general campaign with power and prowess. He somehow managed to remain likeable in spite of the brutality of the campaign.

His relationship with Wright, one has to believe, had prepared him for this moment. Wright had talked with him, mentored him, and supported him. In one appearance that Obama had on *Oprah*, there was Wright, in the audience, whom Obama introduced as his pastor. The love that appeared in that moment was memorable; it was almost as though Obama, the son, was introducing Wright, the father he had missed all his life. The pride that Wright showed in Obama was unmistakable. Wright had done for Obama what he had done for many of his members: he had given sound advice, based on a firm foundation of faith, yet steeped in reality. Obama would grow to love both the spiritual and intellectual depth of his pastor, with his "ability to hold together, if not reconcile, the conflicting strains of black experience."[21] Early in their relationship, Wright, the sage, had told Obama, "Life's not safe for a black man in this country, Barack. Never has been. Probably never will be."[22]

It was a lesson Obama was about to learn firsthand. Obama was making too much headway. Too much of the Republican base was being swayed; even people in the South were leaning toward Obama, and the young man seemed unstoppable. There had to be *something* that could and would stop the momentum . . . and that something, they hoped, would be Jeremiah Wright.

The attack on Barack Obama in an attempt to paint him as a closet radical, full of hatred for white people, came with a fury as sermon clips of Jeremiah Wright were thrown into living rooms of Americans. Obama had proudly said that he had been a member of Trinity United Church of Christ for twenty years. That was okay when nobody knew who Jeremiah Wright was, meaning the American media had not cast him as a religious folk hero or spiritual leader in the way they had Billy Graham, T. D. Jakes, or even Pat Robertson. Wright had built a tremendously successful ministry in Chicago; his church was one of the leading congregations in the United Church of Christ, funneling literally hundreds of thousands of dollars to the denomination for its work with congregations across the country. He was a known and renowned scholar, teaching to whites and blacks in this country and in Cuba and Africa and other countries; he had spoken to and taught people in all denominations . . . and his theme or the thrust of his teaching and preaching never wavered: we lived in a country scarred by racism, militarism, and materialism, and it was the job of Christians to recognize that and to challenge those forces with the gospel of Jesus Christ.

Americans in general, however, did not know any of that, and America was (and is) still very tender and vulnerable regarding race. Talking about race is for the most part avoided, and for many is not considered to be important, as many whites and blacks choose to ignore racism's stubborn insistence on staying alive, and they want to assume that the worst of racism is over. Whites increasingly grow irritated when racism is brought up, accusing those who talk about it of whining and of not looking at and appreciating the gains that black people have made. Many blacks likewise grow irritated talking about it because many want merely to assimilate into American society and be in position to grab onto the American dream. So it was not all that surprising in 2008, since an African American was running for president and was actually making headway, that people, black and white, began to say that there was no more racism in America, and the implication was that things had changed so much that a black man *was even being allowed* to run for president. Nobody wanted to deal with racism, now less than before.

Republican strategists knew that. They knew that many white Americans were nervous about black people in general; because racism has historically been ignored and pushed under the rug, the feelings that made white people nervous and black people angry have never really been discussed and dealt with. The fact that black anger might still exist made many people nervous, and GOP strategists knew it. So it was a no-brainer. If Republicans could tap into that latent, dormant fear and hatred, they might provide a tipping point for the election. The playing of those sound bites was a deliberate, strategic, political move designed to unhinge the Obama campaign. All the GOP base (and many others, strategists hoped) had to see was Jeremiah Wright saying things that many Americans, especially white Americans, would interpret as being hate speech and unpatriotic, and Obama's momentum would be stopped, or at least slowed.

Beginning on ABC in March 2008, viewers saw an animated and angry Jeremiah Wright preaching from the pulpit of Trinity United Church of Christ, criticizing American political actions and policies of the past and present, casting America in a not-so-good light. Here was prophetic preaching in all its power, in the spirit of the biblical prophets who had railed against oppressive governments *and* at "the faithful," God's chosen people, who refused to challenge oppression in the name of Yahweh, who demanded righteousness. As it had been a bitter message to receive by the biblical people, so was it bitter to twenty-first-century Americans, especially white Americans. The clips were played over and over; Dean Reynolds said that "in North Carolina, the Republicans put their ad on the Internet and say they're going to broadcast it as well," and Keith Olberman, in that same conversation, said that the "Republican hit job (in North Carolina) plans a Willie Horton style ad against Obama."[23] Bill Moyers, in an interview he did with Wright in April,

2008, said, "Barack Obama's pastor was in the news again this week. North Carolina Republicans are preparing to run an ad tying Obama to some controversial sound bites from Reverend Wright's sermons. And CBS and MSNBC led their broadcasts with reports about the ad."[24]

That many (not all) African Americans were nonplussed by what they heard was not surprising; they felt, both firsthand and through knowledge of the history of racist policies in this country, that what Wright was saying was *their* truth. According to Mike Green, a *Huffington Post* journalist:

> Wright's messaging . . . delivers penetrating truth, sometimes with a caustic impact that burns through the façade of worshiping America to reveal realities of the past and present. The Christian Church itself has largely become a caricature of itself in both Black and White American societies. Its members are often dutiful followers who share a discontent and disdain for others who don't agree with them, even if those others are professing Christians as well. The church is divided into Black and White experiences that mirror the society in which it languishes, helplessly watching its messaging become ever more irrelevant. . . . Jeremiah Wright's preaching and teaching is tailored to the society in which his audience lives.[25]

Obama knew about that "audience" about which Green speaks—and so did everyone else. Race was still an issue in the United States, Obama's presidential bid notwithstanding. Though some would point to the progress America had made in race relations, the fact was that still, in the twenty-first century, race was rearing its ugly head as an unwelcome permanent presence in American society. In 2008, during the presidential campaign, a story in *The Washington Post* revealed some of what Obama campaigners were encountering:

> In Muncie, a factory town in the east-central part of Indiana, (Danielle) Ross and her cohorts were soliciting support for Obama at malls, on street corners and in a Wal-Mart parking lot, and they ran into a "horrible response," as Ross put it, a level of anti-black sentiment that none of them had anticipated.

> "The first person I encountered was like, 'I'll never vote for a black person,'" recalled Ross, who is white and just turned 20. "People just weren't receptive." For all the hope and excitement Obama's candidacy is generating, some of his field workers, phone bank volunteers and campaign surrogates are encountering a raw racism and hostility that have gone largely unnoticed—*and unreported* [italics mine]—this election season. Doors have been slammed in their faces. They've been called racially derogatory names (including the white volunteers). And they've endured malicious rants and ugly stereotyping from people who can't fathom that the senator from Illinois could become the first African American president. . . .
>
> Victoria Switzer, a retired social studies teacher, was on phone bank duty one night during the Pennsylvania primary campaign. One night was all she could take: "It wasn't pretty," She made 60 calls to prospective voters in Susquehanna County, her home county, which is 98 percent white. The responses were dispiriting. One caller, Switzer remembers, said he couldn't possibly vote for Obama and concluded, "Hang that darky from a tree!"[26]

In other words, W. E. B. DuBois's proclamation that the problem of the twentieth century was the color line was, in fact, *still* the problem now, in the twenty-first century. Obama wasn't coming into the presidential race in a country that had solved its race problem, he was coming into the campaign in a country that had merely covered it up as best it could. While some experts would say racism had gotten so much better from the days of Jim Crow that it was hardly visible or noticeable, other people, especially and including the audience to which Wright preached, knew otherwise. Overt racism was now illegal for the most part, but covert racism still existed in full force. Not surprisingly, more blacks than whites saw racism as a problem, which again may have accounted for the different ways in which many blacks and whites interpreted the words from Wright's sermons played during the campaign. Jack Dovidio, a University of Connecticut professor said in an interview with CNN in 2006 that 80 percent of whites "have racist feelings they may not even recognize. . . . We've reached a point that racism is like a virus that has mutated into a new form that we don't recognize," he said in that article.[27]

But if whites didn't recognize it, plenty of blacks did, and in spite of the charge that Wright suffered from a "cultural lag," meaning that he preached as he did about racism because of the era in which he grew up, statistics, studies, and actual experiences of scores of African Americans showed that no such lag existed.

The testimonies of whites would support that what African Americans felt was not imaginary. In a story that ran on CBS News after Obama won the 2008 election, the wishful thought that America had become a "post-racial" nation was shattered:

> Incidents around the country referring to President-elect Barack Obama are dampening the postelection glow of racial progress and harmony, highlighting the stubborn racism that remains in America. . . .
>
> There have been "hundreds" of incidents since the election, many more than usual, said Mark Potok, director of the Intelligence Project at the Southern Poverty Law Center, which monitors hate crimes.
>
> One was in Snellville, Ga., where Denene Millner said a boy on the school bus told her 9-year-old daughter the day after the election, "I hope Obama gets assassinated." That night, someone trashed her sister-in-law's front lawn, mangled the Obama lawn signs, and left two pizza boxes filled with human feces outside the front door, Millner said.
>
> She described her emotions as a combination of fear and anger.
>
> "I can't say that every white person in Snellville is evil and anti-Obama and willing to desecrate my property because one of two idiots did it," said Millner, who is black. "But it definitely makes you look a little different at the people you live with, and makes you wonder what they're capable of and what they're really thinking. . . ."
>
> Grant Griffin, a 46-year-old white Georgia native, (said), "I believe our nation is ruined and has been for several decades and the election of Obama is merely the culmination of the change.

If you had real change, it would involve all of the members of (Obama's) church being deported."[28]

In spite of the residual, dormant racist feelings among Americans, however, it doesn't appear that what got America riled up about Jeremiah Wright initially were feelings of racism, but, instead, anger at this man who was preaching harsh criticism about America. The fact that this preacher had been the pastor of the would-be president concerned those who heard Wright's words. Was Wright unpatriotic, as they interpreted his words to mean? And if he was, had he preached to Obama that it was all right to be unpatriotic, that God sanctioned such feelings? And could we, then, trust a man to be president who was at his core secretly unpatriotic? When critics of Wright said he preached hatred, they were saying that he was preaching hatred against white people, and they believed that he was preaching hatred against a government that had historically and systematically done him and other African Americans wrong.

Wright got a hit from the same whip of criticism that was cracked after Michelle Obama said in Milwaukee, Wisconsin, in February 2008, "For the first time in my adult life I am proud of my country because it feels like hope is finally making a comeback." Then, though the Obama campaign refuted it, Mrs. Obama apparently said the statement again in Madison that day, "For the first time in my adult lifetime, I'm really proud of my country and not just because Barack has done well, but because I think people are hungry for change."[29]

The reaction to Michelle's words, was swift and brutal, as it was for Wright's. White Americans found her statements offensive, as they found Wright's sermon clips, but African Americans understood instinctively and intuitively what she meant. America's history had not been kind, good, or fair for African Americans. It was hard, as African Americans, to be fully invested in a country that had only marginally invested in them, though the desire to be fully invested and to be regarded as full human beings was always there. No matter where one was in American society, one always knew, if one was African American, that he or she was on the periphery—something Mrs. Obama acknowledged in her senior thesis written at Princeton University. She wrote:

> My experiences at Princeton have made me far more aware of my "blackness" than ever before. I have found that at Princeton, no matter how liberal and open-minded some of my white professors and classmates try to be toward me, I sometimes feel like a visitor on campus; as if I really don't belong. Regardless of the circumstances under which I interact with whites at Princeton, it often seems as if, to them, I will always be black first, and a student, second.[30]

Mrs. Obama, as any African American, felt the racially charged undertow, and it is significant that her thesis, entitled "Princeton-Educated Blacks and the Black Community," was "temporarily withdrawn" during the 2008 campaign. Race was just too explosive a topic to discuss, and the last thing the Obama campaign needed was anyone sounding "too black," a fact that raised the ire of many African Americans. But race was not on the minds of the critics who went after Michelle Obama in February 2008, at least not directly. Michelle was committing the cardinal, unspoken "sin" that any American can commit, free speech and prohibition of censure notwithstanding. She was criticizing the American government.

Michelle Obama distanced herself from her statement as the backlash came, fast and furious. She would be the "First Lady." She had to be American first, and an African American woman who had endured painful experiences due to the color of her skin second, or perhaps not at all. Neither she nor her husband was allowed, so to speak, to talk about the horror and pain of racism.

But Jeremiah Wright could, and did. He had committed cardinal sin of American culture and society in the sermons cited during the 2008 campaign. He had not only criticized America, he had preached that God ought to damn America. He was as far away from the concept of American exceptionalism as a person could be, and using God in the condemnation of America was taken as blasphemy. Interestingly, Martin Luther King preached words that had the same ring of criticism of the government in his sermon, "Beyond Vietnam: A Time to Break Silence," preached at Riverside Church exactly one year before he was assassinated. King was "allowed" to criticize the government as long as that criticism was limited to the way the government had treated black people. But King stepped over a line, the same line that Jeremiah Wright was stepping over, as he began to preach about American foreign policy. Nobody wanted him to do that, not black or white people, but King felt that to keep silent was a betrayal to his call. Those called to "preach good news to the poor . . . to bind up the brokenhearted . . . to proclaim the year of the Lord's favor . . . and comfort all who mourn" were obligated to talk when they would rather be silent. King wrote, in that sermon, "Some of us who have already begun to break the silence of the night have found that the calling to speak is often a vocation of agony, but we must speak."[31] King drew sharp criticism for his words:

> They wander into the towns and see thousands of the children, homeless, without clothes, running in packs on the streets like animals. They see the children, degraded by our soldiers as they beg for food. They see the children selling their sisters to our soldiers, soliciting for their mothers.
>
> What do the peasants think as we ally ourselves with the landlords and as we refuse to put any action into our many words concerning land reform? What do they think as we test our latest weapons on them, just as the Germans tested out new medicine and new tortures in the concentration camps of Europe? Where are the roots of the independent Vietnam we claim to be building? Is it among these voiceless ones?
>
> We have destroyed their two most cherished institutions: the family and the village. We have destroyed their land and their crops. We have cooperated in the crushing of the nation's only non-Communist revolutionary political force—the unified Buddhist church. We have supported the enemies of the peasants of Saigon. We have corrupted their women and children and killed their men. What liberators?[32]

Americans don't like it when their government is criticized. As King was slammed for such criticism, so was Wright. The Republican strategists knew when they heard Wright's words that a good part of America would be incensed. What they hoped was that their anger would be enough to change their minds and vote for Senator John McCain. That did not happen, miraculously.

Even though one could hear Wright saying "No, no, no, God damn America," the last part of the sermon, the hope that is a traditional and important component of the jeremiad, was not blasted across the airwaves. Wright had a call on his life to preach hope to the hopeless. In order to preach hope, he had to identify and call out the reasons for the hopelessness, just as the biblical prophets had done. At the end of the sermon, Wright preached the hope that, if heard during that time, might have reached the souls of grieving Americans:

"Where governments fail, God never fails." That was a resounding note of hope for a people who had known so much failure, brought about in large part by their government. Wright's audience had to have a reason to hope . . . and that hope was God. Wright preached:

> When God says it, it's done. God never fails. When God wills it, you better get out of the way. 'Cause God never fails. When God fixes it, oh believe me, it's fixed. God never fails. Somebody right now, you think you can't make it, but I want you to know that you are more than a conqueror. Through Christ you can do all things, who strengthens you. To the world, it looked like God had failed in God's plan of salvation when the savior that was sent by God was put to death on a Friday afternoon. It looked like God failed. But hallelujah, on Sunday morning, the angels in heaven were singing, "God never fails!" You can't put down what God raises up. God never fails!"[33]

Wright preached a message of hope, salvation, and a promise that with and through God, black Americans could rise from their places of despair. It was a good message, but words of hope had been fully swallowed by the words of frustration that the world, by this time, had heard repeatedly. Obama tried hard not to be thrown off track by his pastor's words. He and his family were a part of the Trinity UCC family. Pastor Wright was his pastor and some would argue that he was also a father figure to the young man aspiring to be elected the most powerful position in the world. Obama stood his ground for a time. He likened his pastor to a relative that all of us have in our families who sometimes say things that are outlandish and ridiculous. He said that though Wright was his pastor, he didn't agree with everything he said. He was criticized severely for not breaking from Wright, but he held his ground. Obama was pressed to distance himself from Wright, to show that he had allegiance to this country, which he wanted to lead. Obama was reluctant. Obama wrote in *The Huffington Post* on March 14, 2008:

> The pastor of my church, Rev. Jeremiah Wright, who recently preached his last sermon and is in the process of retiring, has touched off a firestorm over the last few days. He's drawn attention as the result of some inflammatory and appalling remarks he made about our country, our politics, and my political opponents. Let me say at the outset that I vehemently disagree and strongly condemn the statements that have been the subject of this controversy. I categorically denounce any statement that disparages our great country or serves to divide us from our allies. I also believe that words that degrade individuals have no place in our public discourse.[34]

Obama went on to say he knew Wright as "someone who had served his country as a United States Marine, as a biblical scholar, and as someone who taught or lectured at seminaries across the country. . . . Most importantly, Rev. Wright preached the gospel of Jesus, a gospel on which I base my life. In other words, he has never been my political advisor. He has been my pastor."[35]

While Obama worked on damage control, others criticized the media and the politicians for having a double standard. Plenty of preachers, white preachers, they said, had made incendiary and insulting remarks and plenty of politicians and would-be politicians looked for and sought their support, but never had there been such an uproar, they charged. Frank Schaeffer noted that his pastor/preacher father had said outlandish things and had never faced the excoriation Wright faced. Bill Moyers, who drew sharp criticism after he interviewed Wright on his program *Bill Moyers' Journal,* responded to the criticism both of his interview and of Wright. By the time Moyers wrote this essay, the nation had also seen Wright at the National Press Club, an appearance that did nothing to endear Americans to him, even those who were staunch supporters. Still, Moyers thought the attacks on Wright to be indicative of a double standard in America:

I once asked a reporter back from Vietnam, "Who's telling the truth over there?" "Everyone," he said, "everyone sees what's happening through the lens of their own experience." That's how people see Jeremiah Wright. . . .

Where I grew up in the South, before the civil rights movement, the pulpit was a safe place for black men to express anger for which they would have been punished anywhere else; a safe place for the fierce thunder of dignity denied, justice delayed. I think I would have been angry if my ancestors had been transported thousands of miles in the hellish hole of a slave ship, and then sold at auction, humiliated, whipped and lynched. Or if my great-great grandfather had been but three-fifths of a person in a constitution that proclaimed, "We the people." Or if my own parents had been subjected to the racial vitriol of Jim Crow, Bull Connor and Jesse Helms. Even so, the anger of black preachers I've known and heard about and reported on was, for them, very personal and cathartic. . . .

Behold the double-standard: John McCain sought out the endorsement of John Hagee, the war-mongering Catholic-bashing Texas preacher who said the people of New Orleans got what they deserved for their sins. But no one suggests McCain shares Hagee's delusions, or thinks AIDS is God's punishment for homosexuality. Pat Robertson called for the assassination of a foreign head of state and asked God to remove Supreme Court justices, yet he remains a force in the Republican religious right. After 9/11, Jerry Falwell said the attack was God's judgment on America for having been driven out of our schools and the public square, but when McCain goes after the endorsement of the preacher he once condemned as an agent of intolerance, the press gives him a pass. . . .

Which means it is all about race, isn't it?[36]

The double standard that Moyers pointed out was blatant, but it pointed something out about what religious vitriol is allowed, culturally and societally sanctioned. The difference between what Falwell and Robertson and Schaeffer and Hagee preached or said, and what Jeremiah

Wright preached, was that the former men preached what amounted to a message of bigotry toward certain *individuals*. Their conception and interpretation of scripture seemed to allow for the denigration of individuals if they were judged to be amoral. That type of biblical interpretation was anathema to Wright.

The vilification of individuals *as individuals*, violated the Christian precept to love one's neighbor as oneself. The power of Jesus' ministry, or a good part of the power of his work, was his intentional inclusion of "the least of these." If the Bible is to be believed, he went to the disinherited, the lost, the broken and sick. He talked with the woman who had had five husbands when everyone else ignored her. The whole of Jesus' message was one that was not lost on Wright. What Jesus did do, however, was challenge the Roman government. Obery Hendricks, in his book *The Politics of Jesus*, posits that even the Lord's Prayer was a protest against the government. Hendricks says that Jesus' message, at its core, was that people and the government should "treat the needs of people as holy."[37] He writes: "Howard Thurman lamented that 'too often the weight of the Christian movement has been on the side of the strong and powerful and against the weak—*this, despite the gospel.*'"[38]

While the distinction between what some of the religious right preached and Wright preached is interesting and has validity, it did nothing at all to help Wright, the preacher, or Obama, the would-be president.

After Wright appeared at the National Press Club, his presentation on the importance of the black church totally ignored so that he could be questioned on the now infamous sound bites, things only got worse for both men. Wright was seen as arrogant and disrespectful of America. He was not being criticized and condemned because he was preaching hatred toward white people. He was being demonized because he was criticizing the government. That he was an African American only made things more troubling for those who were prone to worry.

White America (and much of black America as well) didn't want anyone in the White House who didn't love America with all their minds, all their hearts, and all their souls. They were worried, rightfully perhaps, that no black person could love America like that, and Obama's ties to Wright seemed to support their suspicion. Unless Obama completely cut off his relationship with his pastor, he would never make it to the White House.

Reluctantly, it felt, the parishioner publicly cut his ties with his pastor. Some said Obama's speech, "A More Perfect Union," was brilliant, and it was, on one level. But on another level, it had to be excruciatingly painful for both men. America had made two black men, both powerful, both adept and skilled in their fields, both brilliant and both with much to give, one as a politician and the other as a pastor and preacher, square off in a spiritual and emotional dual. What did Obama want? He wanted to be president. Wright had to go. It was the sacrifice he had to make.

The attention given to Wright's words, carefully and skillfully chosen by those who wanted to win the presidency, betrayed the discomfort America still had and has when it comes to race, and also betrayed the willingness of people to play the "race card" in a way that one never had to say the word "race," but everyone knew exactly what was going on.

In an article in *The Monthly Review*, authors Edward S. Herman and David Peterson noted that Wright was not the first to say controversial things, but that his words carried more phlegm, precisely because they spoke to the racial concerns and fears of the American electorate, both white and black. White people could be counted upon to retreat into their latent fear of black people, and blacks could be counted upon to retreat into their desire that racism, and all discussion of it, just go away. In their article, Herman and Peterson noted that John Hagee, embraced by Obama's challenger Sen. John McCain, had said troubling things that never got the mileage that Wright's words received.

Wright asserted that the HIV/AIDS virus was brought intentionally into the black community, drawing on a lingering suspicion about the culpability of the American government using African Americans as guinea pigs in the area of health research, citing the Tuskegee Experiment as proof. That was a horrendous allegation, refuted by almost everyone, including Wright's most ardent supporters. Yet Hagee made a moral condemnation, saying that AIDS was an "incurable plague," "God's curse against a disobedient nation."[39] Many Americans were and are content to define morality in primarily sexual terms, but Wright, as did Martin Luther King before him, tended to define morality more in sociopolitical terms.

A government that ignored the oppressed, the widow, and the fatherless (Isa. 1:17) was unjust and immoral to the biblical prophets and to Wright, but Hagee and others would not agree with that. Peterson and Herman said that the absence of racism and the fiction of equality for all in America were "precisely the myths that powerful Americans cling to most dearly,[40] and Wright had no respect for their reluctance to face his truth and the truth of the oppressed. McCain's religious supporters had quite a bit to say, actually, about *why* AIDS had attacked and killed so many Americans. Jerry Falwell said that "AIDS is not just God's punishment for homosexuals; it is God's punishment for the society that tolerates homosexuals."[41] Both Falwell and Hagee defamed individuals for their sexuality, but personal attacks on groups of people were deemed "moral," and a candidate was not to be looked down upon or viewed with suspicion just because he had an outspoken pastor with personal biases. But Wright was looked at as a traitor, basically, one who spoke against his country. Individual or group criticisms were all right, but not anything that smelled of a lack of patriotism. Government, especially this American government, trumped God. It was that simple.

What GOP strategists were doing was showing their hand, and the hand of America, as concerns race. It would not be difficult to "unseat" and sabotage the forward movement of Barack Obama if they were able to tap into the racial divide. George Wallace said in 1963, following his standoff against black would-be students at the University of Alabama, that "they all hate black people, all of them! They're all afraid, all of them. Great God! That's it! They're all Southern. The whole United States is Southern!"[42] While McCain may or may not have been aware of Wallace's quote, he and the GOP strategists did know how many white people still think about race. Their decision to jump on Wright's quotes was no different in spirit than what GOP strategists did when Michael Dukakis ran for president in 1988, when Dukakis' letting convicted felon Willie Horton go home for a weekend furlough ended tragically. Horton, who was serving a life sentence without parole, was accused of raping, assaulting and robbing a young woman while on that furlough.[43] It was all the evidence some white Americans needed to run toward the GOP.

In the midst of the GOP strategizing and positioning race to undo him, Barack Obama was pressing forward. He successfully beat Hillary Clinton in the primaries and pounded against McCain, winning support from both black *and* white voters. Lurking underneath all that happened in 2008 was the color line, implicitly understood to be there, although nobody dared say it outright—including candidate Obama.

14

AT THE END OF THE DAY

IS WRIGHT'S MESSAGE RELEVANT TODAY?

The foundations of the earth tremble.
The earth is utterly broken,
the earth is torn asunder,
the earth is violently shaken.
The earth staggers like drunkard,
it sways like a hut;
its transgression lies heavy upon it,
and it falls, and will not rise again.

—Isaiah 24:18–20

No matter what, there is always racism. It does not go away.

Americans, both black and white, desperately want to believe that racism is a thing that was. But it has not passed into oblivion. It still rears its ugly head, in all kinds of places, North and South. In spite of the "gains" made by African Americans, there is always the "spirit of racism," if not blatant racism, which far too often moves from a dormant to an active status, scattering the droplets of America's disease like a pesky, untreatable virus. Even now, in the twenty-first century, racism sits stubbornly in the midst of American culture, causing ever more psychic damage to black people, and causing more whites to believe in the concept of the innate supremacy of white people.

Being black is a problem, apparently all over the world. In Mexico, Peru, Brazil . . . all countries where many Africans were brought during the transatlantic slave trade, being black is still a problem; the racism that Afro-Peruvians experience, according to Professor Henry Louis Gates, is worse than much he has seen in the United States. In Brazil, in spite of the fact that more Africans were taken there as slaves than to any other country in the Americas, being black is still the last thing anyone wants to be.[1]

Regarding racism, this writer has wrestled with the notion of how or why a good God would make a people whom the masses in the world would shun. If we call white supremacy "evil," which in this book we do, then why does a good God allow it? The same question may have been asked by Jews, who suffered in the Bible, during the Holocaust, and even to the present day. Philip Yancey in his book *Where Is God When It Hurts?* asks the same question. Can one even trust a God such as this, a God who allows *God's own children* to suffer because of the way God made them? What kind of a God is that? Many gay and lesbian individuals have surely wrestled with confusion about why a good God would have allowed them to be born as they are, only to suffer miserable lives of suffering because of who and how God made them. If we want to keep alive our concept of a good God, what do we do with this God who apparently stands by while God's children suffer just for "being?"

There are many preachers who ignore these difficult and uncomfortable questions. There are stories in the Bible that paint pictures of the personality and character of God that do not gel with the human conception and definition of "good." Some theologians have rejected and ignored, and indeed do not even address, the God of the Hebrew scriptures and so do not force people to deal with God asking Abraham to sacrifice his own son, God allowing Job to unjustly suffer, and don't force them to come face to face with a God who used the enemies of Israel against them. God, it seems, has *allowed* and does allow, certain people to suffer.

The notion of God "standing by" in the midst of suffering is one that really should be dealt with because that is certainly one of the pictures painted in the Christian Bible. The story of John the Baptist, the cousin of Jesus, illustrates how those who endure unrighteous suffering question the ways of God. John has been imprisoned for doing what he has been sent to earth to do . . . prepare "the way" for Jesus. In so doing, he has insulted and infuriated the religious and political superstructures, and thus, is thrown into jail. He sits there and wonders, "Where is God?" He and Jesus, after all, are cousins! He baptized Jesus, even though he hadn't wanted to do that. And yet he sits in prison. He sends people, his own disciples, to find Jesus and ask him, "Are you the one who is to come, or should we expect someone else?" God, through Jesus, was standing by, allowing one of his own to suffer, and despite John's question, did not change the course of John's life. He was not released from prison but was, according to the story, beheaded at the behest of a woman who did not like him.

Viktor Frankl, in his book *Man's Search for Meaning,* brings again to the forefront the image of this God who stands by while people who are being treated horribly just for being who God made them. Could God, should God, have destroyed the Nazi regime that was mercilessly killing innocent people? Many people in the concentration camps found it impossible to hold on and hold out, Frankl contends, not because of the actual, horrific treatment they endured, but because they lost their God-focus and, without such focus, lost their ability to choose how they would respond to their predicament. Rabbi Harold Kushner, who wrote the introduction to the 1992 edition of *Man's Search for Meaning,* said that Frankl offered help to the suffering, showing how to find meaning in life in spite of suffering. Still the idea that God stands by and allows the suffering to continue is troubling. Elie Wiesel offers a recollection of a young boy who asked the difficult questions during the Holocaust: "I remember: it happened yesterday or eternities ago. A young Jewish boy discovered the Kingdom of the Night. I remember his bewilderment, I remember his anguish. It all happened so fast. The ghetto. The deportation. The sealed cattle car. The fiery altar upon which the history of our people and the future of humankind were meant to be sacrificed. I remember he asked his father, "Can this be true? This is the twentieth century, not the Middle Ages. Who would allow such crimes to be committed? How could the world remain silent?"[2]

Did the silence of the world during the Holocaust mean that people were following God's lead? Should the God of the Hebrew Scriptures have done something, made the earth open and swallow the evildoers and their wretched concentration camps, so all the world would see God's wrath? *Was* God bothered?

Likewise, was God bothered, *is* God bothered by the evil of racism? In the presence of evil, there has to be a prophet, one who will speak up and speak out against it. The prophet has the responsibility to clarify what cannot be easily clarified—the actions of God. The prophet must interpret to and for the people God's will, so that evil might be curtailed, while the preacher must explain and reassure the people that, in spite of bad things happening, God is forever with God's children and God cares for them. It is the job of the preacher to inspire the people to hold onto God, even as they do not understand what God is doing or not doing. The prophet/preacher, a rare breed, must do both: explain God's words and inspire the people, and unless and until evil disappears, the need for the prophet/preacher will forever exist. It is the job of the preacher, more so than that of the prophet, to make the people understand how to survive and in fact thrive in the face of evil. "Do not remember the former things, or consider the things of old. I am about to do a new thing; now it springs forth, do you not perceive it? I will make a way in the wilderness and rivers in the desert" (Isa. 43:18–19). The preacher brings hope to those in the grip of evil, causing abject suffering: "When evildoers assail me to devour my flesh—my adversaries and foes—they shall stumble and fall. Though an army encamp against me, my heart shall not fear; though war rise up against me, yet I will be confident" (Psa. 27:2–3). Both the prophet and the preacher are concerned with the souls of God's people, who cannot understand why God does not seem to care when God's own people suffer. Certainly, Jeremiah Wright understood that, and functioned, when he was a pastor, in the dual role of prophet/preacher. But even now, post-retirement, his voice and his message are vital to and for a people who still suffer under the yoke of racism. In the absence of a God who will stop unjust suffering, the people who suffer need a voice, and that voice comes through the prophets. Wright captured the angst and suffering of oppressed people in his sermon "The Day of Jerusalem's Fall:"

> The captives in Babylon asked the question, "How shall we sing the Lord's song in a strange land?" The captives in America answered that question by creating an entirely new genre of music, the spirituals. They sang sorrowfully, "Sometimes I feel like a motherless child, a long way from home." They sang thoughtfully, "Nobody knows de trouble I seen, nobody knows but Jesus." They sang defiantly, "Oh, freedom! Oh Freedom! Oh freedom over me! And before I be a slave, I'll be buried in my grave and go home to my God and be free!"
>
> To quote Dr. Martin Luther King, they took Jeremiah's question mark and straightened it out into an exclamation point. Jeremiah, who saw his people in exile, asks the question, "Is there no balm in Gilead?" The Africans, who were in exile, in a strange land, said, "Oh yes! There is a balm in Gilead."[3]

Those who heard these words, and many like them, were comforted but also immensely empowered to push through racism. What they were experiencing, Wright taught, was no different than what our biblical forebears had. The affirmation of God's presence in the time of suffering was and is a major strength of anyone's preaching, but to a people who have felt marginalized, especially by religion that too often presented God as one who sanctioned their condition, it cannot be overstated.

Wright is obviously not the first prophet/preacher to step up to the call of prophetic preaching in and for the African American community, a people who have been historically traumatized merely by the fact of their births. Without people over the years like Frederick Douglass, Carter G. Woodson, Vernon Johns, Joseph Charles Price, Martin Luther King, Louis Farrakhan, and others, black people in America would be, and would have historically been, voiceless—allowing their pain to well up and spill over, even more often than it has, to the chagrin of whites. In spite of the criticisms levied against Wright in the 2008 presidential campaign, it is a fact that his voice, like that of the prophet/preachers before him, has served to strengthen African Americans and thus the entire American society, by giving hope to a people who have felt the pain of feeling worthless their entire lives. Sunday morning for African Americans is largely therapeutic and cathartic, and without the therapy and opportunity to let out the pent-up pain, the "seething rage" that Dr. Robert Franklin mentioned, which many African Americans carry with them on a daily basis, the world might be different altogether.

It is troubling that conversation and dialogue about racism in this country is so frowned upon. It is equally troubling that those who have suffered because of America's policies are criticized for being angry. Jewish people do—and should—talk about the Holocaust. The Hebrew Scriptures say that God instructed the Jewish people to tell their story to their children, to "write it as frontlets between their eyes" (Deut. 6:8). But African Americans are criticized for their anger, and one wonders why. Anger, followed by knowledge, is empowering and liberating, which is what Wright instinctively knew. It is a great freedom to be able to accept oneself and not feel bad about having been born black! While Wright's ministry had a great impact on black men, it also had a great impact on black women—and on all of the children. It was liberating to just have kinky hair and forget it . . . and know that it was beautiful. It was liberating to hear that African Americans had been trapped in a Eurocentric world—where Europeans had defined and thus relegated a whole race of people to a low berth.

It was liberating to hear that it was okay to hear that African American history was so rich and deep. It was after hearing Jeremiah Wright that this writer realized that, yes, there had been a Jewish Holocaust, but there had also been an African American holocaust as well. Hearing the history, taking the history out of the closet, made it okay to feel certain things, but also opened the door to feel other things—like self-love and racial pride. Listening to Wright served to inspire African Americans not merely to accept their "lower berth" status in life, but to also to think critically about what had gone on for and to them, so as to be able to fight against it with grace and knowledge. One observer, an African American man, noted:

> The importance of Jeremiah Wright's messaging in this land of lies is simply, it delivers penetrating truth, sometimes with a caustic impact that burns through the façade of worshiping America

> to reveal realities of the past and present. The Christian church itself has largely become a caricature of itself, in both Black and White American societies. Its members are often dutiful followers who share a discontent and disdain for others who don't agree with them, even if those others are professing Christians as well. The church is divided into Black and White experiences that mirror the society, in which it languishes, helplessly watching its messaging becoming ever more irrelevant. And if one does not know the two societies have significantly different experiences, one need only try living in one of the other (Black America or White America) exclusively for a time to discover the profound differences.[4]

The man continues, saying, "Jeremiah Wright looks out over a white American landscape and watches it proclaim this nation and institutions it controls as the model for the world to emulate. He sees a nation that proclaims a generation that was hostile to non-whites as its 'Greatest Generation.' He then looks out over a sea of faces in his own church that have been wounded and disparaged by that same nation and who remain disconnected from its professed opportunities today."[5]

This writer would claim that at Trinity, Wright continued to look out over a sea of faces that still carried the signs of hopelessness that they once had, but certainly, as he has preached elsewhere, he has seen those faces, carrying that "sadness" that Barack Obama noted. A continual diet of Wright's preaching and teaching provides spiritual nutrients to time- and history-worn souls. The fact that racism is still a problem, something people do not want to talk about and that too many preachers avoid, means that there are still too many seas of saddened faces, too many people who are still groping for ultimate meaning in their lives here in America. What Wright noted as a young man, that many African American youth did not know their history, did not know the names and work of African American authors, did not know anything about the Middle Passage and how black people got to America, is still a problem today, but less so than it was, not only because of Wright's preaching, but because his preaching spawned a new generation of preachers and teachers who have internalized the teaching and are teaching it to their members.

Following the horrible experience of 9/11, Wright said that he was "nudged" by God to "touch and treat" some very disturbing verses of Psalm 137 "prayerfully, as many of us try to sort out what it is we are feeling and why it is we are feeling what we feel after the trauma and the tragedy of the attacks on the World Trade Center and the Pentagon. Symbols of who America is: the money and the military."[6] We examined some of those verses in an earlier chapter. What Wright wanted to do in that sermon in particular, but in sermons and teaching in general, was to understand governments and the injustices they perpetrate on the masses—not just our government but all governments, hoping to make people understand why their salvation, hope, and power can only come from God. The Israelites were angry at the Babylonians and wanted revenge, but at the end of the day, they endured their exile, looked to God, and survived. Wright's message is that any oppressed group can do the same thing.

Every single oppressed person—be he or she black, gay, developmentally challenged—is capable of handling oppression if God is in the center of all that person does. It is important to note that, while racism was Wright's starting point, he recognized and taught that all oppression was wrong. The same rules apply to any oppressed group. He admitted having once been homophobic but was "nudged" by God to address that issue and stood up for the rights of the LGBT community in spite of sharp criticism from his members and others. Oppression was and is oppression, and wherever it is, it is wrong. Wright believed that from the core of his being, and he spoke it. In his sermon "The Day Of Jerusalem's Fall" he recognized that those who had been oppressed wanted revenge and realized that modern-day oppressed groups would want the same . . . but at the end of the day, he preached:

> This is a time for social transformation. We, we can't go back to doing business as usual and treating the rest of the world like we've been treating them. This is a time for self-examination. This is a time for social transformation. But, then ultimately, as I looked around and saw that God had given me another chance to try to be the man that God wants me to be, another chance to be the person that God meant for me to be, another chance to

try to be the parent that God knows I should be, another chance to try to make a positive difference in a world full of hate, another chance to teach somebody the difference between our God's awesomeness and our nation's arrogance . . . when I looked around and saw that, for whatever reason, God had let me see another day, I realized that the Lord was showing me that this was not a time for self-examination but this is also a time for spiritual adoration.[7]

There was classic Wright, reminding his listeners of the troubles of the day but also the triumph—the hope—possible if anyone who is oppressed looks to God for help and guidance, and the inference is that as one looks to God, God forces him or her to look to him- or herself. Thus, oppression is jointly fought against by the God of us all, and by the God in us all. Wright did bring the focus back to personal responsibility, the need for personal reflection and personal action, only after he had given a broader definition of what social transformation would look like:

Now is the time for social transformation. We have got to change the way we have been doing things. We have got to change the ways we've been doing things as a society. Social transformation. We have got to change the way we have been doing things as a country. Social transformation. We have got to change the way we have been doing things as an arrogant, racist, military superpower. Social transformation. We just can't keep messing over people and thinking that can't nobody do nothing about it. They have shown us that they can and that they will. And, let me suggest to you that rather than figure out who we're going to declare war on, maybe we need to declare war on racism! Maybe we need to declare war on injustice Maybe we need to declare war on greed! . . . We need to declare war on the healthcare system that leaves a nation's poor with no health coverage. Maybe we need to declare war on the mishandled educational system and provide quality education for everybody, every citizen, based on their ability to earn, not their ability to pay![8]

Those types of challenges, however, needed in order for there to be true social transformation, would come when all people, the oppressed included, had looked to God for strength and power. The underlying message was that no person, as long as there was God, had the right to sit in saucers of despair. Even oppressed people had a duty to work to speak truth to power, for themselves and for society at large.

Wright's ability to minister to the too-often sublimated pain, anger, and disenchantment of African Americans was key to the success of his ministry. His ability to meld biblical stories with present-day realities gave African Americans an anchor to grasp and a means to propel themselves out of despair and into places where they dared hope to be. The racism was and is always there, but with the hope-filled messages of Wright, which validated their perceptions of what went on in their lives on a daily basis, there was enough spiritual propulsion to push them forward.

To critics who said and still say that racism is gone and there is no need to talk about it, reality rebuffed their argument. Even in a day when an African American was elected president of the United States, racism continues to rear its head. The case of Shirley Sherrod, the one-time Georgia State Director of Rural Development who was accused of being racist in remarks she made to the NAACP, is a very recent case in point. Racism, for purposes of this book, isn't just name-calling and bigotry. It is a system of economic and political oppression held by one race over another. According to that definition, there is no way Sherrod could be a racist. That didn't matter, however. When Sherrod was attacked due to the antics of the late conservative media personality Andrew Breitbart, who wanted to disrupt and uproot the presidential bid of Barack Obama, there was the charge that she was being "racist" because in an edited version of remarks she made, it looked as though she was saying she refused to help a white farmer save his farm twenty-four years before.

Though she had not said what had been alleged, though she asked state and, later, federal officials to listen to the entire tape, she was ignored; they would not and did not listen to her side of the story. She was put on administrative leave, and was later asked by the U.S. Secretary of Agriculture, Tom Vilsack, to resign. (Sherrod maintains that it was the

White House who asked her to resign.) It was wrong and she knew it. The Obama administration was walking on thin ice; it didn't want to appear to be "too black," and to defend a woman who had apparently "been racist" would have undercut its credibility. Ignoring the entire economic and political components of racism, the Obama administration apparently feared being accused of showing favoritism to black people. That could not work; the president was to be president of *all* the people.

Breitbart played it right; he intuitively knew that the administration would be forced to take action, and he could help shift the attention of racism off whites and onto blacks. His strategy worked; Sherrod resigned, pulling over to the side of the road and submitting her resignation via her Blackberry. She kept asking her employers to listen to the entire tape, but they did not, and not even the appearance of the white couple to whom she had referred could help her as they explained, on national television, that she had helped them save their land. It was only after she was out of a job that the entire statement she'd made was released. It turned out that she was explaining how she for a moment wrestled with the idea of not helping the white farmer, but did what she knew was right and actually helped the farmer and his wife save their land. The incident, which she explained had happened twenty-four years prior to the airing of the story, helped her understand her own feelings about racism and how to work through them. The White House was embarrassed; she was offered her job back, but she refused. Said Sherrod when asked if racism was still something she'd be talking about in the twenty-first century, she said, "I certainly did not. I thought we would really get beyond this years ago, as we started having more gains during the civil rights movement. I certainly thought we would be beyond this point. It seems we go forward, and we move back. We go forward, and we move back. We dealt with the issues of Jim Crow and segregation, but we didn't deal with the issue of racism, and I don't know how we can ever do that."[9]

Shirley Sherrod knew racism well. She grew up in Newton, Georgia, where her father, Hosie Miller, was fatally shot by a white man, Cal Hall Jr. The two men had apparently had a dispute over cows; Miller was shot in the back and died. There were repeated failures by grand juries to indict Mr. Hall, and the case went cold. There was no justice for her family, but that was common not just in the South but throughout the country.

Sherrod had seen the injustice supported by racism and fought against it her entire life. It was tragic and ironic that she would be booted out of her job, accused of being racist . . . and yet, that was and is the fabric of the lives of many African Americans.

Wright quickly and soundly dispelled the notion that, following Barack Obama's election to the presidency, America was "post-racial." There was still work to do. Black men were still being picked up and thrown into jail for offenses for which whites were let go. He preached that America still has the highest incarceration in the modern world. He implored people to pay attention to economic policies that were helping them to stay in economic slavery; encouraging people not to shop at stores, for example, that had horrid wages for workers with no benefits. He taught them that they were better than that—they deserved better! He made people aware that the Prison Industrial Complex (PIC) is the fastest growing, or one of the fastest growing industries in this nation. If there are more prisons being built, he would remind listeners, then you need to think about who is going to be targeted to fill the cells! He soundly criticized African Americans in positions of power who did little or nothing to help other African Americans. (One of his most frequent targets was United States Supreme Court Justice Clarence Thomas.)

He reminded people to continue to study who they were, to study their history. He continued to teach that injustice anywhere is injustice everywhere; as long as black workers in South Africa were being exploited in order to produce the diamonds that Americans (and the world) likes too much, he taught, there was a need to fight the injustice by not buying diamonds. He taught that the world could not be post-racial if everyone kept doing the same things, accepting what had always been, giving into their material wants at the expense of other people, even if those people happened to be children in a far-away place called South Africa. He took people to Africa so they could *see* the land of their ancestors, see the "Door of No Return" that led from a slave castle in Ivory Coast, see the Christian church that was planted right in the midst of a slave castle. His mission was not over just because Barack Obama had made it to the White House.

When young Trayvon Martin was shot and killed by George Zimmerman, it seemed that Wright's message to listeners to beware of saying

American was "post racial" shot into the forefront of American thought as a truth that could not be ignored. Wright reached the souls of African Americans embittered and angry about the case, with George Zimmerman being acquitted of second-degree murder:

> Wright got the biggest reaction when speaking on the persistence of racism in America, saying that black people are letting those in power tell them racism is over when it is still alive and well in "so-called post-racial America."
>
> "Ask Trayvon Martin's parents if racism is a thing of the past," he said as many in the audience nodded or murmured in agreement. Wright used the coming anniversary of the assassination of Martin Luther King Jr. to remind the audience that King stood for peace and the country's poor. America today, with its "militaristic philosophy," would be King's nightmare, Wright said.
>
> "King is repackaged and made powerful for the people who oppose everything he stood for," Wright said. "We let folks repackage King."[10]

The words of Tim Wise, reflecting on the Trayvon Martin case, were posted on Wright's blog:

> And this is what brings us to the terrifying present, a period of some 155 years later, but during which time it appears there are still far too many in the white community (and even among some persons of color) who would return us to the logic of *Dred Scott.* This they make clear from their hateful and bigoted musings about Trayvon Martin, a 17-year old black male who made the mistake, in their mind, of forgetting that he had no rights which white men (or even Latino white-male wannabes like George Zimmerman) need respect. No right to go where he pleased, "without molestation," no right to be treated like a citizen, indeed like a human being. No rights to due process, to peaceably assemble on a public street, to free speech (which he foolishly tried to exercise by asking his pursuer, Zimmerman, why he was following him) to be free from cruel and unusual

> punishment (such as extra-judicial execution for being black in a hoodie and thus arousing the suspicions of a paranoid negrophobe). No rights at all.
>
> And not even the well-established right to self-defense—the very right Zimmerman would now claim for himself, but which apparently did not extend to the young man whose life he ended. . . . The active and putrescent campaign of defamation now in full swing against this dead child is a reminder of just how little black life matters to some. No matter the facts, their deaths are always justified.[11]

Even now, the "seething rage" at the persistence of racism is palpable. It is not only Trayvon Martin's death that brings home the pain of racism. There are stories about young black men meeting violent deaths at the hands of law enforcement officers daily. Another young African American boy, sixteen-year-old Kimani Gray, was shot and killed by police officers in the Flatbush section of Brooklyn, who said the youth had a gun, but again, there was great suspicion that the police had not been honest and that there would be no justice for Gray's death. Forty-six protesters, peaceful protesters, were arrested. It felt like "the same old thing," and frustration built among blacks. Blacks rioted in Los Angeles after the late Rodney King was brutally attacked by white police officers, an attack caught on video, which still did not result in those officers being disciplined.

Few African Americans have confidence in the American justice system. There is a sense in African American communities that police just do not care. This writer experienced a situation in Columbus, Ohio, where during a community event, shots rang out. Women with little babies in strollers were seen scurrying, dropping packages in their quest to find safety for themselves and their children. Mothers near a station where free produce was being given out were heard to say to their children, "Get down, get down." Older women prayed out loud . . . but in all of the confusion, *no police ever came.* This writer asked if police were called, and the answer was, "Yes, three times." One woman said, "I called 911 and got a recording." Later, the women gathered together, furious. "If this had happened in a different zip code," one said, "the police would have been here, and not just one police car, either. There would have been SWAT units, a helicopter—the full brigade.

As she spoke, a tear ran down her cheek. "They don't care about us," she said. "They just don't care."

The rage bubbles beneath the surface of all that seems calm, quiet, and changed, because those who live in urban areas know that, for them, very little has changed. If there are not voices for the voiceless, the rage will bubble up and boil over. The ministry of Jeremiah Wright can rightfully be credited with addressing some of that rage and helping people divert it into positive energy. His voice, and others like it, are still sorely needed.

Wright's foundation for all he does and teaches is theological, but the very theology that is part of the foundation for Wright and was the foundation for others, including Martin Luther King, is frequently under attack by some white people. Former Fox News host Glenn Beck is reported to have said in 2012 that liberation theology, which Beck called "black liberation theology," is "the theological tradition based in hate, intolerance and black nationalism."[12] Such pronouncements by those who have no interest in knowing what works to empower the oppressed take a special place in the spirits of people who are tired of having others decide what is good for them, and what they believe. James Cone, who is generally considered to be the father of liberation theology, says that this theology is "an interpretation of the Christian gospel from the experience and perspectives and lives of people who are at the bottom of society—the lowest economic and racial groups."[13] Yet another theologian, Shannon Crago-Snell, says that "liberation theology, at its most simple, is the Sunday school Jesus who healed the sick or took care of the poor people. . . . It isn't something people should be afraid of unless they're invested in poor people not getting fed or sick people not getting healed."[14]

Wright knows and preaches liberation theology, though he acknowledges that he does not agree with everything Cone says, but understanding the theology and the impetus behind it might have helped take some of the panic and angst out of whites who heard the clips of Wright's sermons in 2008. Black liberation theology was always at the core, in the foundations, of black preaching and speaking. The God that blacks came to know was a God of justice, a God who did not approve of the powerful trampling on the lives of the poor. In July of 1966, fifty-one black pastors put a formal name on what had been being preached for a long time. They took out a full-page ad in the *New York Times* "demanding a more aggressive approach to eradicating racism."[15]

In his sermon "The Audacity to Hope," Wright drew upon the tenets of liberation theology to offer to his listeners his belief that God, who had been misused by organized religion in order to justify and sanction not only discrimination against blacks, but against women, Jews, and the LGBT community, offered hope to all, no matter who they might be. Thus, God, and God in Jesus, transcended traditional religious values and beliefs, which have done so much to keep discrimination in place. God was who people were to listen to, Wright preached, because God, not religion, gave hope. He tells the story of Hannah in this sermon, describing Hannah as a woman devoid of hope because what she had always wanted had been denied her: a child. Wright drew his listeners into the story, because he knew that all people, no matter how religious they might be, feel, at times, the loneliness of hopelessness. He preached:

> What Hannah wanted most out of life had been denied to her. Think about that. Yet, in spite of that, she kept on hoping. The gloating of Peninnah did not make her bitter. She kept on hoping. When the family made its pilgrimage to the sanctuary at Shiloh, she renewed her petition there, pouring out her heart to God. She may have been barren, but that's a horizontal dimension. She was fertile in her spirit, her vertical dimension. She prayed and she prayed and she prayed and she kept on praying, year after year. With no answer, she kept on praying. She prayed so fervently in this passage that Eli thought she had to be drunk. There was no visible sign on the horizontal level to indicate to Hannah that her praying would ever be answered. Yet, she kept on praying. And Paul said something about that, too. No visible sign? He says, "Hope is what saves us, for we are saved by hope. But hope that is seen is not hope. For what a man sees, why does

he have hope for it. But if we hope for that which we see not [no visible sign], then do we with patience wait for it."[16]

The message was not lost on the congregation. One had to be liberated from all that had worn one's spirit down over time in order to hope. Wright used illustrations in the sermon that spoke of various situations requiring hope—like broken marriages or people strung out on drugs or sex or money. No matter how dire one's situation, Wright preached, if one could hold onto hope, one could survive and eventually thrive. Hannah had been denied the one thing she wanted most; African Americans, in spite of being religious, had been denied the thing they wanted most—dignity, fairness, and a level playing field. In terms of what America offered, the "American dream," too many African Americans were far from it and many felt trapped in lives that would never help them to even be in position to reach for the dream. Discriminatory practices in hiring made it difficult for black men to support their families the way they wanted to, and made the lives of single-parent households sometimes insufferable. But Wright drove the point home: that if the people could hold onto hope, one could make it up and out of the cultural and societal doldrums that had bound them for so long. He urged his listeners to keep looking up—to God, the vertical dimension of their lives—rather than straight on at their horizontal levels. The message literally inspired people from despair to hope, just in that time of listening.

Because racism is not yet gone, and because America has been reluctant to even talk about it, it remains an unresolved issue in this country and there is still a need for the prophetic voice of Jeremiah Wright. As we have already mentioned, many to most of the people who sat in Wright's pews while he was pastor at Trinity United Church of Christ had tasted and experienced personally the peculiar type of racial hatred directed toward them as they grew up in the South, and others had experienced it perhaps more subtly in other ways, especially after the Great Migration. And it appears that most African Americans suffered from the effects of racism, even if they said they had not personally experienced it. These people were all a part of Wright's generation and before.

Even though many people would not talk about their experiences with racism (in many families it was taboo to talk about, and in white communities, people who brought up incidents of racism were accused of "stirring up" the people, an act which could get one killed), most of them knew what it looked like and felt like. Little African American girls grew up thinking they were ugly because they did not look white, and little black boys "got it" early on that life would be harder for them and that they should be careful, because the "good policemen" were not always so good, so nice, or so fair with black people. As much as black parents wanted to believe that the threats to their lives due to racism were a thing of the past, they knew it was not true. To be black in America was and still is, unfortunately, a liability.

The author Richard Wright, who grew up in Mississippi in the 1920s, was just one of many black boys who learned the ugliness of racism. There were four pivotal events that happened in his life, which helped him shape what it meant to be black in America: the murder of his uncle, seeing a chain gang, a friend of his getting him a job in Jackson, and later on-the-job conflicts he had in Memphis. Wright's mother tried to shield from him the ugliness of racism, much as had the parents of Jeremiah Wright, but when Richard Wright's uncle was killed by whites only because they wanted a part of his liquor business, the reality of the power of racism hit him in ways he never forgot. When he saw a chain gang and noticed there were not any whites, he asked his mother why and she reportedly said that "whites are just harder on black people."[17]

That was the message given to many black children. Children, even in the twentieth century, reported being sorely disappointed and hurt by white teachers who put them down or ignored them. This writer had a white teacher who ignored her hand waving frantically because she wanted to go to the bathroom. After waving her arm in the air for the longest time, this writer just ended up not being able to hold it, and relieved herself in her seat. It caused extreme humiliation, and some anger, because the white students in the class who raised their hands were always called up and were always allowed to go to the bathroom. Black children were passed over for solo parts in glee club performances, and they began to understand why. Some of those children may never have talked with anyone about their experiences in school but held the results of being discriminated against in their hearts.

Those people made up part of Jeremiah Wright's flock. It may very well be that black people in general ended up cultivating a "false self" as described by David Benner. People of all races and ethnicities are guilty of doing this, according to Benner, but because African Americans wanted so desperately to be accepted as equal, to have access to "the American dream," it may be that this group of people, more than any other, developed a "false self" in order to survive in a country that used their labor and skills but did not particularly want them as citizens or neighbors. According to Benner, people who live with the "false self" get their security and significance by what they have or can do, and by what others think of them. One who cultivates a false self seeks happiness autonomously, apart from God; one's identity is one's idealized self, which is defined as who one wants others to think one is. The person living in and with a false self gets that sense of self by pretense and practice, the false self is maintained by effort and control, and the person embraces illusion as a means of attempting to become a god.[18] There was definite pressure in my neighborhood, at least, to "act right," which was a euphemism meaning that we were to act as white as possible because it would help us get farther along. Many African Americans, because of racism, were forced to live with a "false self."

So Jeremiah Wright, knowing that, helped release people from mental slavery. The physical release from slavery meant nothing as long as the minds and spirits of the people were still in chains. Being released from that pressure, ironically, helped release the possibility and capacity for hatred and bitterness to spill over. Howard Thurman said hatred cannot be described; it can only be defined, but he wrote: "Hatred, in the mind and spirit of the disinherited, is born out of great bitterness—a bitterness that is made possible by sustained resentment which is bottled up until it distills an essence of vitality, giving to the individual in whom this is happening a radical and fundamental for self-realization."[19]

"Hatred becomes the way by which one defines him- or herself, writes Thurman. "Hatred becomes for you a source of validation for your personality."[20] Hatred becomes a way for the disinherited to get a sense of significance—a false self, so to speak. Because they are despised, says Thurman, they despise themselves.[21] Thus, the preacher/prophet has a behemoth job before him or her. The word and will of God must be preached and people held accountable, but at the same time, that same word and will of God must be able to penetrate hardened souls.

Wright was able to that. His message was powerful and unique, empowering and liberating, fit for young, old, and in-between. There was a special brilliance that seeped through everything he preached and taught, so that whoever was listening would be able to benefit. Said one of the members:

> What made the Trinity experience so awesome to me was that I had never seen or heard of a worship experience that was so engaging to so many different types/ages of congregants. For example, it was so crazy at one point in the old church that we were doing a service on Saturday night, and four on Sunday (8:00 a.m., 10:00 a.m., Noon and 6:00 p.m.) I remember when Rev had to start preaching the SAME sermon at each service just so that people would go home and free up seats for the next service."
>
> When he preached different sermons in each of those sermons, these (members) would NOT leave! LOL! They would stay in those seats and people couldn't get in for the next service. Who ever heard of such fervor???? When have we ever heard of church worship affecting people like that? I know I have never seen or heard of anything like it.
>
> My Dad was never that big on anybody's church or preachers in general. One day, he started going on and on about Trinity and this Rev. Wright. He started bringing home tapes, going to church every Sunday and kept trying to get me to listen to these tapes of Rev. Wright that he was buying like crazy. I remember thinking who is this Rev. Wright and what the heck is going on over there on 95th Street? What have they done to my father? Why is he trying so hard to get me over there? Well, long story short, I went to visit to find out what had taken over my father's mind! Shoot, I ended up joining before he and my mother did!!![22]

What this member mentions was true. It was nothing to hear Wright, in the middle of perhaps the most engaging theological discourse, break out into a contemporary R&B song or rap; in so doing, he thrilled those listening and was able to draw them even more deeply into the theological lesson he was trying to teach. His use of music was intentional; it was an amazing tool to get all ages engaged. One sat with a sense of awe that he could know so much about so many things in ways that would enable him to connect with as many people as possible. His use of contemporary music also allowed people to know that being "religious" didn't mean that one had to cut oneself off from the things in pop culture that they loved. He made it understood that all things were created from and created by God; therefore, to use what God had allowed to be created, especially if it made people more curious, serious, and intentional about knowing what God said and God wanted, was a good thing. It was amazing to watch.

Wright could be talking about Moses at the Red Sea one moment and break out into a song by the Four Tops the next. The congregation would go up in flames, everyone singing along. There was total engagement—and then, while they were so engaged, Wright would skillfully lead them back into the scriptural message, the Bible story, that was being presented to them. It was brilliant. Here was a man who could and would use whatever tools God provided to bring people closer to God and give them a hunger to want to serve God.

The use of music also helped to dissipate the anger felt by many African Americans over the way they'd been treated in America. Yes, he'd remind them of what the country had done to them. They needed to know that. But he would, through using music in conjunction with the word of God, draw their attention away from what they could not change to the things they *must* change, like dealing with gangs, pulling those young men into the fold of Christ, not putting them or pushing them out "in the name of Jesus." He needed for people to understand that God was love . . . they could be reminded of romantic love through the singing of a pop hit, followed by an old hymn of the church, which reminded them of God's love . . . and then, he'd direct them to use the love they craved (romantic) with the love that they needed (God's love) to draw people to the Christ. Thus, middle class and upper middle class, lower middle class and poor were drawn to his ministry. The very young looked forward to hearing what "Rev" was going to say next; the very old, perhaps tainted by life and tired out by it, would come to hear what this young man would say, whose words were an elixir, it seemed, to those who had long given up on expecting their lives to change.

Wright would use biblical illustrations to drive points home, but he would also single out members in his congregation who were living lives he believed God would be pleased with. In a sermon entitled "Good News for Good Parents," Wright taught that his congregation needed to know what a good parent was, and he made no bones about going to examples of what he believed bad parenting to be . . . but he also then made a point of using some Trinity members to show the contrast:

> We hear so much news about bad parents. We hear so many instances of bad parenting and poor choices made by parents. We hear so many people hiding behind the cop-out "Well, I ain't never been a parent before," as if that exonerates them somehow from the criticism they so richly deserve for some poor decisions they have made. We are always hearing about bad parents: absentee daddies and abusive mommies, daddies who drink too much and mommies who work too much, daddies with two or three chicks on the side and mommies with "cousins" who keep saying, "You can't miss what you can't measure." We're always hearing about bad parents who had no time for their children, who kept the streets hot and let love die; parents who robbed their children of their heritage and history and kept their children away from their grandparents; parents who robbed their children of a religious upbringing; parents who confused their children by saying one thing and doing another, promising one thing and never delivering on their promises. . . .
>
> We are always hearing horror story after horror story about bad parents, sexually abusive parents, spouse-abusing parents, parents who were kids when they had kids and now that their kids are grown up, they're still kids—grown kids—trying to look younger, act younger, and sleep younger than their own grown kids. We are always hearing so much about the bad par-

> ents that we ignore God's word for those who are trying to be good parents.
>
> I see Val and Ethel Jordan, who raised all their children in the church. They didn't send them; they brought them. Good parents. I see Mike and Cheryl Brown. I see Michael and Carol Jacobs. They are *with* their children in church every Sunday. Good parents. I see my mama and my daddy, who helped us with homework and taught us to do housework; who took us to Sunday school and BTU; who took the time to teach us the Word of God at home; who introduced us to the Lord and showed us how to pray; who proved to us that when you call on the Lord you will get an answer; who drilled into us that God cares, God hears, God can, and God is. Good parents.[23]

It was Wright's unique gift to be able to show compassion to whomever was in the congregation; he was attuned to the fact that many in the African American community felt the criticism by society for being single parents, and yet, he knew, many single parents did amazing jobs, with little or no support. In that same sermon, Wright took note of them: "I also see many single parents who are good parents. I see Pierre, a single daddy, raising his family in the fear and admonition of the Lord. I see Elizabeth and Brenda, Janet and Jeri, I see Denise and Leslie—fathers and mothers who have learned how to trust the Lord and take him at his word. Good parents."[24]

What was remarkable was that Wright was calling names out of a congregation not made up of forty or fifty members, but by that time, having more than thirty-five hundred members! He had an amazing gift of being able to make people feel personally important to him. No matter where he was in the world, he was in contact with his members. Members were known to get personal letters from him even when he was as far away as South Africa. Members got personal letters for the milestones in their lives; they got personal letters encouraging them when they or a family member fell on hard times. It seemed that nothing escaped him, and the members, in spite of the huge membership, bonded closer to him, to God, and with each other because of his gift of being a pastor.

That must have made it easier for his members to receive the hard lessons he knew he had to bring to them. Yes, Wright talked about the havoc American culture had wrought in the lives of African Americans, but he also identified and addressed the havoc that African Americans brought on themselves. In the same sermon quoted earlier, he preached:

> Good parents not only take seriously the responsibility of shaping character, they take seriously the responsibility of sharing crises. When crises come into our children's lives, we too often brush them aside as unimportant or trivial. So often we do untold damage that will take years to repair. We need to share in our children's crises. I don't mean just the major trauma that can lead to antisocial behavior; I mean crises of identity and crises of personality development. The world tells them something different from what you've been telling them. That creates a crisis. You are trying to raise your child one way, telling your daughter one thing, and then some little hard-legged boy whispers something else in her ear, and all the while the hormones are raging. You've got a crisis in your home. When you are telling your son that this is what it takes to be a man, and his partners are telling something else (peer pressure is a pistol) you've got a crisis in your home.[25]

Wright shepherded his flock with a tough tenderness and a love that was noticeable. He pushed them to embrace their African American identities, but would not let them slip into barrels of self-pity or debilitating anger. In the name of the God who had brought them thus far, they had work to do. And so his messages were laced with cultural and historical information, biblical lessons . . . and practical instruction on how they should live their lives as African Americans. He said to them, for example, that they as African American parents had huge responsibilities to parent their children in a way that would equip them to handle the challenges of their world. It was their responsibility. Oppression, racism, discrimination—none of that excused them from their responsibilities as men, women, spouses, and parents.

Wright's personal illustrations in his sermons had immense power because they (1) showed he was willing and able to present himself as no better than anyone else; that he hadn't always been a preacher and in fact had been quite far away from being a theological poster child, and (2) engaged the audience, his listeners, on a personal level, allowing them to laugh, allowing them to see a fuller dimension of their pastor, and forcing them to look at themselves. The lessons Wright taught were usually hard lessons, things people might not necessarily want to hear, but once they were able to meld biblical lessons with laughter and a sense of being connected with their very human pastor, the lessons were more easily accepted.

What was being offered was not just a lot of religious rhetoric or dribble. It was food, spiritual food and water for spirits that had long been dried out and famished. Wright offered his members the opportunity and privilege to embrace "everlasting life" or, more accurately, "new life" while they were yet alive. They didn't have to wait to die in order to experience a sense of power and peace. They had an opportunity to experience heaven and God while alive, if they would listen, if they would learn from their pain, put their experiences in perspective, which was easier as they understood the cultural, social, and historical factors that they had been dealing with without even knowing it, and if they would be willing to let God turn their mourning into dancing, as the prophet Isaiah preached that God would do.[26]

That Wright preached lessons of hope and empowerment in the twentieth and twenty-first centuries and was not ashamed or afraid of bringing the reality of racism front and center is central in understanding the power of his work. He would not listen to the myths that said racism was gone; he would not bow to the desire of some that he leave well enough alone. Regardless of what politicians and even other religious leaders would say, criticizing him for being so bold in his denouncement of racism as a cultural and historical reality, he dealt daily with people who lived it. In an article in *The Christian Post* entitled "Black and White and Red All Over: Why Racial Justice Is a Gospel Issue," author Russell D. Moore wrote in 2012:

> One of my earliest memories is of a substitute Sunday school teacher in my Southern Baptist church chastening me for putting a coin in my mouth. "That's filthy," she said. "Why, you don't know if a colored man might have held that." It might just be

my imagination playing tricks on me, but it seems as though she immediately followed this up with, "Alright children, let's sing 'Jesus Loves the Little Children, All the Children of the World.'"

Now, this lady probably didn't consciously think of herself as a white supremacist. She almost certainly didn't think of herself as subversive of the gospel itself. She never thought about the hypocrisy of holding two contradictory worldviews in her mind. She probably didn't see how her dehumanizing of African Americans was a twisted form of Darwinism rather than biblical Christianity.[27]

Moore makes a compelling argument in this article that the civil rights movement created a dilemma for religious people. "Politically, Americans had to choose: be American (as defined in the Constitution and the Declaration of Independence) or be white supremacist; you can't be both."[28] Governmental powers, likewise, had to choose, said Moore: be a Christian (as defined by the Scripture and the small "c" apostolic tradition) or be a white supremacist; you can't be both.[29] The whole black-white gridlock, or the gridlock caused by the white power structure wanting to maintain absolute power over black people, had a religious dimension that some knew of and many did not—but a dimension, nonetheless that was going to have to be reckoned with. According to Moore, "How can white supremacy be true . . . if humanity is made from 'one blood' in the creation of Adam? How can one segregate evangelistic crusades if the cross of Christ atones for all people, both white and black? If God personally regenerates repentant sinners, both white and black, how can we see people in terms of 'race' rather than in terms of the person? If we send missionaries across the seas to evangelize Africa, how is it not hypocrisy not to admit African Americans into church membership?"[30]

While many black and white theologians, preachers, and pastors ignored the obvious contradiction between the written gospel and the practice of that gospel, Wright did not. He met it head-on; it was, after all, a Goliath for his people. The God he loved had been boxed into a religion that kept black people a safe distance away from God, arrogantly suggesting, if not saying outright, that the Bible ordained and sanctioned it. Such a contradictory message was confusing and debilitating to a great many people, and Wright sought to correct what he saw as a blatant misrepresentation of God's good news.

Thus, in spite of us being in the twenty-first century, Wright's voice and message are still relevant, still needed, and still timely.

15

A TRAGEDY OF SHAKESPEAREAN PROPORTIONS

Men at some time are masters of their fates:
The fault, dear Brutus, is not in our stars, but
in ourselves, that we are underlings.

—SHAKESPEARE, *JULIUS CAESAR*

At the end of the day, what happened to Jeremiah Wright and to the relationship between him and Barack Obama can only be seen as a tragedy of Shakespearean proportion.

Wright, for scores of oppressed peoples, African American and others as well, was a hero. He had heeded his call—as had the prophet Isaiah—to "proclaim good news to the poor. He has sent me to bind up the brokenhearted, *to proclaim freedom for the captives and release from darkness for the prisoners . . .*" (Isa. 61:1–20; italics mine). The pastor/preacher/prophet effectively did just that by stepping far away from the norm of preaching heard in the black church. Because of his prophetic preaching, people were freed from beliefs that had caused them to remain enslaved in spite of the Emancipation Proclamation. And as Wright knew, no temporal freedom was or is possible if one's mind is held captive.

Blacks were held captive by white supremacy and by the attendant hatred, racism, and discrimination that came with it. God was good; black people knew that. But black people needed to find their place in the world and specifically, in this country—which was founded on the words "all men are created equal." Blacks believed that this equality also applied to them, but history showed otherwise. The equality Jefferson and the other founding fathers spoke of was for white, land-owning males. Not even women were included. The myth of equality was the point of contention, not only for Wright, but for preachers and prophets before him. Frederick Douglass, Rev. Martin Luther King, and countless others, quoted the precious words. Historically, there had been an outcry for myth to meld into reality, for the two to become one, but it had not, and Wright saw the discrepancy and dealt with it, head-on.

Somehow, Wright had to meld politics and religion. The questions were, "Where was God in a racist world?" and "Why was God allowing racism and hatred and overt discrimination and bigotry to survive?" Historically, God had ignored hatred. God had allowed more than six million Jews to be murdered by a demagogue named Adolph Hitler. God's inaction and silence, however, didn't make white supremacy in America any easier to take.

In order for blacks to get to God and be empowered by God, they had to be free. Wright's ministry, therefore, sought to free blacks culturally, socially, and politically. Then they would spiritually be free. Wright was a hero. Wright was a hero of Shakespearean proportion because he sought—and succeeded—in freeing scores of African Americans from mental slavery. This was brought to a horrible crash, however, in the light of the 2008 presidential election.

In college, this writer learned that Shakespearean tragedies had certain qualities. One quality was that a hero is a person of high estate who is brought low. The hero experiences a reversal of fortune that arouses all kinds of emotions in the audience or reader of the play, emotions including fear, anger, and pity. Much of what happens to the hero hinges on chance, and the central impression of the hero's life is one of waste. The great Shakespearean tragedies include *Macbeth, Othello, King Lear,* and *Hamlet*. In each of these tragedies, this writer felt a sense of sadness for the hero because he had "fallen." My professors were adept at pointing out the flaw of each hero, perhaps to make his fall more palatable, but for me, it was not. It was just sad.

Jeremiah Wright was, and is, a hero for people who have needed help to loose themselves from white supremacy, not only in the United States but also in Africa and Cuba. For them, he was and is a great man. He is a hero. He is a person who risked being criticized and ostracized because he spoke the truth as he had known it, lived it, and as he had seen people experience it. His goal was to free them—and he did. Thus, to see him pulverized by a media hungry for ratings and by a political campaign hungry for a historic victory, was to watch him get slapped in the face and spit upon. He knew far too many African Americans could not fully sing Lee Greenwood's "I'm Proud to be an American." Yes, African Americans *were* American; they had built much of this nation and were and are responsible for America's thriving economy, in large measure. But still, African Americans were not free, as Greenwood's lyrics described. African Americans were America's stepchildren; a group of people who had been used and then criticized for resenting being used and denied full rights of American citizenship. For the most part, African Americans could not truthfully sing they were proud to be an American, *"where at least I know I'm free"*[1] (italics mine). Yes, it was good to be an American, but African Americans were American in name only. Not even being American citizens was enough to guarantee justice and equal opportunity.

Thus, throughout his ministry, Wright worked to empower and inspire all African Americans who had historically borne the brunt of racism's injustice. Under his leadership, young African American men came off the streets and into the church, only to return to their communities with a new-found sense of themselves and their worth. Wright, who, as you remember, was disappointed by how little black history was known by African Americans, dedicated his life to teaching them about African Americans whom God had made, who had done great things, and who had beaten the odds. His was a ministry of inspiration and hope. Wright reminded all his listeners, but especially youth, that they had been given much and were required to give much back. Young boys became fascinated as they listened to Wright preach about the Bible, then heard him communicate with them in their "street" language, then discuss his thoughts about the latest R&B, rap, and/or hip-hop song. They saw a role model the likes of which few of them had seen before. They were taught not only about the injustice that was going on in America, but also about the injustice all over the world. They knew people such as Nelson Mandela, Steve Biko, and Archbishop Desmond Tutu. On any given Sunday, they might see some well-known celebrity grace the sanctuary of Trinity UCC. People—like the Staples Singers, Kirk Whalum, or Gladys Knight—who amazed the world were really not far away from them. They were taught African American literature and poetry. They performed in annual oratorical contests, learned how to present themselves in the public arena, and also became aware of the wealth of talent within their own culture that they simply had not been taught.

Wright had a passion for people; all people, yes, but especially for his people. He groomed and prepared them to go out into the world and meet their difficulties head on because they had been taught that God would surely help them through it. Never was God out of the picture. Without God, there could be no triumph over the evil of racism. Wright taught them that it was okay to be a Christian. Moreover, he taught it was *good* to be a Christian. Jesus, he taught, was as powerful a savior as anyone could want, and it wasn't necessary to migrate to Islam to feel empowered. (He had no issue with Islam, however.)

Wright taught African Americans to love themselves, to love God, and to love their race, to throw down the shackles of shame, and to stop believing the stereotypes that just because they were black, they were "less than." "Different does not mean deficient," he would say throughout his ministry and, indeed, still says to this day. He taught young males the definition of being men, of being fathers, differentiating between making babies and raising children. He taught them that a man could be sensitive and strong at the same time. In everything he said and taught, he pulled people toward a God who really did not have any favorites, as the Bible said. African Americans should not hold their heads down but instead, high. He taught them about the African origin of biblical people; he taught that the Cushites and Hittites and the other ethnic groups mentioned in the Bible lived in Africa, and not in Italy or on the shores of the Mediterranean. With every sermon—even with critiques of American policies that affected black people and other oppressed groups—Wright had sound teaching to dispel misconceptions and leave people with a sense of pride and a desire to know about who and *whose* they were.

He was "Rev" to the young people; he could be seen joking and bantering with them, but he was a father figure to many. He knew many of them were being raised by single mothers, and he knew the value of having a strong male presence in one's life. The young boys and the older boys flocked to him; in him there was security, there were answers, there was encouragement and a demand that they be the best they could.

Wright taught them that they could be religious and still be cool. For many it seemed that if one was religious, one was already at a disadvantage in a city filled with gangs, daring young men to stand up for themselves. But they could come to Wright and talk to him about not wanting to be in a gang. They could be reassured that Wright would guide them on how to keep their hands in God's hand and be assured they would have the strength to resist the temptation and the threats presented to them on the streets of Chicago.

He asked the parents of the young people to whom he ministered to tell them their history, an admonition not unlike that given to the Israelites in Deuteronomy where Moses said, "Keep these words that I am commanding you today in your heart. Recite them to your children and talk about them when you are at home and when you are away, when you lie down and when you rise. Bind them as a sign on your hand, fix them as an emblem on your forehead, and write them on the doorposts of your house and on your gates" (Deut. 6:6–90). Indeed, even as little babies were brought to the altar to be dedicated to God, Wright reminded the parents and godparents:

> The circular shape of this wristlet suggests continuity and infinity. It represents the sacred link, the *Sasa*, which means the present, with the *Zamani*, which is the past! This wristlet is an ever constant reminder to this child that he/she is a descendant of a people who have a rich spiritual and cultural heritage. We did not begin in slavery! We began on the shores of Africa! We began at the beginning of time! We began when civilization first dawned, and God breathed into the nostrils of humankind God's own breath and we became living souls!

This wristlet shows our connectedness to the past and our hope for God's future! Your child(ren) and godchild(ren) will not remember this day, but we encourage you to begin today to tell him/her of the commitment that you have made; of the rededication of your lives that you have made; of the importance of the African American community and the Church which the Lord Jesus Christ gave his life for, and of the prayers said on his/her behalf, this day!"[2]

Gently, yet consciously and persistently, the people whom Howard Thurman called "the disinherited" were brought into the presence of a loving God who, in spite of what the world said to them and about them, loved them and expected great things from them. Like the parents of the Israelite parents were instructed to do, Wright instructed the parents to do something differently, to ingest the truth of their own inherent worth and value and to pass it onto the children. As the little babies in the dedication services were given small amounts of salt, pepper, water, vinegar, and honey, and then finally anointed with oil, one could almost see the history of a people who had endured the scourge of racial discrimination being written as an emblem, "as frontlets," between their eyes.

It is not a surprise that Wright reached the tall, lanky community organizer who aspired to be a politician. It is not surprising that Barack Obama gravitated toward Wright, listened to his messages, and received his teaching. Wright took the time with young people that so many others did not, would not, or could not. He was inspiring, his knowledge was so vast, and yet he was down to earth. It was what the young man who had a white mother and an African father needed in order to navigate the waters of racial discrimination in Chicago. Obama needed guidance. He needed instruction and he needed someone to help him understand the things he would not have been able to quickly understand. Further, as his aspiration to be a politician became apparent, Barack Obama needed someone with connections to help him get started.

It is safe to say that had it not been for the presence of Wright in Obama's life, his ascendancy might not have been as rapid. Why? Because of the confidence Wright instilled in young people as he taught them "who" they were and "whose" they were. Wright didn't demand that a person dispose of or diminish his or her intelligence in order to be "right" with God. On the contrary, he taught that God had given such intelligence so that people would use it for the building of the realm of God. Wright would have been able to help Obama understand what he must in order to organize communities around issues of social justice; social justice was one of the components of Trinity UCC's mission statement. Yes, it is quite safe to say that had it not been for the presence of Wright in Obama's life, his ascendancy to political power might not have been as rapid.

Thus, the tragedy was that as Obama was at the point of running for president of the United States, the relationship between the two men was shattered, manipulated by media overkill of Wright's sermon clips in an effort to derail Obama's campaign. Obama's ascendancy was, it seemed, Wright's prototype of what he had worked for his whole life—to get African American men to realize their worth and power and go for it. Obama had done that. He admired his pastor and gave him much credit for where he was. But the media was ruthless in painting Wright as one who was "incendiary" and "divisive," not good qualities for the pastor of a would-be president. Obama, ever the politician, ended up denouncing his pastor, who in large part was responsible for where he was.

It was a tragedy of Shakespearean proportion.

Not only was the media dismantling a relationship between two powerful men, it was also attacking Wright's life's work. His entire ministry was being called into question; it was being demonized, and he was being described as some out-of-touch lunatic. The characterization was wrong, but those seeking political victory did not care. Obama had to be stopped, and if Wright was the tool to do it, then so be it. Wright was attacked not only by white people, who perhaps feared him, but he was attacked by black people, some of whom he had helped along the way in their careers. It became uncomfortable to be associated with Wright; those who wanted to be in cahoots with the president saw their chances slipping away. Some of the most scathing words and attacks against Wright were brought by black people.

In Shakespeare's tragedies, good men are brought down by their flaws. In some plays, it's the quest for power that brings a man down, in others, it's greed or jealousy or naiveté. To this writer, what brought Wright down was not any of those. Indeed, after a very powerful interview with Bill Moyers and a presentation at the NAACP Annual Convention in 2008, many people who had been bothered by the sound bites had been quieted. Wright, it seemed, spoke a truth, an unpleasant truth, but a truth nonetheless. They were able to see him as a human being with sound opinion and much scholarship.

It was the presentation at the National Press Club that provided the ax to fell Wright's career. Where the Moyers interview had presented Wright as a complex human being with many dimensions, his appearance at the National Press Club led people to see him as an object and not as a person. His presentation on the black church was stirring and stimulating, but the moderator seemed not to have heard and instead went on the attack for those now infamous sound bites.

But the flaw that got in Wright's way on that day was anger. The seething anger I have talked about in this book—the anger that lies just below the surface—reared its head. It wasn't just anger at the young moderator at the Press Club. It was built-up anger, similar to that of many blacks, an anger that exists because of the capacity and tendency of some white people to see African Americans as objects and not as human beings with feelings who deserve dignity. The very thing Wright had sought to teach people to control and put into other avenues, was the thing that was seen that day—and rightfully so—in April 2008. The moderator's dismissal of Wright's speech and her choice to hone in on the political turmoil for the Obama camp caused by the sermon sound clips brought on the anger. Once it started, it kept coming. It was painful to watch, but those of us who knew Wright knew exactly what it was. There was the familiar arrogance that African Americans have sensed and borne from white people throughout history, staring him and his supportive audience in the face.

It is important to note that America has seemingly always had a problem with African Americans being angry. The notion of African Americans being angry seems to frighten much of white America. Even after the election, many reporters and pundits watched uneasily to see if Obama would turn out to be an "angry black man." Even though there is more than enough reason for the anger to exist, America has resisted acknowledging and affirming that anger. The sense and the sentiment has been that racism "used to be," that black people can do anything they want. As segregation has become less and less the reality in America, far too many have shrugged their shoulders and have wondered out loud why African Americans continue to complain. What they don't understand is that racism, this "spirit of racism," has never gone away. Bandaids have been put on gaping emotional and spiritual wounds.

Martin Luther King became an "angry black man," wrote John Blake of CNN, when he was cooped up in a Birmingham jail and read an ad that had been placed in a newspaper by white clergy. White clergy were angry and disturbed that King continued to push against the current of society, pressing for equality and dignity for African Americans.[3] They called King an outsider and an agitator and they wanted him to stop what he was doing, go away, and let the process of gaining equality take its course. These clergy were not arch-conservatives; they were *moderate*. They were of the group that King and others thought would understand and support the struggle that was going on. But instead, these ministers were critical of King's work. Their ad made King angry, yes, but that anger was not something that just appeared, as Blake suggests. It was always there. The supposition by white America that African Americans have complained and whined with no reason, and that they should be content with what they have, has always been insulting. King merely let his irritation and anger out in the form of his famous "Letter from a Birmingham Jail," but the notion that he "became" an angry black man is as ludicrous as it is erroneous.

Wright knew, as did King, Tutu, and others who have fought racism, that opposing racism is and was about justice. Indeed, Bishop Desmond Tutu wrote in *God Is Not a Christian: And Other Provocations* that opposing not only racism, but apartheid, discrimination against women, or discrimination against people on the basis of sexual orientation—are all matters of justice, as well as love.[4] Tutu wrote that "there can be no superior or inferior race. We are all born of equal worth."[5] That's the message Wright drove home to those who heard him; whether the audience was black, white, or mixed, Wright's message stayed the same.

Yes, Wright was pushing against the current of American mores and beliefs that produced anger. Although that anger is being called a flaw, it is only a flaw in the eyes of white America. Righteous anger is and has been necessary to fight discrimination of all kinds. Without it, things may not have changed for African Americans, as Frederick Douglass said: "power concedes nothing without a struggle." Anger at an oppressive British government was the impetus that resulted in the struggle called the Revolutionary War . . . which led to the freedom and independence of Americans. Frankly, it is puzzling that anybody can expect any less outrage from a group that is being oppressed or discriminated against. Thus, the flaw that reared its ugly head at the National Press Club in 2008, righteous anger, was seized upon and Wright was further vilified. His anger, however, like that of the prophets before him, was precisely the "flaw" that had helped bring about social change.

Wright's angry retorts to the Press Club moderator were justified, yet it was sad for Wright and sad for Obama who, as a politician, had to cut himself off from his pastor in order to win the election. It was also extremely sad for those who knew Wright's work and understood how that work had gotten Obama, or at least had helped get Obama, to where he was.

The spirit of racism exists. Even as this book goes to print, America still wrestles with that spirit that pervades nearly everything we do. A jury found George Zimmerman, a white vigilante and the alleged murderer of Trayvon Martin, not guilty in the shooting of an unarmed black teenager. The case had sparked familiar anxiety in the hearts and minds of many African Americans—will another African American life be thrown away as being undeserving of justice? A report in *The New York Times* said that the work done to promote diversity may very well be going backward.[6] Historian David Blight has written about the origin of Memorial Day and how that day was really begun by African American soldiers who fought in the Civil War and who wanted a proper burial for white Union soldiers whose bodies had been thrown in a mass grave in South Carolina.[7] Another article reported that the poorest of the poor, many of who are African American, will still not be able to afford health insurance.[8] In Chicago, President Obama's home town, the Board of Education voted to close fifty inner-city schools. Mayor Rahm

Emmanuel approved the closing of these schools in May 2013 in spite of an outcry of protests from angry parents.[9] The reason, at least partially, was that enrollment in the targeted schools was low; from an outsider's point of view, smaller classes in urban schools is probably a good thing, but apparently not. The spirit of racism will not go away. It lingers, hovering over everything we do in this country.

Statistics show that African Americans are still disproportionately jailed, still disproportionately receive the death penalty, and are still more apt to get arrested for offenses than whites. Public schools for urban youth, most of whom tend to be African American, are still struggling, and the education given at many of them is still subpar. In Philadelphia, public schools are being closed while at the same time $400 million is being used to build a new prison.

Obama won the presidency, but it was not without cost. President Obama, too, knows the anger, the seething anger, that exists in many African Americans. Some argued that when Henry Louis Gates was arrested by a white police officer for trying to get into his own house Obama showed that same anger when he said what the police officer had done was "stupid." As the politician, President Obama had to back down and ended up having the infamous "beer summit" with Gates and the officer, but again, those who live under the spirit of racism knew exactly what President Obama was feeling.

Wright, the pastor, teacher, preacher, and prophet, continues to do his work. President Obama, the politician in a second term as president, might now feel free enough to deal with "the least of these" in ways he may have been reluctant to do in his first term. Neither man, Reverend Wright or President Obama, can feel good about what happened in 2008. In a very sad way, even though President Obama won the presidency, he lost perhaps one of the most important influences of his life.

Some said that when President Obama was elected that racism was gone. Not yet. We've got a way to go.

Shakespeare could not have written this story any better.

Notes

PREFACE

1. See http://memory.loc.gov/cgi-bin/query/r?ammem/llst:@field %28DOCID+@lit%28llst022div3%29%29. The opinion was read on March 6, 1857.

2. 1 Cor. 13:12. In the NIV translation of the Bible it reads, "Now we see but a poor reflection as in a mirror; then we shall see face to face."

3. See www.ncbi.nlm.gov/pubmedhealth/PMH0001923/.

4. Rachel Yehuda, "Post-Traumatic Stress Disorder," *New England Journal of Medicine* vol. 346, no.2 (January 10, 2002),108, http://www.nejm .org/doi/full/10.1056/NEJMra012941.

5. Ibid.

6. William Sloan Coffin, "A World Fit for Children," in *The Collected Sermons of William Sloan Coffin: The Riverside Years,* vol. 1 (Louisville: Westminster John Knox Press, 2008), 10.

7. "Soon-ah-will–be-done," Negro spiritual.

INTRODUCTION

1. Barack Obama, *Dreams from my Father: A Story of Race and Inheritance* (New York: Three Rivers Press, 1995), 282.

2. Ibid, 283.

3. Ibid, 284.

4. Ibid.

5. Ibid, 285.

6. Ibid.

7. Ibid, 293.

8. This was shared with me by Jeremiah Wright.

9. *New York Times* transcript, www.nytimes.com/2008/04/28/us/politics/28text-wright.html.

10. Ibid.

11. Ibid.

12. Ibid.

13. Ibid,

14. Ibid.

15. Ibid,

16. Ibid.

17. The "Ham Doctrine," found in Genesis 9, was used by ancient rabbis and later by Christian ministers to justify racism and the enslavement of Africans. The story tells of Ham finding his father Noah naked in his tent. Ham informs his brothers, Shem and Japheth. They back into the tent, so as not to see their father naked, and cover him. Noah awakens and curses Ham's son, Canaan (not Ham). In the Bible, the land of Canaan was thought to be what is known today as black Africa.

18. "Our Church's Wider Mission" is a fund into which congregations of the UCC contribute to assist the work of the larger church.

19. Peter Gomes. *The Scandalous Gospel of Jesus: What's So Good about the Good News?* (New York: Harper Collins, 2007), 12.

20. Ibid.

CHAPTER 1

1. H.W. Brands. *Traitor to His Class: The Privileged Life and Radical Presidency of Franklin Delano Roosevelt* (New York: Doubleday, 2008), 579–80.

2. Jeremiah A. Wright Jr., "What Makes You So Strong?" in *What Makes You So Strong? Sermons of Joy and Strength from Jeremiah A. Wright Jr.,* ed. Jini Kilgore Ross (Valley Forge, Pa.: Judson Press, 1993), 144.

3. Jeremiah Wright Jr., *A Sankofa Moment: The History of Trinity United Church of Christ* (Dallas: St. Paul Press, 2010), 2.

4. Wright, "What Makes You So Strong?, 143.

5. Ibid.

6. Ibid., 142.

7. Ibid., 36.

8. Jeremiah Wright Jr., "Good News for Good Fathers" in *Good News: Sermons of Hope for Today's Families,* ed. Jini Kilgore Ross (Valley Forge, Pa.: Judson Press, 1995), Kindle edition, loc. 714–24.

9. Ibid.

10. From a personal letter sent to the author of this book in response to wishing Wright a "Happy Father's Day."

11. Arlen Parsa, "Interview with Jeremiah Wright" (2009), Oral Histories, paper 17, http://digitalcommons.colum.edu/cadc_caam_oral histories/17/.

12. Wright, "Unhitch the Trailer," in *What Makes You So Strong?* 28.

13. Ibid.

14. Ibid.

15. Ibid.

16. Parsa, "Interview."

17. Wright, "Good News for Good Parents" in *Good News: Sermons of Hope for Today's Families,* Kindle ed., loc. 435.

18. Wright, "The Audacity to Hope," in *What Makes You So Strong?* 106.

CHAPTER 2

1. Adapted to gender-neutral language from Henri Nouwen, *The Wounded Healer* (New York: Doubleday, 1979), 4.

2. Martin Luther King Jr., *A Testament of Hope: The Essential Writings and Speeches of Martin Luther King Jr.,* ed. James Washington (San Francisco: HarperCollins, 1986), 290.

3. Jeremiah Wright, *Africans Who Shaped Our Faith: A Study of 10 Biblical Personalities*, ed. Colleen Birchett (Chicago: Urban Ministries, 1995), 260.

4. Ibid.

5. Parsons, "Interview."

6. Wright, *Africans Who Shaped Our Faith*, 261.

7. Ibid.

8. Parsa, "Interview," lines 357–65.

9. Ibid., lines 366–76.

10. Ibid.

11. Ibid., lines 395–400.

12. Ibid., lines 384–85.
13. Ibid., lines 401–10.
14. Ibid., lines 621–34.

CHAPTER 3

1. Carter G. Woodson, *The Mis-Education of the Negro* (Washington: Associated Publishers, 1933; Kindle edition used for this work: Seven Treasures Publishing, 2010), 4.
2. Ibid.
3. Ibid., 5.
4. Ibid, 7.
5. Wright, "When God Is Silent," in *What Makes You So Strong?* 112.
6. Woodson, *Mis-Education of the Negro*, 113.
7. Ibid.
8. James Cone, *God of the Oppressed* (Maryknoll, N.Y.: Orbis, 1979), xvii.
9. Romans 6:1–4 is generally quoted and listed as our directive to imitate the Christ. We are to imitate the Christ in his death, burial, and resurrection.
10. Cone, *God of the Oppressed*, 26.
11. Ibid.
12. Ibid.
13. Ibid.
14. Ibid., 5.
15. Washington, *A Testament of Hope*, "Letter From a Birmingham Jail," 295.
16. Cone, *God of the Oppressed,* 9.
17. Ibid.
18. Woodson, *Mis-Education of the Negro*, 102.
19. Ibid.
20. Ibid.
21. Woodson, *Mis-Education of the Negro,* 10.

CHAPTER 4

1. Wright, "When You Forget Who You Are," in *What Makes You So Strong?* 66.

2. Ibid.

3. David Von Drehle, *Time*, April 18, 2011.

4. Randall Robinson, *The Debt: What America Owes to Blacks* (New York: Penguin Books, 2000), 2.

5. Ibid.

6. Ibid.

7. Ibid.

8. Forrest G Wood, *The Arrogance of Faith: Christianity and Race in America from the Colonial Era to the Twentieth Century* (New York: Alfred Knopf, 1990), 89.

9. Wright, "Unhitch the Trailer," in *What Makes You so Strong?* 27.

10. Wright, "When You Forget Who You Are," in *What Makes You So Strong?* 72.

11. Edwin Black, *War against the Weak: Eugenics and America's Campaign to Create a Master Race* (New York: Four Walls Eight Windows, 2003), Kindle ed., loc. 72.

12. Ibid., Kindle ed., loc. 66.

13. The words were penned some sixty years ago by Big Bill Broonzy (June 26, 1903–August 15, 1958), who was a songwriter, singer, and guitarist. His words were quoted by the late Reverend Joseph Lowry at President Obama's inauguration, setting off a firestorm of criticism. Broonzy, born in Arkansas, is said to have written and sung about his experiences in the U.S. Army and his experiences in Arkansas and Mississippi upon his return.

14. "We'll Understand It Better By and By," words and music by Charles Albert Tindley, ca. 1906.

15. Wood, *Arrogance of Faith*, 72.

16. Ibid.

17. Ibid., 89.

18. Ibid., 20.

19. Ibid.

20. Ibid.

21. Peter Gomes. *The Good Book: Reading the Bible with Mind and Heart* (New York: William Morrow, 1996), 29.

22. Ibid., 50.

23. Wright, *Sankofa Moment*, 74.

CHAPTER 5

1. Gomes, *Good Book*, 50.

2. Paul Lawrence Dunbar, "We Wear the Mask," in *Lyrics of the Lowly Life* (Charleston, S.C.: BiblioLife, 2009), 167; the poem appeared in Dunbar's first published poetry volume, by the same title in 1896.

3. Woodson, *Mis-education of the Negro*, 86.

4. Joy Degrury Leary, *Post Traumatic Slave Syndrome: America's Legacy of Enduring Injury and Healing* (Milwaukie, Oregon: Uptone Press, 2005), 7.

5. Edwin Black, *War against the Weak: America's Campaign to Create a Master Race* (New York: Four Walls Eight Windows, 2003), xv.

6. Ibid.

7. Ibid., xvi.

8. Ibid.

9. Ibid., xvii.

10. *Race: The Power of an Illusion*, produced by California Newsreel, 2003.

11. Thomas Jefferson, *Notes on the State of Virginia*, 94.

12. Ibid., 95.

13. Ibid., 97.

14. Wood, *Arrogance of Faith,* 99.

15. Ibid.

16. Howard Zinn, *A People's History of the United States, 1492–Present* (New York: Harper Collins, 1999), 35.

17. Wood, *Arrogance of Faith*, 99.

18. Ibid., 59.

19. Ibid.

20. Ibid., 66.

21. Alexis de Tocqueville, *Democracy in America* (New York: Doubleday, 1969), 639.

22. Ibid., 342.

23. Ibid., 343.

24. Ibid.

25. Harry Emerson Fosdick, *The Meaning of Prayer* (New York: Abingdon Press, 1915), 69.

26. Ibid.

27. Ibid., 101.

28. Gomes, *Good Book*, 98.

29. Ibid., 5.

30. Jeremiah Wright, "The Day of Jerusalem's Fall," sermon, taken from transcript.

31. Gomes, *Good Book*, 96–97.

32. From interview with Bill Moyers, http://www.pbs.org/moyers/journal/04252008/transcript1.html.

33. Renita Weems, "Reading Her Way through the Struggle: African American Women and the Bible," in *Stony the Road We Trod* by Cain Hope Felder (Minneapolis: Fortress Press, 1991), 162.

34. Wright, "Ain't Nobody Right but Us," in *What Makes You So Strong?* 18.

35. Ibid., 23.

CHAPTER 6

1. Wright, *Sankofa Moment*, 18.

2. Ibid., 37.

3. Wright, "Ain't Nobody Right but Us," in *What Makes You So Strong?* 17.

4. Wright, *Sankofa Moment*, 37.

5. Ibid., 33.

6. Ibid., 32.

7. Ibid., 39.

8. Woodson, *Mis-Education of the Negro*, 90.

9. Wright, *Sankofa Moment*, 51.

10. Ibid., 52.

11. Ibid., 55.

12. Leary, *Post Traumatic Slave Syndrome*, 162.

13. Ibid.

14. Wright, *Sankofa Moment*, 64.

15. Ibid., 68.

16. Ibid., 81.

17. Ibid., 83.

18. Ibid.

19. Renita Weems, "Reading Her Way," 57.

20. Wright, *Sankofa Moment*, 107.

21. Ibid., 108.

22. Ibid., 260–61.

23. Ibid., 312–13.

24. Jonathan Alter, *The Promise: President Obama, Year One* (New York: Simon & Shuster, 2010), 139.

25. Ibid.

26. Wright, *Sankofa Moment*, 146–49.

27. Ibid., 148–49.

28. Jon Meacham, *American Gospel: God, the Founding Fathers, and the Making of a Nation* (New York: Random House, 2007), 118.

29. Wright, *Sankofa Moment,* 104.

CHAPTER 7

1. Abraham Heschel, *The Prophet: An Introduction* (New York: Harper Torchbooks, 1962), 6.

2. Ibid.

3. Ibid., 7.

4 Ibid., 11.

5. David J. Garrow, *Bearing the Cross: Martin Luther King, Jr. and the Southern Christian Leadership Conference* (New York: Vintage Books, 1986), 135.

6. Gomes, *Good Book,* 97.

7. Isabel Wilkerson, *The Warmth of Other Suns: The Epic Story of America's Great Migration* (New York: Random House, 2010), 186.

8. Leary, *Post Traumatic Slave Syndrome*, 145.

9. Damani Davis, "Slavery and Emancipation in the Nation's Capital: Using Federal Records to Explore the Lives of African American Ancestors," *Prologue Magazine* 42/1 (Spring 2010), www.archives.gov/publications/prologue/2010/spring/dcslavery.html.

10. Wright, *Sankofa Moment*, 312.

11 Heschel, *Prophet*, 15.

12. Ibid.

13. Gomes, *Good Book*, 37.

14. Heschel, *Prophet*, 16.

CHAPTER 8

1. The Declaration of Independence.

2. "George Mason's Views on Slavery," www.gunstonhall.org/georgemason/slavery4.html.

3. "Rediscovering George Washington: George Washington and the Problem of Slavery, www.pbs.org/georgewashington/classroom/slavery4.html.

4. The Thirteenth Amendment to the U.S. Constitution.

5. Douglas Blackmon, "The World War II Effect," *Wall Street Journal,* March 29, 2008online.wsj.com/article/SB120674498432473091.html.

6. Ibid.

7. Meacham, *American Gospel*, 11.

8. Ibid., 125.

9. Ibid.

10. Wright, "What Makes You So Strong?" in *What Makes You So Strong?* 147.

11. Ibid.

12. Wright, "What Makes You So Strong?" in *What Makes You So Strong?* 155–56.

13. Ibid.

14. Ibid., 156.

15. Ibid.

16. Ibid., 157.

CHAPTER 9

1. Paul Tillich, *The Courage to Be* (New Haven: Yale University Press, 1952), 3.

2. Timothy Egan, *The Worst Hard Time: The Untold Story of Those Who Survived the Great American Dust Bowl* (Boston: Houghton Mifflin, 2006), 227.

3. Cone, *God of the Oppressed*, 10.

4. Ibid., 5.

5. Ibid., 9.

6. "In the Garden," words and music by C. Austin Miles, 1913.

7. Wright, "The Audacity to Hope," in *What Makes You So Strong?* 97.

8. Ibid., 101.

9. Obama writes of hearing the sermon and how it impacted him in his book *Dreams from My Father* (New York: Random House, 1995, 2006), 293–94. The title of the president's second book is *The Audacity of Hope*; Wright's sermon title, as noted, was "The Audacity to Hope."

10. Cone, *God of the Oppressed*, 7–8.

11. Ibid., 19.

12. Ibid., 19–20.

13. Peggy McIntosh, "White Privilege: Unpacking The Invisible Knapsack," http://www.nymbp.org/reference/WhitePrivilege.pdf.

14. Wood, *Arrogance of Faith*, 9.

15. Ibid., 208.

16. Ibid., 210.

17. Ibid.

18. Ibid.

19. Wright, "What Makes You So Strong?" in *What Makes You So Strong?* 155.

20. Ibid.

21. Cone, *God of the Oppressed*, 37.

22. Ibid.

23. Ibid., 39.

24. Ibid.

25. Ibid.

26. Wright, "Faith in a Foreign Land," in *What Makes You So Strong?* 134.

27. Tillich, *The Courage to Be*, xxii.

28. Ibid.

29. Cone, *God of the Oppressed,* xii.

30. Ibid., xi.

31. "Glenn Beck: Liberation Theology and Social Justice," www.glenn beck.com/content/articles/article/198/42891/.

32. Jim Wallis, *God's Politics: Why the Right Gets It Wrong and the Left Doesn't Get It* (New York: Harper Collins, 2005), 4.

33. Cone, *God of the Oppressed,* 42.

34. Ibid., 43.

35. Wright, "What Makes You So Strong?" in *What Makes You So Strong?* 150.

CHAPTER 10

1. Jeremiah Wright, "Confusing God and Government," http://www.blackpast.org/2008-rev-jeremiah-wright-confusing-god-and-government.

2. David Howard-Pitney, *The African American Jeremiad: Appeals for Justice in America* (Philadelphia: Temple University Press, 2005), 5.

3. Sacvan Bercovitch, *The American Jeremiad* (Madison: University of Wisconsin Press, 1978), 18.

4. Ibid.

5. Howard-Pitney, *African American Jeremiad,* 5.

6. Ibid., 6.

7. Ibid.

8. Bercovitch, *American Jeremiad*, 82.

9. Howard-Pitney, *African American Jeremiad,* p. 4

10. Ibid., 8.

11. Ibid.

12. Ibid., 25.

13. Ibid.

14. Ibid., citing George Fredrickson, *The Black Image in the White Mind* (New York: Harper & Row 1971, Torchbook ed., 1972), 98.

15. Howard-Pitney, *African American Jeremiad,* 26.

16. John Baer, *The Pledge of Allegiance: A Revised History and Analysis, 1892–2007* (Annapolis, Md.: Free State Press, 2007); see also Baer's "The Pledge of Allegiance: A Short History," http://www.oldtimeislands.org/pledge/pledge.htm.

17. Ibid.

18. Howard-Pitney, *African American Jeremiad,* 4.

19. Ibid., 5.

20. Ibid., 6.

21. Ibid., 12.

22. Ibid., 20.

23. Ibid., 16.

24. Ibid., 35.

25. Ibid., p44.

26. Frederick Douglass, "What to the Slave Is the 4th of July?" speech given at Rochester, N.Y., July 5, 1852, in Stephen Prothero, *The American*

Bible—Whose America Is This?: How Our Words Unite, Divide, and Define a Nation (New York: HarperOne, 2012), 4.

27. Howard-Pitney, 203.

28. Ibid., 205.

29. Ibid.

30. King, *A Testament of Hope,* 299.

31. "A Testament of Hope," in *A Testament of Hope,* 327–28. Essay was published posthumously.

32. King, "Where Do We Go from Here?" in *A Testament of Hope,* 250.

33. Ibid.

34. Martin Luther King Jr., "Beyond Vietnam: A Time to Break Silence," speech at Riverside Church in New York City, April 4, 1967; see http://www.hartford-hwp.com/archives/45a/058.html.

35. Ibid.

36. Ibid.

37. Ibid.

38. Ibid.

39. Heschel, *Prophet,* 109.

40. Ibid., 112.

41. Ibid., 114–115.

42. Ibid., 119.

43. King, "Beyond Vietnam."

44. Children and young adults were primary participants and victims in the Connor attacks on "the Children's Movement"; the events were influential in pushing forward the civil rights movement.

45. Howard Thurman, *Jesus and the Disinherited* (Boston: Beacon Press, 1976), 22.

46. Ibid., 23.

47. Wright, "Confusing God and Government," 3.

48. Ibid.

49. Ibid.

50. Ibid.

51. Ibid.

52. Ibid.

53. People for the American Way, "Statement on Divisive Comments by Religious Right Leaders, " U.S. Newswire press release, September

13, 2001, partial transcript of Jerry Falwell and Pat Robertson on Robertson's "700 Club," http://www.freerepublic.com/focus/news/523202/posts?page=151; see the interview at http://www.youtube.com/watch?v=H-CAcdta_8I.

54. Wright, "Confusing God and Government."

55. Ibid. See Deuteronomy 27:15–26 and Deuteronomy 28. The biblical understanding of to be cursed or damned is to be removed from God's favor. The Hebrew verbal root for "cursed" is *arr*; it is the opposite of blessed. In English, the best equivalent for the Hebrew *arr* is "damn." It means a person shall be removed from God's protection and favor.

56. Frank Schaeffer, "Obama's Minister Committed 'Treason' But When My Father Said the Same Thing He Was a Republican Hero," March 16, 2008, http://www.huffingtonpost.com/frank-schaeffer/obamas-minister-committed_b_91774.html.

57. Ibid.

CHAPTER 11—THE OPPRESSOR AND THE OPPRESSED, UNITED

1. From Studs Terkel interview with James Baldwin, 1961.
2. Ibid.
3. Ibid.
4. Jeremiah Wright, "The Proof, the Promise, and the Proclamation," sermon preached April 3, 2005.
5. Howard-Pitney, *African American Jeremiad,* 28.
6. Ibid.
7. Terkel, interview with James Baldwin.
8. Thurman, *Jesus and the Disinherited,* 17–19.
9. Ibid., 20.
10. Ibid., 22–23.
11. Ibid., 29.
12. Elie Wiesel, *Night* (New York: Hill and Want, 1958), 76.
13. Excerpt from John Jasper's sermon, "De Sun Do Move," http://www.gjwn.net/news/2012/02/20/de-sun-do-move-by-john-jasper/.
14. Jasper sermon transcript, "De Sun Do Move," http://www.archive.org/stream/cu31924101095226/cu31924101095226_djvu.txt.
15. "Yes, It Was About Slavery," Baptists and the Civil War in Their Own Words, http://www.civilwarbaptists.com/featured/slavery/.

16. Weisel, *Night,* 76–77.

17. Ibid., 77.

18. Leary, *Post Traumatic Slave Syndrome,* 129.

19. Ibid., 152.

20. Gary Schmidt, *Lizzie Bright and the Buckminster Boy* (New York: Clarion/Houghton Mifflin, 2004), 218.

21. Ibid.

22. Ibid., 219.

23. Fred L. Standley and Louis H. Pratt, *Conversations with James Baldwin* (Jackson and London: University Press of Mississippi, 1989), 95.

24. Wright, "Faith in a Foreign Land," in *What Makes You So Strong?* 133.

25. "We'll Understand It Better By and By," words by Charles Findley, ca. 1906.

26. Wright, "Faith in a Foreign Land," 134.

27. Michele Norris, *The Grace of Silence* (New York: Pantheon Books, 2010), 96.

28. Ibid., 93.

29. Ibid., 98.

30. Ibid., 101.

31. Ibid., 126.

32. Stanley and Pratt, *Conversations with James Baldwin,* "Ida Lewis and Lewis Baldwin, 1970," 85.

CHAPTER 12

1. Interview with Dr. Robert Franklin, December 27, 2012

2. Ibid.

3. Dr. Wright at the National Press Club, April 28, 2008, transcript, http://www.nytimes.com/2008/04/28/us/politics/28text-wright.html?pagewanted=all&_r=0.4. Ibid.

5. Ibid.

6. Franklin interview.

7. Wright, NPC speech.

8. Prothero, *American Bible*, 34.

9. Ibid., 35.

10. Ibid., 36.
11. Ibid.
12. Ibid.
13. Bonnie Kavoussi, "The One Percent Is 288 Times Wealthier Than the Median U.S. Household," citing "The State of Working America," a report by the Economic Policy Institute, September 11, 2012, http://www.huffingtonpost.com/2012/09/11/one-percent-vs-median-household_n_1873673.htm.
14. Prothero, *American Bible*, 37.
15. Ibid., 38.
16. King, "Beyond Vietnam."
17. Prothero, *American Bible*,254.
18. Ibid., 38.
19. Franklin interview.
20. Ibid.
21. Ibid.
22. James Baldwin, "Interview with Eve Auchincloss and Nancy Lynch, 1969," in Stanley and Pratt, *Conversations with James Baldwin,* 75.
23. Richard Wright, "How 'Bigger' Was Born," essay included in some editions of *Native Son*, and found at http://xroads.virginia.edu/~ma01/white/anthology/bigger.html.
24. Wright, NPC speech.
25. Ibid.
26. Ibid.
27. Ibid.
28. Ibid.
29. Richard Wright, "How 'Bigger' Was Born."
30. Ibid.
31. J. Wright, NPC speech.
32. Kevin Tyson, interviewed, January 4, 2013.
33. Ibid.
34. Ibid.
35. Ibid.
36. R. Wright, "How 'Bigger' was Born."
37. Ibid.
38. Ibid.

39. Rick Bragg, "Chain Gangs Return to the Roads of Alabama," *New York Times*, March 25, 1995, http://www.nytimes.com/1995/03/26/us/chain-gangs-to-return-to-roads-of-alabama.html.

40. Ibid.

41. Wright, "What Makes You So Strong?" 151.

42. Ibid., 155.

CHAPTER 13

1. Barack Obama, *The Audacity of Hope: Thoughts on Reclaiming the American Dream* (New York: Random House, 2008), 207.

2. Wright, *Sankofa Moment,* 170.

3. Ibid., 197.

4. Ibid., 170.

5. Ibid., 171.

6. Martin Marty, "The Truth about Trinity United Church of Christ," blog, March 26, 2008, http://truthabouttrinity.blogspot.com/2008/03/rev-wrights-teacher-and-friend-martin-e.html.

7. Wright, *Sankofa Moment,* 175.

8. Ibid.

9. Interview with Richard Sewell.

10. Dianna Bass, "Putting Rev. Wright's Preaching into Perspective," blog, The Truth about Trinity United Church of Christ, March 28, 2009, http://truthabouttrinity.blogspot.com/2008/03/dianna-bass-putting-rev-wrights.html.

11. Obama, *Audacity of Hope,* 233.

12. Ibid., 236.

13. King, "The Strength to Love," in *A Testament of Hope,* 491.

14. Ibid., 492.

15. Ibid.

16. Ibid., 513.

17. Obama, *Audacity of Hope,* 203.

18. Ibid., 205–6.

19. Ibid., 207.

20. Marty, "The Truth about Trinity."

21. Obama, *Dreams from My Father,* 282.

22. Ibid., 284.

23. Transcript of Bill Moyers' interview with Wright, http://www.pbs.org/moyers/journal/04252008/transcript1.html.

24. Ibid.

25. Statement from Michael Harris, *Huffington Post* journalist.

26. Kevin Merida, "Racist Incidents Give Some Obama Campaigners Pause," *Washington Post,* May 13, 2008, A1.

27. "Poll: Most Americans See Lingering Racism—in Others," CNN.com, December 12, 2006, http://www.cnn.com/2006/US/12/12/racism.poll/.

28. Jesse Wahington, "Obama Election Spurs Race Crimes around the Country," *USA Today*, November 16, 2008, http://usatoday30.usatoday.com/news/nation/2008-11-15-2960000388_x.htm.

29. "Michelle Obama: For the First Time in My Adult Life, I'm Really Proud of My Country," ABC News, February 18, 2008, http://abcnews.go.com/blogs/politics/2008/02/michelle.obam-1-2/.

30. Jeffrey Ressner, "Michelle Obama Theses Was on Racial Divide," *Free Republic*, Febraury 22, 2008, http://www.freerepublic.com/focus/f-news/1974896/posts.

31. King "Beyond Vietnam.

32. Ibid.

33. J. Wright, "Confusing God and Government."

34. Barack Obama, "On My Faith and My Church," *Huffington Post*, March 14, 2008, http://www.huffingtonpost.com/barack-obama/on-my-faith-and-my-church_b_91623.html. 35. Ibid.

36. Bill Moyers' essay, "Reflections on Jeremiah Wright," May 2, 2008, http://billmoyers.com/content/bill-moyers-essay-reflections-on-jeremiah-wright/.

37. Hendricks, *Politics of Jesus*, 103.

38. Ibid., 46.

39. Edward S. Herman and David Peterson, "Jeremiah Wright in the Propaganda System," Monthly Review, http://monthlyreview.org/2008/09/01/jeremiah-wright-in-the-propaganda-system.

40. Ibid.

41. Ibid.

42. Ibid.

43. Horton was granted the furlough in 1986, two years before the 1988 presidential race.

CHAPTER 14

1. PBS's Black in Latin America series, "Brazil: A Racial Paradise?" http://www.pbs.org/search/?q=black+in+latin+america%2C+brazil.

2. Wiesel, *Night,* 118.

3. Jeremiah Wright Jr., "Day of Jerusalem's Fall."

4. Statement given by Mike Green, a journalist, in response to the question, "What is the importance of Jeremiah Wright's preaching/teaching in today's world?"

5. Ibid.

6. Wright, "Day of Jerusalem's Fall."

7. Ibid.

8. Ibid.

9. Erin Williams, "Shirley Sherrod Pens New Memoir, 'The Courage to Hope,'" Washington Post, September 18, 2012, http://www.washingtonpost.com/blogs/therootdc/post/shirley-sherrod-pens-new-memoir-the-courage-to-hope/2012/09/18/32aad236-fdd9-11e1-a31e-804fccb658f9_blog.html.

10. Arika Herron, "Jeremiah Wright, Obama's former minister, had crowds on their feet Saturday night," *Winston-Salem Journal,* March 23, 2013, http://www.journalnow.com/news/local/article_561c9992-9425-11e2-ab8c-0019bb30f31a.html.

11. Tim Wise, "Trayvon Martin, White America, and the Return of Dred Scott," March 27, 2012, http://www.timwise.org/2012/03/trayvon-martin-white-america-and-the-return-of-dred-scott/.

12. Barbara Bradley Hagerty, "A Closer Look at Liberation Theology," NPR.com, March 18, 2008, http://www.npr.org/templates/story/story.php?storyId=88512189.

13. Ibid.

14. Ibid.

15. Ibid.

16. Wright, "The Audacity to Hope" in *What Makes You So Strong?*

17. "The Insidious Racism in 'Black Boy,'" http://www.megaessays.com/viewpaper/10086.html.

18. David Benner, *The Gift of Being Yourself: The Sacred Call to Self-Discovery* (Downers Grove, Ill.: InnerVarsity Press, 2004), 66.

19. Howard Thurman, *Jesus and the Disinherited* (Boston: Beacon Press, 1976), 79.

20. Ibid., 80.

21. Ibid.

22. E-mail received from Larry Whitman, former member of Trinity United Church of Christ.

23. Jeremiah Wright, "Good News for Good Parents," Kindle ed., loc. 70.

24. Ibid.

25. Ibid., Kindle ed., loc. 399.

26. Ibid., Kindle ed., loc. 435.

27. Russell D. Moore, "Black and White and Red All Over: Why Racial Justice Is a Gospel Issue," *The Christian Post,* CP Opinion, June 13, 2012, http://www.christianpost.com/news/black-and-white-and-red-all-over-why-racial-justice-is-a-gospel-issue-76558/.

28. Ibid.

29. Ibid.

30. Ibid.

CHAPTER 15

1. Lee Greenwood. "I'm Proud to be An American," 1984. Lyrics can be seen at www.elyrics.net/read/l/lee-greenwood-lyrics/i_m-proud-to-be-an-american-lyrics.html.

2. Words taken from baby dedication service traditionally done at Trinity UCC under Wright's leadership.

3. John Blake, "How MLK became an angry black man," CNN.com, April 16, 2013, www.cnn.com/2013/04/16/us/king-birmingham-jail-letter-anniversary/.

4. Bishop Desmond Tutu, *God Is Not a Christian: And Other Provocations* (New York: HarperCollins, 2011), 50.

5. Ibid., 53.

6. Nathan D. Schwartz and Michelle Copper, "Racial Diversity Efforts Ebb for Elite Careers, Analysis Finds," *New York Times*, May 27, 2013, http://www.nytimes.com/2013/05/28/us/texas-firm-highlights-struggle-for-black-professionals.html?emc=tnt&tntemail0=y&_r=1&.

7. David Blight, "Forgetting What We Remember," *New York Times,* May 29, 2011, http://www.nytimes.com/2011/05/30/opinion/30blight.html?pagewanted=all.

8. Robert Pear, "States' Policies on Health Care Exclude Some of the Poorest," *New York Times,* May 24, 2013, http://www.nytimes.com/2013/05/25/us/states-policies-on-health-care-exclude-poorest.html?pagewanted=all.9. Bob Secter and Noreen S. Ahmed-Ullah, "Hearing Officers Oppose 13 of Closings Proposed by CPS," *Chicago Tribune*, May 8, 2013, http://articles.chicagotribune.com/2013-05-08/news/chi-chicago-public-schools-closings-20130507_1_hearing-officers-closures-closing-schools.

Other books from The Pilgrim Press

GOOD NEWS PREACHING

Offering the Gospel in Every Sermon

GENNIFER BENJAMIN BROOKS

ISBN: 978-0-8298-1822-2/paper/144 pages/$20.00

Brooks asserts that every sermon needs to be intentional and explicit in its offering of good news, regardless of the scripture or occasion. Based on her years of preaching and teaching, she provides preachers with practical guidance on how to identify good news in scripture texts and how to connect that news with today's situations. As a tool, she includes four "good news sermons" she herself preached that she believes embody her methodology and techniques.

THE GOSPEL ACCORDING TO THE WIZ

And Other Sermons from Cinema

OTIS MOSS III

ISBN: 978-0-8298-1991-5/paper/144 pages/$17.00

The Gospel According to The Wiz is a powerful connection between the good book and the silver screen. The honest, thought-provoking sermons in this book from renowned preacher Otis Moss III are based on popular films "juxtaposed to the Bible," he says, to "help us illuminate a variety of insights about human nature." In addition to *The Wiz,* other sermons are based on the films *Avatar, The Book of Eli, The Color Purple,* and more. Includes stimulating reflection questions that make this a compelling Bible study.

I REFUSE TO PREACH A BORING SERMON

Engaging the 21st Century Listener

KARYN L. WISEMAN

ISBN: 978-0-8298-1956-4/paper/128 pages/$17.00

One of the reasons preachers give boring sermons, says Wiseman, is because they haven't moved into the modern world and connected with their members. Here she shares many insights and strategies gleaned from years of experience teaching courses in homiletics, liturgical studies, and worship. Preachers will learn how to make their sermons come alive with social media, narrative techniques, technology, imagery, and imagination. Each chapter includes a "Things to Try on Your Own" section.

PREACH!

The Power and Purpose Behind Our Praise

OTIS MOSS III AND OTIS MOSS, JR.

Foreword by Andrew Young

ISBN: 978-0-8298-1907-6/paper/128 pages/$16.00

Dynamic father-son preaching team—Otis Moss, Jr. and Otis Moss III—share their sermons on social justice and other progressive Christian topics in this interactive book. Read each sermon, then scan the code at the end of each chapter to download and listen to the sermon. Topics include: "God Loves the Lost," "The Greatest Invitation: RSVP," "From Moses to Joshua," "Called to Make a Way," and more.

THEY LIKE TO NEVER QUIT PRAISIN' GOD

The Role of Celebration in Preaching

Revised and Updated

FRANK A. THOMAS

ISBN: 978-0-8298-1978-6/paper/192 pages/$16.00

Revised and updated edition of a popular preaching resource. According to Thomas, preacher and professor, all good preaching has strong elements of celebration, which is the genius of African American preaching. He explores this rich tradition and shares his findings to empower students and preachers to transform the impact of their preaching. Includes new sermon illustrations, strategies, and more.

THOSE SISTERS CAN PREACH!

22 Pearls of Wisdom, Virtue, and Hope

VASHTI MURPHY MCKENZIE, EDITOR

ISBN: 978-0-8298-1984-7/paper/144 pages/$15.00

A remarkable collection of sermons from twenty-two highly esteemed African American women preachers, edited by Vashti Murphy McKenzie, best-selling author and first female bishop in the African Methodist Episcopal (AME) Church. Each sermon has the corresponding scripture(s) and addresses issues Christian women face. Titles include: "It's a Set-Up," "What You Have . . . Is More Than Enough," "Cut It Off and Cut It Loose," "Push Past Your Pain," and more. Will inspire a new generation of prophetic female voices.

UNEXPECTED GRACE

Preaching Good News from Difficult Texts

GENNIFER BENJAMIN BROOKS

ISBN: 978-0-8298-1938-0/paper/160 pages/$20.00

Building on the success of her previous book, *Good News Preaching: Offering the Gospel in Every Season,* Brooks offers here a new, constructive approach to not only preaching challenging gospel texts, but how to do so with authority and passion. Her strategies will help preachers recognize the intentional good news of God revealed in the Bible and breathe new life into their sermons.

To order these or any other books from The Pilgrim Press call or write to:

THE PILGRIM PRESS
700 PROSPECT AVENUE EAST
CLEVELAND, OH 44115-1100

Phone Orders: 1-800-537-3394
Fax Orders: 216-736-2206

Please include $6.00 shipping charge for first book and $0.75 for each additional book.
Or order from www.thepilgrimpress.com
Prices subject to change without notice.